Je

Y0-AFT-439

MASTER
MEDIA
LIMITED

MasterMedia books are available at a discount with bulk purchase for educational, group, premium, or sales promotion use. For information, please write to:

Special Sales Department
MasterMedia Limited
333 West 52nd Street
Suite 306
New York, New York 10019

BEYOND

Success

*How Volunteer Service Can
Help You Begin Making a
Life Instead of Just a Living*

BY

JOHN F. RAYNOLDS III

AND

ELEANOR RAYNOLDS, C.B.E.

MASTER
MEDIA
LIMITED
New York

Copyright © 1988 John F. Raynolds III and Eleanor Raynolds, C.B.E.
All rights reserved,
including the right of reproduction
in whole or in part in any form.
Published by MasterMedia Limited

MASTERMEDIA and colophon are registered trademarks of
MasterMedia Limited
Designed by Irving Perkins Associates
Manufactured in the United States of America

10 9 8 7 6 5 4 3 2 1

Library of Congress Cataloging-in-Publication Data

Raynolds, John F.
  Beyond success.

  Bibliography: p.
    1. Voluntarism—United States.   2. Volunteers—
United States—Attitudes.   3. Executives—United
States—Attitudes.   4. Professional employees—
United States—Attitudes.   I. Raynolds, Eleanor.
II. Title.
HN90.V64R39   1988   361.3'7   88-23043
ISBN 0-942361-04-0

The authors gratefully acknowledge permission to reprint excerpts appearing on the following pages:

pp. 16: Material from *What Lies Ahead: Looking Toward the '90s* (United Way of America, 1987) used with permission from United Way of America. P. 22: Extract from *Democracy in America* by Alexis de Tocqueville (translated by Henry Reeve; New York: Alfred A. Knopf, 1976) reprinted with permission from the publisher. P. 55: Quotation from *Making a Difference: The Peace Corps at Twenty-Five* is reprinted courtesy of the Peace Corps. P. 41: Quotation from "The Difficult Art of Giving," by John D. Rockefeller, from *Random Reminiscences of Men and Events* (Sleepy Hollow Press), is reprinted with permission from the publisher. P. 46: Flow chart from Second Harvest reprinted with permission of Second Harvest National Food Bank Network. P. 45: Quotation from *Why Charity? The Case for a Third Sector* by James Douglas (Newbury Park, Calif.: Sage Publications, 1983) is reprinted by permission of Sage Publications. Pp. 54, 59: Quotations from *The Recovery of Confidence* by John Gardner (New York: W. W. Norton, 1970) are reprinted with permission from the publisher. Pp. 56, 294: Quotations from "Americans and the Cause of Voluntarism" by Kathleen Kennedy Townsend (*The Washington Monthly*, October 1983) are reprinted with permission from *The Washington Monthly*. P. 66: Quotation from *Working* by Studs Terkel (New York: Pantheon, 1972) is reprinted with permission from the publisher. Pp. 73–295: Quotations from *Everything to Gain: Making the Most of the Rest of Your Life* by Jimmy and Rosalynn Carter (New York: Random House, 1987) are reprinted with permission from the publisher. P. 239: Remarks by John M. Richman are reprinted with the permission of Kraft, Inc. P. 237: Quotation from an essay by Clifton C. Garvin in *Corporate Philanthropy: Philosophy, Management, Trends, Future, Background* (Washington, D.C.: The Council on Foundations, 1982) is reprinted with permission from The Council on Foundations. P. 253: Remarks by John F. Akers are reprinted with permission from International Business Machines Corporation. P. 288: Information from *Volunteer to Career: A Study of Student Voluntarism and Employability* by Jeremy Bentley-Kasman (New York: The Mayor's Voluntary Action Center, 1983) is reprinted with the permission of the Mayor's Voluntary Action Center. P. 298: Extracts from "The Durham Statement," published in *Campus Outreach* (Sept.–Oct. 1987), are reprinted with the permission of the Campus Outreach Opportunity League (COOL). P. 300: Quotations from "What Colleges Ought to Do to Instill a Voluntary Spirit in Young Adults" by Brian O'Connell (*The Chronicle of Higher Education*, April 15, 1987) are reprinted with the permission of *The Chronicle of Higher Education*.

This book is dedicated to our families, loved ones, and friends. For at the end of the day, those we are close to and those whose lives we have touched by love, kindness, or service give our lives their real meaning.

ACKNOWLEDGMENTS

We first want to thank our publisher, Susan Schiffer Stautberg, for her excellent ideas and consistently high enthusiasm.

On a personal level, we are deeply grateful to our late mentors Carl Voss and Francis R. Stoddard, Jr.; in our younger days, they set us on the path of service.

Susan Gulla spent hundreds of hours transcribing our conversations with the people whose words appear on the following pages. Susan Gill, Kathi Simendinger, and Maddie Byer helped with countless details.

Throughout the project, staff members at VOLUNTEER—The National Center, United Way of America, and Independent Sector answered questions and provided information.

Our greatest thanks, however, go to Patricia Fogarty, who worked with us in all phases of the book's creation. Her contributions have been invaluable.

CONTENTS

Contents

BEYOND SUCCESS

INTRODUCTION:

WHY YOU NEED THIS BOOK

You're saying, "Wait a minute. I thought this book was about volunteer service. Doing things for needy people and worthy causes. Why do I need this book? Why does the category on the jacket say *self-help*?" Bear with us a moment, and we'll explain.

Our lives today can be incredibly busy, full of rushing and doing, seeing friends, making deals, exercising and playing sports, helping our kids grow up, advancing our careers, enjoying the fruits of our successes. Yet in our private moments, many of us have felt a gnawing sense of incompleteness. Amid our abundance, we're bothered by a paradoxical little voice that whispers, "Is that all there is?" We take a quick personal inventory and are puzzled: "I have so much. What's wrong? Why do I feel that something is missing?"

As have millions of other Americans, we've discovered a cure, an answer to these questions. And once we realized that no book had been published on this cure—no secret, surely, since so many people take advantage of it—we got to work.

The cure is volunteer service. It isn't bought with money—although active philanthropy is a rewarding way of "giving back"—but with a giving of ourselves: of our time, our hands and feet, our ideas, our ability to help another person, our problem-solving skills, our professional knowledge.

One of the nicest things about service work is that you are the one who decides how you will participate and what skills and talents you will contribute. And the return, the psychic income, from giving of yourself is so unique, so special, that we urge you to try it.

Beyond Success will lead you through a process of thinking about yourself, about the world of not-for-profit service organizations and activities, and about the roles that people play in making them work. Our book is not the traditional pitch about how badly volunteers are needed, about how much there is to be done. Our focus is on *you*: on the rewards that service work will bring to your life.

In the pages that follow, we'll talk about

- Locating and investigating organizations, evaluating their activities, and determining which role is the right one for you;
- How to become a dynamic and effective volunteer who makes a high-quality contribution;
- The ways that service work can make important contributions to your sense of self-worth, to your relationships with family and friends, and to your career.

The book is full of stories of people whose lives have been enriched by service, descriptions of familiar and unusual programs and projects, and the accounts of friends and acquaintances who have made service an essential part of their lives. The testimony of the volunteers themselves is the simplest and best way to convey our message. We've placed these personal accounts between chapters, in sections titled "In Their Own Words."

WHO WE ARE

We don't claim to be the world's foremost experts on the not-for-profit world, but our experiences have given us a perspective on life with and without service involvement. We were both active in various organizations in early adulthood but, as often happens, found that children and careers made such overwhelming demands on our time that we stepped away from those activities. When we became reinvolved, during the past decade or so, we were struck by the extraordinary value that this work holds for our psychic well-being. And our experience is echoed by that of many others.

Throughout the book, we speak as "we," except when one of us wants to talk about an experience that is not shared but individual, when it's "I." The speaker's name heads these passages. You'll find this same structure used for the "In Their Own Words" sections after each chapter, where you'll read first-person accounts of the experiences of many volunteers.

John: *I've been a lifelong mountaineer and backpacker. During the Korean War, I was a Navy frogman and one of the founders of the SEAL teams [the Navy's sea, air, and land commando force]. At age twenty-five, a merchant in a small California town, I became president of the Monterey County Red Cross chapter and later president of the Salinas Rescue Mission, a shelter and way station for migrant workers. I was active in the local Junior Chamber of Commerce, Rotary Club, and other nonprofit activities, and helped found a preparatory school, the York School.*

I've been active in church affairs, having served as chairman of the board of trustees of the New Canaan, Connecticut, Congregational Church. While in New Canaan, I helped start a chapter of A Better Chance, a Boston-based organization that places promising inner-city students in college preparatory high schools, and served as a foster parent for two years to a student in the program. I am currently finance chairman and cochairman of the Steward-ship Campaign of the Second Congregational Church of Greenwich, Connect-icut.

During my business career, I have been a corporate president, an invest-ment banker, and director of corporate development for one of America's largest privately held corporations.

Today I thoroughly enjoy a role that combines true adventure, vigorous exercise, the application of entrepreneurial business skills, and service to others. Having been involved since 1974 as a board member and chairman of the fund-raising and expedition committees, in 1982 I became the full-time president of Outward Bound USA, the world's largest and oldest nonprofit adventure-based educational organization. I often speak before business, cul-tural, and educational groups on the process of personal growth through challenge and pushing through one's self-imposed limits in outdoor adven-ture.

Ellie: *I am a partner in the New York office of the executive search firm Ward Howell International, having worked previously in a high-technology corporation and a Fortune 500 company. Because of my business and service involvements, as well as my lifelong commitment to women's issues, I'm often asked to appear as a panelist and speaker in New York, Washington, and London. One of my favorite activities is chairing a luncheon discussion and support group of my female business peers.*

During my teenage years, I was introduced to service work as a candy striper. Stationed with my first husband at Fort Benning, Georgia, I taught modern dance to disadvantaged children and was active in church work. When I moved to San Francisco, I became involved in teaching crafts at the Florence Crittenden Home for Unwed Mothers and in volunteer work for the Crippled Children's Society of San Mateo, subsequently heading a major fund-raising extravaganza for the Multiple Sclerosis Society.

Back East, on Long Island, I became a Cub Scout mother (to my dismay, my son remained in the troop only six weeks before moving on to other pursuits) and was voted PTA president. I worked with Holiday House, bringing New York City kids out to a camp in Cold Spring Harbor. I have worked professionally for a not-for-profit organization, as head of individual and corporate fund-raising at the New York Botanical Garden.

I sit on the advisory board of Outward Bound USA and have taken it as my special mission to make women more aware of Outward Bound and to see more women involved at the policy-making levels. I run church fellowship groups for working women and teenagers.

In 1983 and 1984, I served as president of the British-American Chamber of Commerce—the first woman and only the third American to lead this nonprofit organization that promotes healthy trade between the two countries and serves as a platform for issues of mutual interest. During my two terms, I spent about 50 percent of my time on Chamber business, running offices in both countries and meeting with British and American officials. I was thrilled when Queen Elizabeth II awarded me the title Commander of the British Empire (C.B.E.) in recognition of my service as president of the Chamber.

Outward Bound

Outward Bound is an important part of our lives. It has informed our thinking on many aspects of service: challenge, opportunity, satisfaction, friendship, and compassion. Throughout the book, we'll come back repeatedly to what we've learned and enjoyed in our work with this exciting organization.

The courses offered by Outward Bound are designed to develop and enhance self-confidence and self-esteem, leadership qualities, teamwork and empathy, service to the community, sensitivity to the environment, and compassion for others. Based on the concept of placing people in value-forming experiences, the courses emphasize personal growth and teamwork.

In philosophy, Outward Bound is an interpretation of the thinking of Kurt Hahn, an innovative German-Jewish educator who was devoted to the concept of experiential education. He said, "No student should be compelled into opinions, but it is criminal negligence not to impel him into experiences." Hahn emphasized developing and maintaining "strong awareness of responsibility for others along with the belief that strength is derived from kindness and a sense of justice. . . . Compassion is learned through the opportunity and ability to help others in distress."

Young people are at the core of Outward Bound's mission, but programs have also been developed to serve adults and those with special needs, among them youth at risk, alcohol and drug abusers, the handicapped, Vietnam veterans, battered wives, and cancer patients. At this time, one of every five students receives some form of financial aid. Our goal is to offer financial aid to at least 40 percent of young applicants.

The philosophy and methods pioneered by Outward Bound have been adapted by more than 3,000 American public and private schools, colleges, and universities. We encourage imitation and provide help and consultation for those who wish to develop similar programs.

For the next ten years, Outward Bound will direct a major part of its innovative energies toward influencing the American high school education process. In the fall of 1987, this work exists primarily as a few developing model programs and as a vision rather than as a fully articulated approach, but we've begun to take concrete steps toward this goal. We are running alternative high schools in several locations, as well as working with school systems to design courses as part of the curriculum. And we're training teachers, who tell us that Outward Bound changes the way they teach.

As part of this long-range vision, rather than taking kids out into the mountains, we are coming into the inner cities to run urban Outward Bound programs. We are under way in Baltimore and Minneapolis, have begun a new Outward Bound Center in New York City, and are developing a program for Boston.

ABOUT THE SCOPE OF THIS BOOK

The private nonprofit sector includes more than 800,000 (some analysts say up to 2 million) organizations; in order to provide a focus, we have excluded here whole sectors of that universe.

Although we will occasionally mention an organization with a religious affiliation, we won't give any systematic attention to the huge numbers of religious groups. We hope that our rationale is obvious and forgivable: it would be nearly impossible to give equal coverage to all religious groups, and we feel that readers who maintain a strong religious orientation will have both knowledge of and ready access to the service work that takes place within their church, synagogue, mosque, or other group.

Volunteering for political candidates and causes, essential to the health of our country, is a most important way for people to contribute their energies and ideas. However, as with religious groups and for similar reasons, we won't specifically address political volunteering.

Because their activities are mainly intended to benefit their memberships, we have also largely excluded professional associations, labor unions, fraternal organizations, neighborhood and civic associations, and mutual-interest and self-help groups. The activities of such groups are often explicitly or implicitly philanthropic or charitable, and they unquestionably perform service for their members and often to the community in general. Yet we have chosen to concentrate on types of organizations whose missions are centered around outreach programs.

The groups and programs that we mention throughout the book and that are listed as categories in chapter 3, "A Service Sampler," are the following:

· Umbrella groups
· Social services

- Education
- Culture
- Health
- Environment/animal protection
- International organizations
- Groups of interest to children and youth
- Groups of interest to senior citizens and retired people.

We'll say this here and repeat it throughout the book: we don't intend to provide a definitive survey or directory of the not-for-profit world. Our goal is to provide an overview of the broad outlines of the independent sector, particularly in the categories mentioned above. When we mention an organization, it is to give an example of a type of activity or program. We do not endorse one educational, cultural, or social service organization over another, but give examples to provide an idea both of the scope and of the particular types of groups that exist.

WHY WE'VE WRITTEN THIS BOOK

Many people sense that something is missing in their lives and in the overall quality of contemporary life. And while large numbers of Americans are already involved in the special world of service, many—around half the adult population—are not.

We want you to try what we believe is a reliable way out of feelings of incompleteness, of alienation from society. You see, the involvement that comes with service work provides a sense of satisfaction like no other.

We feel that we have grown, and we know that we have found an energizing sense of fulfillment from our service activities—and we want to share these benefits with others. Service work is not an impersonal dispensing of programs and funds, but a dynamic interaction in which individual parties—and the cause, community, nation, and even the world—are rewarded. Not only is it okay to be honest about what each individual has to gain, but we also want to go beyond that and shout the message that service is something you can't afford to pass up. Do *yourself* a great service— get involved!

CHAPTER ONE
THE INDEPENDENT SECTOR

ONE way to think about the world of volunteer service is to think of it as independent, and, in fact, the term "independent sector" is becoming the one most commonly used to describe this large, diverse part of American life. More specifically, nonprofit organizations exist independent of business and government (although some are partly funded by and sometimes work in cooperation with them). The activities of nonprofits most often focus on needs that are not met or satisfied by the two larger sectors.

Almost any list would do, but consider these facts:

· **The Montgomery County [Maryland] Hotline,** staffed by trained volunteers who work four hours a week, is in operation twenty-four hours a day, seven days a week, helping on an immediate and confidential basis with such problems as child abuse, depression, drug and alcohol abuse, pregnancy, problems of the homeless, and suicide. Since 1970, hotline volunteers have received more than 40,000 calls and have made more than 3,200 referrals to area agencies and programs.

· **Habitat for Humanity,** an ecumenical, grass-roots Christian group, uses the labor of volunteers and of the people who will live in the homes to build decent houses for the poor, at an average cost of $25,000 in the United States and $1,000 to $3,000 overseas. Mortgages, on a no-profit, no-interest basis, are issued over a fixed time period.

· **Wheels,** in Philadelphia, is one of thousands of local volunteer agencies nationwide that provide the elderly and handicapped with low- or no-cost transportation to and from doctors' offices and hospitals.

· **Reading Is Fundamental** (RIF) works for a literate America by inspiring young people to read. With the help of more than 85,000 volunteers, RIF conducts imaginative activities that make reading a meaningful experience. Since 1966, it has brought more than 78 million books to American families.

· **Northwest Medical Teams** is an emergency medical relief agency that dispatches volunteer physicians, nurses, medical technicians, and staff to meet the immediate short-term health needs of people overseas who are stricken by natural disaster and social strife. After the earthquake that struck San Salvador in October 1986, the agency sent in a specialized team of surgeons, nurses, and technicians to repair the bodies of victims who otherwise would have been crippled for life.

· **The Holiday Project** sends volunteers into hospitals, nursing homes, orphanages, prisons, and shelters, to bring gifts and celebrate Christmas and Chanukah with confined people. In 1986, more than 19,600 volunteers shared the holidays with nearly 172,000 people in 1,829 institutions.

· **The American Museum of Natural History** in New York City has a volunteer staff of more than 500 people, equal to 10 percent of the staff. Volunteers work cataloging artifacts and specimens; on animal behavior studies; conducting tours; performing clerical and administrative functions; at the Museum Shop; and in so many other ways that they have become a vital part of this wonderful institution.

· **Children of the Night,** in Hollywood, California, is dedicated to reaching out to "throwaway" kids who are selling themselves on the street just to have a place to sleep and food to eat. More than 100 children come in each month to escape the vicious circle of drugs and prostitution.

· **The Friendly Visitor Program** in Napa County, California, like many similar programs across the country, sponsors regular visits and ongoing relationships between volunteers and residents of nursing homes. People in many groups have expanded their responsibilities to become ombudsmen who look after the finances of the residents and the details of their care.

Whether it is to improve the quality of life, to ease the pain of loneliness, or to break a cycle of desperation, efforts like these respond to needs that the public and commercial sectors have left unanswered. Sometimes, as in the case of stress hotlines or visitors to nursing homes, the need is not monetary but a simple human need for someone to care.

Recent budget cuts notwithstanding, government in this country has become increasingly involved since the 1930s in providing social services, and sometimes, without really thinking about what we're saying, we wish that local, state, or federal officials could come up with the solutions to our society's problems. Yet when you get right down to it, public programs can't be expected to meet all the various needs of our society.

It is probably far more efficient for local needs to be met by local organizations, with private individuals involved in managing and providing the services. Inefficiency is almost synonymous with bureaucracy, and public administration almost always lacks the special character of the volunteer worker or private financial contributor, who not only gives money and time but also can monitor and evaluate firsthand the results of the service.

We will return again and again in this book to the consideration of quality, for quality is what the independent sector, the nonprofit world, stands for. When the quality has drained away from any situation—the elderly living sad lives in nursing homes, 27 million Americans unable to read and write, children who have lost faith in their schools and families—groups of private individuals tend to form and react to the need. Others work proactively to ensure that people have the wherewithal to improve and enrich their lives, that institutions such as libraries, museums, and orchestras can continue to contribute to our overall well-being.

SOME STATISTICS

In 1984, the not-for-profit sector had annual funds totaling about $253 billion, had 6.7 million paid employees, and owned about 9 percent of private property in this country. There were more than 800,000 nonprofit groups, of which about 350,000 had tax-exempt and tax-deductible status.

In economic terms, the American philanthropic and voluntary sector is much smaller than the governmental and commercial sectors. Business totals about 79 percent of national income, government 15 percent, and the independent sector about 6 percent. Philanthropy alone, meaning all giving by foundations, corporations, and individuals, amounts to only 2 percent.

Sources of Support

Very roughly speaking, at mid-decade private contributions and government funding were about even as sources of support for the independent sector, each contributing 25 to 30 percent. (These statements describe the sector as a whole. Many organizations are completely private and accept no government funding. Others depend heavily on government grants and contracts.) The remaining 40 to 50 percent is generated by the organizations themselves.

Many of today's nonprofits are run like businesses, with ventures to generate income that range from selling calendars and T-shirts to collaboration with consumer product and credit card companies, which contribute to the nonprofit each time a consumer buys their product or uses their service. Some organizations charge fees for their services, and many have the support of endowment and other investment income.

Here's how private philanthropy in the United States broke down in 1987:

- Total giving was $87.22 billion. (In 1985, it was $80 billion; in 1984, $73.3 billion.)
- *Nearly 90 percent of giving was by individuals:* 82.2 percent through living gifts, 6.38 percent through bequests.
- Foundations gave 6.81 percent of the total.
- Corporations gave 4.80 percent of the total.

People are often surprised by the size of personal contributions as compared with the amounts provided by foundations and corporations. It's not that these institutions don't give large sums; it's that individuals give a lot more than we assume they do.

Here's more that may surprise you. Of contributions from individuals, about half the total amount comes from families with incomes of less than $39,000. Nine out of ten adults are regular givers, and the current average gift is a little more than 2 percent of their income. The 20 million Americans who give at least 5 percent of their income are on the cutting edge of a national movement that promotes this level of giving on the part of all Americans. The "Give Five" campaign was kicked off in 1987 by the Advertising Council and Independent Sector, a nonprofit coalition of 650 corporations, foundations, and voluntary organizations. The campaign challenges Americans to collectively double their charitable giving and increase volunteering 50 percent by 1991.

Religious organizations receive the greatest portion of donations: 46.9 percent in 1986. Education benefited to the tune of 14.6 percent, and health-related causes took 14.0 percent. Ten and a half percent went to human services, and 6.7 percent went to the arts, culture, and the humanities.

A Loss of Government Funding

Since 1980, "federal budget cuts have simultaneously left more of the burden of meeting human service needs on the nonprofit sector while reducing the important stream of revenues that nonprofit organizations receive from federal program sources."*

More specifically, between 1980 and 1987, federal spending in areas of interest to nonprofits was down a total of 10 percent (excluding Medicare and Medicaid), with a 31 percent drop in education, training, employment, and social services, and a 46 percent reduction in community and regional development. For the same period, the total reduction in direct federal support to nonprofit organizations was 26 percent (excluding Medicare and Medicaid), with a 34 percent drop in education, training, employment, and social services, a 38 percent decline in community development, and a 14 percent reduction in international assistance.

* "Nonprofit Organizations and the Fiscal Year 1988 Federal Budget," a report prepared by Lester M. Salamon of The Johns Hopkins University and Alan J. Abramson of the Urban Institute.

The idea that state and local governments would pick up the slack has thus far worked better as a concept than it has in actual practice. In the reapportioning process, many services and agencies lost funding at state and local governmental levels as well.

We've read about two dramatic examples from California of the independent sector stepping in to fill a need. In 1979, the Food Bank in Santa Clara County was 97 percent federally funded. Within four years, all that grant money had dried up. The good news is that the organization rolled up its sleeves and developed new sources of funds. By 1986, it had tripled the amount of food it handed out and was using 1,250 volunteers to distribute meals or packages of food to 63,000 people monthly.

In Fresno, in 1981, when the school system lost city and county funding for street crossing guards, 350 volunteers came forward, *saving taxpayers $250,000 annually.*

The Volunteers

According to a 1985 Gallup poll commissioned by Independent Sector, 89 million Americans fourteen years old and older (48 percent of the population) reported *volunteering an average of 3.5 hours per week,* up from 2.6 hours in 1980. Fifty-one percent of women volunteer, and 45 percent of men. The 23 million Americans who volunteer five hours per week have met the second goal of Independent Sector's "Give Five" campaign.

In 1985, volunteers contributed a total of 16.1 billion hours. The value of volunteer time given to private nonprofits was estimated at $84 billion, the equivalent of about 5 million paid employees. In terms of total employment in the sector, volunteer time represents roughly 40 percent: around 60 percent in arts and cultural organizations, 50 percent in social services, 20 percent in education, and 14 percent in health services.

THE FUTURE: PROBLEMS TO SOLVE

What Lies Ahead: Looking Toward the '90s is the 1987 report of the United Way of America's Environmental Scan Committee. In abbreviated form, here are some of the facts and trends they see as they plan for the final decade of the century:

- While the rate of erosion of the middle class will slow, greater economic growth will occur in high-income households than in low-income households.
- With almost half the mothers of children under age three in the work force, the United States is the only industrialized nation that lacks a national child care policy.
- The number of children who live in poverty will grow. In the late 1980s, one-third of the children born in the United States will spend some time living below the poverty line.
- Many children will be in crisis because of poverty, child abuse, suicide, and running away from home.
- The number of single-parent families will grow.
- As the role of caregiver becomes more complex—with many people caring for an elderly relative as well as children—services directed at the support of families will become increasingly important.
- The tragedy of homelessness will continue.
- The problem of hunger is getting worse. Approximately 20 million Americans go hungry at least two days a month.
- The dropout rate for high school students indicates a serious social problem. Presently, one out of four freshmen fails to graduate.
- The teacher shortage will increase at the primary and secondary levels and will become particularly severe in science and mathematics.
- Questions will continue to be raised about the quality of public education. Some experts feel that today's younger generation of Americans may be first to receive a lower standard of education than the generation that went before.
- Increased attention will be focused on illiteracy.
- Teenage pregnancy will remain a problem.
- The AIDS epidemic will become increasingly critical.
- The drug abuse issue will become even more visible.
- The number of legal and illegal immigrants will grow.
- Environmental issues such as indoor and outdoor air pollution, water shortages, and toxic waste will demand continuing attention.

We are not sociologists or philosophers, but it must be fair to say that the way Americans respond to these and other issues will determine the future direction and quality of our society. Do we want to live and work in cities where we encounter people in terrible trouble whenever we leave our homes or offices? Do we want to sit by as a social underclass is allowed to grow, poorly nourished, badly educated, and unmotivated? Will we allow our dance companies, theaters, and artists to abandon their creative efforts for lack of support?

You're saying, "I knew they'd get around to the part about how much there is to be done." Yes, but we still stand by the basic thesis of our book: that being involved in service work, in reaching out to improve the lives of people or the life of the community, is one of the best things you can do for yourself.

Living in an industrialized society that is threatened by serious problems and not helping to solve them has got to be one of the most demoralizing aspects of modern life. The person who thinks that seeing a half-dozen men and women begging for spare change on his way to the subway every morning doesn't affect him is very mistaken. If we assume that the plight of the poor is their own lookout, we are worse than mistaken: we are self-defeating.

Helping others and helping ourselves are just different ways of doing the same thing. Modern life has become so fragmented and compartmentalized that it is sometimes hard to see the connectedness, but when we can get past the trees to a broad view of the forest, we understand that when we help someone learn to read, enjoy an afternoon outing, experience the comfort of a hot meal and a safe place to sleep, we are also helping ourselves.

OUR HERITAGE OF SERVICE

Altruism, or attention to the welfare of others, has throughout history been tied to the welfare and growth of communities, to the advancement of civilization. While there probably have been cultures and societies that ignored the virtues we have come to call humane, it is a safe generalization that, as primordial hunting bands formed tribes and as tribes established villages, some early people indulged and formalized their impulses to care for the ill, the elderly, and orphans. They began to provide for the overall well-being of the community.

Two forms of altruism have coexisted throughout history: aid to needy individuals (the word "charity" is often used) and a more general focus on social conditions that affect society as a whole (the word "philanthropy" reflects the broader implication of this proactive orientation). During different periods, one or the other may dominate, yet they are related, almost like two sides of a coin.

An interesting historical theme is the trading off, the sharing, the flowing back and forth of charitable and philanthropic activity among various sectors of society. Another theme, especially in recent history, has been the assumption by government of many services that formerly had been provided by independent organizations.

Service in Ancient Times and the Old World

The service ethic exists far back in recorded history. In China, two thousand years before Christ, families cared for orphans and elderly widows and widowers without children. In ancient Babylonia, the Code of Hammurabi ordered justice for widows, orphans, and the poor. The ancient Egyptians provided for the disadvantaged members of society, apparently at least in part to guarantee favor with the gods.

The ancient Hebrews tithed—either in money or crops—as *tsedaka* (justice, righteousness). They espoused an ethic of mutual help that has extended through the centuries, so that today the Jewish community around the world supports an extraordinary network of humanitarian services.

To the limited extent to which it existed, Greek and Roman altruism took the form of actions to benefit the populace as a whole. Typical examples of this type of philanthropy were water storage and delivery systems, schools, theaters, public baths, parks and gardens, temples, and festivals, feasts, and games.

Christian doctrine tied together the concepts of love of God, love of self, and love of neighbor, urging people to be their brother's keepers, to follow the example of Christ and the Good Samaritan. Based on Christ's urging to minister to the needs of "the least of my brethren," emphasis fell most heavily on aid for the individual needy. In the fourth century, the church became the principal channel for charitable activity when the emperor Constantine allowed citizens to bequeath money or property to it.

During the Dark Ages, the monasteries, as they did with the traditions of learning, helped in keeping such ideals alive. Aid was given to the poor, the old, and the sick. Orphanages, almshouses, schools, and hospitals were built.

Throughout the Middle Ages, the Christian ethic of aid to the poor was uppermost, with little emphasis on social reform. As monasteries grew in number, the church, sometimes aided by lay groups, continued to sponsor foundling hospitals and institutions for the care of the indigent. Feudal lords looked out for the individual welfare of the people in their charge. Through the Crusades, a consciousness was born of the needs of the imprisoned. The growth of trade and commerce brought the medieval era to a close, and as cities grew and thinking became more liberal, citizens began to look to the needs of their neighbors.

The Reformation allowed increased freedom of association, and parishes in Germany set up "common chests" of food, clothing, and money for the needy. Throughout Europe, as the medieval church was superseded, governments or newly organized state churches stepped in to provide support for schools and hospitals. Because King Henry VIII had secularized the monasteries and convents, there was a need in England for an alternative method of caring for the poor. In 1601, Parliament enacted the Poor Law, which provided for the indigent through taxes. In various forms, this legislation lasted into the 1800s.

The Industrial Revolution brought large numbers of people together in cities and made more dramatic the plight of the urban poor. During the second half of the nineteenth century, various efforts were made to improve their health, education, and living conditions. Among the private nonprofit societies that were formed, the important Charity Organization Society, established in London in 1869, orchestrated the activities of private and public charities. Its approach was the somewhat revolutionary one of helping people to help themselves.

Service as Part of the American Ideal

Mutual help was essential for the success of the early American settlements. The colonists reached out to one another with hands willing to clear land, build houses and barns, and bring in the hay and the harvest. The women held sewing and quilting bees and annual housecleaning parties. In the absence of doctors and trained midwives, they helped each other in childbirth. Woodsmen blazed trails, and townsmen created roads. Public protection was guaranteed by freely made associations of citizens, as were many of the civic and what we would today call human service functions of society.

Perhaps because so much mutual help was required in building the new settlements, there was not much tolerance for the poor, particularly when the poverty was the result of an avoidable mistake or personal weakness. The English colonies continued the traditions begun by the Elizabethan Poor Law, although in the New World charity took the form not of almshouses but of "outdoor relief": food, clothes, and fuel. While the churches provided help, in general aid to the unfortunate was to fellow religionists. However, the Quakers in Pennsylvania and the Catholics in Maryland aided people outside their congregations.

The early colonies generally did not establish orphanages, hospitals, and asylums; the citizens provided help in other ways. The old and infirm were boarded in private homes, and the hosts were paid with tax money. Orphans and illegitimate children were apprenticed until age twenty-one. In a practice called "taking in," families took turns housing and feeding a poor person of the community.

The more philanthropic side of early American altruism is exemplified most fully in the life of Benjamin Franklin, who helped create a free lending library, the first volunteer fire department, and a plan for paving, cleaning, and lighting the streets of Philadelphia. He established America's first hospital, the Pennsylvania Hospital, the Academy of Philadelphia, later to become the University of Pennsylvania, and the American Philosophical Society.

In the spirit of mutual help, the early colonists provided each other with disaster relief. When Charleston, South Carolina, suffered a devastating fire in 1740, donations of money and materials came from as far away as Massachusetts. Similar aid arrived from neighboring towns and colonies after the great fire in Boston in 1760.

"School societies" that were created around the turn of the nineteenth century were the basis for the later public schools supported by taxes. More than 3,000 local lyceums—societies for adult education—were created in the 1820s and 1830s.

After Alexis de Tocqueville, French statesman and philosopher, traveled through the United States in 1831, he wrote:

> Americans of all ages, all conditions, and all dispositions constantly form associations. They have not only commercial and manufacturing companies, in which all take part, but associations of a thousand other kinds, religious, moral, serious, futile, general or restricted, enormous or diminutive. The Americans make associations to give entertainments, to found seminaries, to build inns, to construct churches, to diffuse books, to send missionaries to the antipodes; in this manner they found hospitals, prisons, and schools. If it is proposed to inculcate some truth or to foster some feeling by the encouragement of a great example, they form a society. Wherever at the head of some new undertaking you see the government in France, or a man of rank in England, in the United States you will be sure to find an association.
>
> I met with several kinds of associations in America of which I confess I had no previous notion; and I have often admired the extreme skill with which the inhabitants of the United States succeed in proposing a common object for the exertions of a great many men and in inducing them voluntarily to pursue it.*

As the country moved westward, the themes of mutual help and freely made associations continued, with community activities helping to maintain the momentum of the advancing settlements. Settling ungoverned and lightly governed territories often meant providing protection of people and property through vigilantism. Citizens frequently set up courts of law that had no real connection with official national law.

During the nineteenth century, life in the United States was shaped by several important events: the Civil War and the abolition of slavery; the continuing Industrial Revolution; the move away from an agrarian society to a concentration of population in cities; the birth of labor unions; the founding of many private schools and colleges; the improvement of health services; and the establishment of many voluntary social service organizations.

In New York, the Asylum for the Deaf and Dumb was founded

---

* From *Democracy in America,* by Alexis de Tocqueville. Reprinted from the edition translated by Henry Reeve and published by Alfred A. Knopf, Inc., New York, 1976.

in 1827 and the New York Institution for the Blind in 1831. In 1853, the Children's Aid Society was founded to resettle urban street children with families in the West. Cooper Union, organized in 1859 by Peter Cooper, provided educational opportunities for workingmen in New York City, offering free courses in science, chemistry, electricity, engineering, and art. During the mid-1800s, Dorothea Dix was well known here and in Europe for her work in urging more humane treatment for the mentally ill.

The United States Sanitary Commission was established in 1861. A private effort to "combat filth and disease" in Union army camps during the Civil War, it pointed the way for the organization of state departments of public health.

Some American organizations modeled themselves on European ones, three examples being the American YMCA, the Salvation Army, and the American Red Cross. Nonprofit organizations became so numerous that umbrella groups were formed. In the late 1800s, the National Conference on Social Welfare came into being, and the Charity Organization Society was founded here to coordinate the many groups and to promote "scientific charity" that would attack the causes of poverty. The Society for the Prevention of Cruelty to Animals was formed, followed by the Society for the Prevention of Cruelty to Children. Four churchmen in Denver created a united Community Campaign that later became the United Way of America; John Muir founded the Sierra Club.

Jane Addams's Hull House in Chicago was one of the most important of the settlement houses. These centers, established in low-income neighborhoods, aimed to improve the overall quality of life by providing a range of social service activities, including education, health, and recreation. Today government and the private sector have taken over various of the functions—especially kindergartens, other educational facilities, and the health clinics—formerly provided by the settlement houses, which continue to exist in some of our largest cities.

Addams was a pioneer in the growing effort to address the causes of illness and abuse, rather than merely to care for the needy. As the twentieth century dawned, there was a general trend away from asylums for orphans and abandoned children and toward adoption and foster care. Reformers attacked the system of child labor and urged educational reform and the rehabilitation of juvenile delinquents.

The early twentieth century saw the founding of many of the major American organizations directed at the cure of diseases: the National Tuberculosis Association, now the American Lung Association; the American Society for the Control of Cancer; the Association for the Prevention and Relief of Heart Disease of New York City.

By this point in American history, vast personal fortunes had been accumulated by the great men of industry. These fortunes led to the establishment of foundations, reservoirs of capital assets available for good works. One of the purposes of foundations was to guarantee a family tradition of philanthropy, and many wealthy American families have instilled a strong sense of duty in their members.

Andrew Carnegie, who made a fortune in the steel industry, undertook at age fifty-four to give away his wealth. One of his greatest works was the founding of approximately 2,800 libraries in this country and Canada. Carnegie paid for the building and outfitting, while the community was required to donate the site and maintain the library. In 1911, he established the foundation called the Carnegie Corporation.

John D. Rockefeller, who created the foundation bearing his name, began in a small way as a philanthropist. Born in 1839, he kept account books that show that in 1857 he donated $28.37 to several churches and the YMCA; a dozen years later, the amount had increased to $5,489.62. In 1889, he contributed $600,000 to the founding of the University of Chicago, plus $1 million per year for the next two years. In all, Rockefeller gave away $531 million during his lifetime.

In 1936, Henry Ford and his son Edsel created the Ford Foundation to manage their charitable giving in the Detroit area. Reorganized along national and international lines in 1950, the foundation annually donates more than $100 million to a wide variety of American and foreign cultural, human rights, educational, feminist, and development reforms.

During the Great Depression of the 1930s, the federal government undertook large measures of responsibility for the needs of the poor, the unemployed, the aged, and the ill. The first Social Security legislation was passed in 1935. As the welfare state grew, not-for-profit organizations were able to expand their reach to additional client groups and issues, and to refine their focus for more effective action.

The welfare state had a second, though temporary, resurgence during the 1960s, with President Lyndon Johnson's vision of the Great Society and his war against poverty. Medicare was established to provide free medical care to the aged under Social Security. Federal aid to education at all levels was greatly expanded. Antipoverty programs were funded by federal money. The Department of Housing and Urban Development was created. Partly because of the financial drain and the divisiveness of the Vietnam War, government's role as the answer to all social problems started to be questioned, and many human services programs begun in the 1960s were phased out for lack of funding.

Throughout the twentieth century, the social base for charitable giving and voluntarism has greatly broadened and become less elitist and more popular. The expansion began with the fund drives during the First World War, followed by university alumni fund-raising campaigns in the 1920s and the development of local community chests. Money was raised through mass appeals and the work of large groups of volunteers, such as the March of Dimes. This expansion has continued, and today groups of people, such as those with low incomes and the physically handicapped, who were once thought of as client populations are increasingly coming forward and being welcomed as volunteers.

Today human service and social welfare activities are shared by religious organizations and other not-for-profit groups, government at all levels, private business, and, as always, individuals from all walks of life—the many who give relatively small amounts and the few who return to society large parts of their fortunes.

Our Lives in Service Today

As our living conditions become more and more complicated and as population densities increase, the old traditions of individual human service, of helping another person, can become diluted. In urban areas, drivers whose cars break down generally have to look to their own resources. People just don't stop to help other people. There has been a fragmentation of the basic human instinct to help

THE PRESIDENT'S VOLUNTEER ACTION AWARDS

Created in 1982 to call public attention to the contributions of our nation's volunteers and to demonstrate what can be accomplished through voluntary action, the President's Volunteer Action Awards are cosponsored by VOLUNTEER—The National Center, a private nonprofit organization, and ACTION, the domestic federal volunteer agency. Funding for the program comes from private corporations and foundations.

For the 1987 awards, approximately 2,000 nominations were received from local, regional, and national voluntary organizations and public agencies, corporations and labor unions, civic and neighborhood groups, and fraternal organizations. Awards are made in ten categories: arts and humanities, education, environment, health, human services, international volunteering, mobilization of volunteers, public safety, youth volunteering, and the workplace.

Judges from VOLUNTEER and ACTION submit about seventy finalist nominations to the president for his final selection. Eighteen to twenty awards are given each year. The president presents the award, a sterling silver medallion, at a White House ceremony.

Winners have included established national organizations with thousands of volunteers, newly developed grass-roots movements with national scope, fraternal organizations, employee volunteer programs, local organizations and groups, individuals, and labor union volunteers. Some award winners are well known; others are known only to those with whom they work.

Several of the organizations mentioned in this book have received the award. They are the **Americares Foundation,** the **Campus Outreach Opportunity League, Mothers Against Drunk Driving**, the **Oregon Shakespearean Festival Association** (see chapter 3); and the **Corporate Angel Network, Levi Strauss & Co.,** and the **Shell Employees and Retirees Volunteerism Effort** (see chaper 6).

our fellowman. Social service organizations have stepped into this void, providing on an institutional basis what formerly was accomplished in a much more individual way.

Paradoxically, today it is often through a large and sophisticated organization or institution that people are enabled to reach one another with warmth, human kindness, and a willingness to improve each other's lives. While certainly a great many people regularly help family members, neighbors, and friends in an informal way with meals, shopping, transportation, or essential medical care, still a huge number of Americans find that an excellent way to give of themselves is through the formalized programs of the independent sector.

And although sadly many people are now directly asking for money on the streets of our cities, most financial giving is done through organized religious or not-for-profit groups, some as large as the United Way of America, which in 1987 collected $2.6 billion from individuals, corporations, small businesses, and foundations.

As we look forward to the last decade of the twentieth century, we sometimes wonder how we will cope with the problems that we already see, not to mention ones that are yet to announce themselves. In the United States, despite the many social and economic problems that we face, we are among the most fortunate people on the planet. We have a governmental system that allows great personal freedom of action and expression, and a strong and resilient economy that has developed vast resources of wealth for the country. And we have a healthy and growing independent sector.

> "Today Americans no longer look to government to answer every problem. Individuals and organizations are taking the initiative to mold the future of their communities. Volunteerism is an integral part of our national character. America is the big winner when citizens of all backgrounds willingly give their time, energies, talents, and money to better their lives and those of fellow citizens. The generosity of the American people provides a powerful vehicle for community improvement. I believe that voluntarism is crucial to our future, and that Americans are rallying to meet the challenge."
> —*Donald Hodel, U.S. Secretary of the Interior*

Nonprofit organizations in this country complement the activities of government and business, providing substantial benefits to the nation as a whole, as well as valuable personal benefits for the individuals who join in their work. Hundreds of thousands of large and small nonprofit organizations in this country have made major contributions to the evolution of our culture, and they will continue to do so. The strength and impact of that contribution, and the extent to which you will be part of the effort and the rewards, will depend partly on your awareness of the independent sector.

What we plan to do in this book is to show the beauty of the not-for-profit world, and to inspire you to take part in running it.

IN THEIR OWN WORDS

"[Businesswomen] don't have time to take care of themselves, and they don't consider being involved with service work as taking care of themselves. They are suffering from emotional and spiritual bankruptcy, an emptiness that I believe can only be filled up with relationships and causes beyond making money. Giving something away—you know, open hand, open heart—is what it is really all about."

—Tessa Warschaw

"I've had some thoughts over the years about experimenting with a career change. I feel the satisfaction of having realized more in my life than simply meeting my own personal needs. Reaching out to others has brought a deeper, richer, far more enjoyable reward than what I could have achieved by continuing to focus entirely on my business career."

—Michael Shimkin

"I hold them, mostly. I feed them. I change them. I talk to them, Hello, I call them by their names. I try to walk with them. I'm a big music person, so I like to sing to them, and I like to sort of dance with them, you know, give them some rhythm. I know that somewhere along the line this is going to make an effect on this child."

—Karen Lindauer

Tessa Warschaw: *A psychotherapist with a private practice in New York and a consultant to corporations across this country and Canada, Tessa Warschaw specializes in interpersonal negotiations. She runs seminars that teach businesspeople how to negotiate with clients, customers, and colleagues, and that show parents how to negotiate with children. She is the author of three books:* Winning by Negotiation, Rich Is Better, *and* Winning with Kids.

I grew up with the concept of service, and I don't think of it as work. I think of it as participation; that's my philosophy on it. I participate in it, I bring something unique to it—my creativity, my energy, and my desire to contribute.

Most important, however, is to find a cause that is crucial and beyond yourself. You find a lot of people, especially in the city, who are so caught up in what they will get out of it. Are they going to participate in a fund-raiser because it will be great networking? A better question to ask yourself would be: are you doing something that you love to do so that you can approach it with an open hand and an open heart? I think that is very crucial—that you find something that you love to do that goes beyond yourself.

Service work helps you in your job because you are put into an experience of absolutely working with a team. You don't do any of it alone, unless you are writing a check, and we are talking here about involvement. You're working on a team.

It has nothing to do with you except to fill up your heart—it doesn't have to do with filling up your profits. And it puts you in a position of not being in charge. I mean, I am in charge once a month of creating a meal for Meals on Wheels, but I can't do it alone, so I never actually think of myself as bossing it. I think of myself as part of the team.

I do the cooking for Meals on Wheels once a month, and I fill in when they need me. For example, I always fill in on the holidays. Even if the meals are catered, you still have to organize it, pull people together, get it packaged and wrapped. I plan and coordinate and cook the meal for between sixty-five and eighty-five homebound people.

I do it according to the season. For example, in the summertime, for those people who can't go outside, I try to bring the outside inside. I'll pack a picnic lunch and I'll put in daisies. In the fall, I will use the fall colors of leaves, that type of thing. Every season I try to add something special.

I really get excited when the food comes out great. They only give you $1 or $1.25 per person to feed the people, and I just contribute whatever is left out—whatever we need I just pay for it. So that I don't have to think, well, I can't do lamb chops, I have to do hamburgers, or I can't throw in flowers because there's no money. I just do it.

I also participate in the Madison Square Boys and Girls Club. I'm on the planning committee for their fund-raiser that is coming up in October, which is a dinner-dance, at $300 a person, which is a lot for many people. So they came up with an idea to sell dolls for Christmas. I'm going to have a sack of them here— to offer to clients and people who come into my life, and at the dinner-dance I'm going to work the booth. It has never been enough for me just being a passive contributor. I am a doer, not just a talker.

The interesting thing is that I have stopped some friendships because I know a lot of people, a lot of successful women, particularly, and they don't have time for service or a need for it. They say yes, and then they never show up. It's not that they have to do what I do. But it tells me a lot about their values and their need to contribute and their need to participate and their priorities.

I'll say to a friend of mine, listen, I'm going down to cook for Meals on Wheels and three people couldn't show up, do you want to give me a hand? She says, well, I don't have time, I'm busy. I say, okay, I'll be through about one o'clock. She says, great, I'll meet you for lunch. You hear the difference.

My advice would be to stop talking about it and do it. But test it out: you may not find that it is something in harmony for you. Find something, test it out. People think that if they get involved in something and they don't like it, they are stuck with it. They gradually withdraw, rather than to say, I tested this out and it just isn't for me.

I think that businesswomen today are overwhelmed with survival. In the major cities, the high-level professional woman is into survival, that's number one. Number two is the issue of time. As it is, they don't have time to take care of themselves, and they don't consider being involved with service work as taking care of themselves. They are suffering from emotional and spiritual bankruptcy, an emptiness that I believe can only be filled up with relationships and causes beyond making money. Giving something away—you know, open hand, open heart—is what it is really all about.

I grew up with a blue can on the sink, and I still have a blue can on the sink, for the Asthmatic Foundation, because I was a very sick child and that was an organization my mother was very involved with. So I just fill up a can and take it with me every time I go back to L.A. My deal with myself is that at the end of each day I just dump all my change, no matter how much it is, into the jar. Sometimes you have no idea what you are giving, but the point is that I know I'm doing something that's going to be helpful.

Service work has to become a priority. I think that a lot of women would be willing to do it if they could see it as a priority in their lives. You see, they are all scheduling now. They don't know what it is that's gnawing on them. Is it my job? Well, I'm already earning six figures. Is it my love life? Well, there aren't any men around. My kids are gone, so I'm not so close to them. They don't see that service contribution is a priority.

Women have to look both inward and outward. They have to look inward and say, what is it that is going on in my life, why do I feel a gnawing feeling? Women who don't go beyond themselves are so unhappy. They don't have loving relationships, they don't have friendships in their lives. It is only other people that bring you the true satisfactions of life. I believe in that whole thing about taking paper and pencil to your life—saying, what are the five most important things to me, and seeing if you are doing them.

In one of my books, I have written about three responsibilities we have, which are to optimism, to life, and to others. We really do have that responsibility, to go beyond ourselves.

If I were to choose one word that describes the time I spend in service work, it would be "joyous." It can mean cutting onions and garlic, but you really want to do it, you want it to be good.

Michael Shimkin: *Michael Shimkin spent the first part of his adult life as a publishing executive, with Simon & Schuster and with several companies that he founded. In 1978, he decided to reorder the priorities of his life, restructuring his time commitments so that he now spends 75 percent of his work week in service work and 25 percent on income-producing business.*

When I find somebody who is financially comfortable and who is working hard to be rich rather than being just comfortable, often they are not really happy doing that. They've reached their monetary goals, but they don't know how to change. They have a sense of malaise and they don't understand what it is, and they don't understand what they're not fulfilling in their lives. They respond very well when I suggest that maybe something along the lines of what I've done would fill their needs.

Nine out of ten times, people say, yeah, that's exactly what I want to do, but I don't know how to do it. There are so many things to do, how do I find the one I'm interested in. My days seem to get so busy with my business and my children and friends that I never find time to figure out for myself what I want to do.

How to do it is really a question of positive thinking. If you say to yourself when you wake up in the morning, this is the most important thing to me right now, I'm going to get this done, you're going to do it. I try to do that. Like so many people, I have fifty things on my list to do every day. But there are only a few things I can do well. If finding a new area of my life, a change of career, is paramount, I have to say, OK, I'm going to focus on that and get this whole process started.

Don't worry whether you're going to find your ultimate new career the first time out. If you sense in your heart that this is what you want to do, just follow your interests and they will take you to the right place eventually. Even if the people you work with or the distance from your house or something else becomes a problem, at least get started, get out there and try some things out.

For me, after I decided to take on voluntary service work, the first experiences were interesting, but I didn't hear that call that comes when you know you have found just what you want. But they were helpful. They made me familiar with how a not-for-profit organization works, its reason for existence, its operations and relationships. My early experiences also made me familiar with how a board of directors of a not-for-profit organization works, and how it relates to the staff director and the staff itself.

Then, after six years of experimenting, it came to me. On October 22, 1984, along with millions of other people, I saw the BBC broadcast of the Korem feeding camp in Ethiopia. I was astounded and overwhelmed by the enormity of the tragedy, about which I knew very little up to that point. I remember the feeling of simply knowing, right then and there, that this was the job I was looking for.

So I worked up a résumé and sent a letter to the executive directors of several international relief and development organizations, and then I interviewed with them, with the idea that I would match my interests and skills with the needs of these organizations.

I chose Oxfam America, located in Boston, for several reasons. They are free from external influences, such as having a parent religious organization. They do not receive U.S. government funds and are therefore free to speak out about government policy. And they had a wonderful reputation for being effective in their overseas work. Also, it was a small enough organization so that I felt I could have an impact. It felt good, so I went for it.

I've been associated with Oxfam America since November 1984. And my interest there led me to a special interest in Central America. In June of '85, I traveled with a small group to Nicaragua. We traveled in the cities and deep into the countryside, into the war zone, far into the mountainous area, where people live in very small, isolated settlements. I began to experience a very different Nicaragua than had been portrayed in the press in the U.S.

I've had some thoughts over the years about experimenting with a career change. I feel the satisfaction of having realized more in my life than simply meeting my own personal needs. Reaching out to others has brought a deeper, richer, far more enjoyable reward than what I could have achieved by continuing to focus entirely on my business career.

There have been so many benefits. For me, volunteer service has brought a marvelous education in a new and fascinating field. When I started in international development and relief work, I knew nothing about the field. To work for Oxfam as a volunteer and director was for me a straight-up learning curve. And it's very exciting and stimulating to learn again with a real intensity. It's better than going back to school, because you can do all of your learning out in the field.

My search took a long time, but it certainly was worth it.

Karen Lindauer: *Karen Lindauer, a video editor at CBS, volunteers in the boarder baby program at St. Luke's/Roosevelt Hospital on Manhattan's Upper West Side.*

I found out about the boarder baby program through my job at CBS. I'm a videotape editor, and I happened to do a story on dead-end street kids—what happens to these kids after they leave home, kids who end up on 42nd Street. We looked at them and asked, What is their future? It was scary to watch eight- or nine-year-old kids hanging out in the video arcades. We interviewed and got involved with these kids. Some of us were taking them to karate classes and buying them clothes, and we really got attached to them.

We ended up looking back and asking ourselves where they came from, and we found out that many of them were boarder babies—babies who have been taken away from their parents, many of whom are drug addicts or are not capable of taking care of them. Many of the mothers are twelve and thirteen years old. Most of them are cocaine or heroin addicts.

The boarder babies just fit in for me because of my age—the chronological time clock that was saying, "Okay, go!. . . Be with babies. . . . I want a baby, I want a baby!" I couldn't have a baby, I'm not married, so the idea of working with babies was perfect for me. When I put one baby down, there was another baby to go to, and it was just so much release for me. I was singing to them, I was talking to them. I had never held a baby in my life.

They're newborn, about a week to a month old, and, they're small because most of them are preemies. So you have to take care of them a little bit differently. They're not healthy babies.

I hold them, mostly. I feed them. I change them. I talk to them, Hello, I call them by their names. I try to walk with them. I'm a big music person, so I like to sing to them, and I like to sort of dance with them, you know, give them some rhythm. I know that somewhere along the line this is going to make an effect on this child. Of course, sadly enough, a lot of these kids are going to end up like the dead end kids, tossed around from foster family to foster family, with no roots, but I feel that it's really important because it's an initial bond.

I really love doing it. My job is not a person-to-person job, it's all technical, it's rush rush rush, and it has nothing to do with helping people, except that it's giving information to people. And so it's very exciting to work with the babies. I don't even have breakfast those days that I go down to the hospital. I just run down there, because I can't wait to do it again.

I do it on Wednesdays and Thursdays, which are my days off. And I do it between two and four hours. And, of course, I'm not getting paid, so people are so appreciative that I'm there in the first place and keep coming back. A lot of hospitals that don't have programs will not allow volunteers in because a lot of them get scared off and go away, and it's a shame, because there's something in my heart that I can't believe that people won't come back. It's so fulfilling to me as an individual doing this.

I love being a part of another group, in a hospital. I love being respected for the fact that I come weekly. And I get information about how to take care of children. I'm not doing it for a preparation for myself, I'm not doing it so that when I have a baby I'll know how to take care of it. But there was something lacking in me, in my job, and being able to release all the stuff, all the love, and all the feelings, it was just like glue. It just worked, it was the right thing for me to do.

As a result of this, I was also looking for a career change at the time, and since then, I don't need a career change, I really don't. Because it fulfills everything. What I really wanted to do was work with people. I was getting no person-to-person interaction with my job, and now, six months later, I don't need to do anything more than I'm doing, this has such a hold for me. When I have children, maybe the whole situation will be completely different, maybe I won't need to volunteer. But right now, my life needed that other half, it really did, and it worked out well.

And I guess I didn't come with a whole lot of expectations. I didn't know how big a deal this would be for me. I kind of did it on a whim. Someone suggested it, and I knew I had needs that weren't being fulfilled. It ended up working, it ended up being just what I wanted.

I saw a sign on the bus about abused children and abused families, that if you wanted information about how to volunteer to crisis intervene with families that abuse their children, send away for this information, and I've done that also. That is really something that I want to pursue, because it's a real challenge.

I've never had so much feeling in my life, and, really, it's an overflowing of love, and when you don't get that in your life you tend to really be kind of a dull person. What's nice for me is that I am becoming a woman I really admire, and just the job can't do that. I didn't want to take a painting class, or take a dance class. I just don't want to deal with filling up my basket more. I really wanted to give it back, I really wanted to give it out, and I feel so lucky that I found something.

I would never—now that I've got it all in my life—I would never take any of it away. I feel like I have got it all.

CHAPTER TWO

WORKING ON THE SIDE OF THE ANGELS

$\mathcal{M}$ANY Americans perceive that our country is experiencing, at the end of the 1980s, a crisis of values. We're writing at the end of 1987, and it has been an amazing year: insider trading on Wall Street, conflict-of-interest scandals at all levels of government, presidential candidacies rocked because of extramarital affairs or plagiarism, critics wondering whose responsibility it is to teach our children values.

In the 1980s, people stopped apologizing for "going for" as much as they could get for themselves. Among some sectors of society, incomes rose to new levels, and people went on a spending spree—on themselves, on homes, vacations, cars. The BMW generation was upon us. To one degree or another, materialism sounded its theme throughout the middle and upper-middle classes.

Yet at the end of this decade, we face massive challenges as a society. The economy is threatened by unstable financial markets and national deficits; a growing number of our citizens can't afford a place to live; 25 percent of high school students—50 percent in some inner-city districts—drop out before graduation; many environmental problems are growing more critical.

And we sense that, on a personal level, many people are wondering whether they are really happy. We seem to have reached a point, as individuals and as a nation, at which we are questioning some of the assumptions we have been living by.

We don't know what to do about the trade deficit and we're not prepared with a plan for toxic waste disposal. What we do know something about is how to put some value, some quality back into our lives, and that is through service, through reaching out to an involvement with other people and causes. *We believe in this method so strongly that we've come to think of service as working on the side of the angels.*

The great humanitarian Albert Schweitzer made a statement that captures the essence of what service work can mean in the life of an individual: "One thing I know: the only ones among you who will be truly happy are those who have sought and found how to serve."

FILLING THE GAP LEFT BY MATERIALISM

A quote from Gertrude Stein is relevant to the pursuit of happiness through materialism: "When you get there, you discover that there isn't any 'there' there."

Many young people properly feel a real sense of purpose in achieving success in business or professional life and providing for their families. As they attain goals and financial security, however, further accumulation can become an end in itself—a numbers game. As they continue to accumulate, they may not find the process as satisfying as it was in the past. That is just the time to break that pattern in favor of activities that are directed toward others and that at the same time can satisfy personal values.

We see numbers of men in their mid-forties who have made enough money so that money is no longer a goal. They're suddenly looking ahead and saying to themselves, "I really don't want to spend the rest of my life putting money in the bank. I have found that it is no longer by and of itself a fulfilling goal. I want to do something else, something more." Coming to this conclusion often leads to the change from merely making a living to dynamically building a life.

"The mere expenditure of money for things, so I am told by those who profess to know, soon palls upon one. The novelty of being able to purchase anything one wants soon passes, because what people most seek cannot be bought with money."—*John D. Rockefeller, in an essay entitled "The Difficult Art of Giving"*

Making a Life Instead of Just a Living

What we're talking about is finding ways to achieve greater inner satisfaction. Instead of being outer-directed, concerned with our wealth or reputations, we can become more inner-directed, concerned with the integrity of our attitudes and actions. Psychologists say that such a transition is the true achieving of maturity. We believe that happiness is not static, centered on comfort or material things, but a dynamic involvement in the processes of life, in which individuals exercise their abilities on behalf of a greater good.

When people make a life instead of just a living, they think about and refine their priorities, they find a new definition of success. Their goal becomes a feeling of wholeness. They tend to see the connection of their personal values and family lives with public policy on education, medical care, aid to people in trouble, environmental issues, and to act on those perceptions. They expand the small circles that revolve around themselves into larger ones that revolve around others.

Many people who are extremely busy, who honor many commitments of their time and attention, weave service into their daily activities, into their professional and family lives. And it is possible to do this without losing ground with your family or with your job. In fact, because of the considerable amount of psychic income that service provides, it is most likely to enhance your professional life as well as your relationships with your family.

The tricky thing about service is that it often blends naturally and unobtrusively into the flow of daily life. While a few large organizations stand out with well-publicized fund-raising drives and public-education campaigns, we tend to take many groups and activities for granted. They are features of community life, like the PTA, the local library, and the committee that tends the garden in the town square, or of our kids' after-school and weekend activities, like 4-H, Junior Achievement, Little League, and Camp Fire.

Even if we're aware that an activity is not-for-profit, we may not think much about it, because it is a small, local effort, one that our neighbor Jane spends a few hours on each week. We miss the fact that, at the local crisis center, Jane's sustained caring is the primary motivation for a sixteen-year-old girl who is trying to stay off drugs; that one person's tutoring one other person in a literacy program is part of a nationwide effort to stamp out illiteracy by the year 2000; that board members at local Red Cross chapters make policies and oversee budgets that ensure their readiness to provide shelter, first aid, food, and clothing to accident and disaster victims; that volunteers in hospitals often bring patients the warmth that can make long days bearable.

Each service activity is like a small stitch in a very large quilt that is worked on by many different hands. It's the kind of quilt with patterns and pictures, and borders, and lots of different colors. But the best thing about it is that people made it, close up and with care. They all know which parts they worked on, and most of them really like the way those parts look.

WHAT SERVICE DOES FOR US COLLECTIVELY

Nonprofit service may often be local and personal, so that we sometimes take it for granted, but service activities are a most important part of American life. In the first chapter, we mentioned the special role that mutual help played in the early history of the United States. Today service work performed by individual people and private organizations makes a major contribution, one that is far out of proportion to the size of the independent sector, in enhancing our public and private lives.

Collectively and individually, Americans from time to time become critical of government and business, and at any given moment it is easy to find people who can speak against one or both large sectors. We like the American system when it's working as it is designed to work, and we especially admire free enterprise when it includes components of humanity and responsibility. Yet there are moments when neither one provides the right channel for forces and energies that are trying to find expression in us.

The independent sector is an alternative, an arena in which quality and excellence can thrive largely unhindered by considerations of profit or bureaucracy. There's a special feel to "value-driven" organizations. The fact that not-for-profit activities play such a strong part in our national culture benefits our society in a number of related ways.

Fostering Innovation

Ideas that are controversial, unpopular, or just plain unfamiliar often have little chance of prospering in the commercial or political marketplaces. The independent sector is a wonderful seedbed, a testing ground for new notions of all kinds. In the past, private initiative has pioneered creative approaches to individual and societal needs, in education, care for the mentally ill, and material support for the needy. Today innovation remains a primary hallmark of the not-for-profit world.

Volunteers for Medical Engineering (VME), founded in 1981, is a Baltimore-based volunteer organization devoted to aiding the handicapped and furthering medical science. More than 200 highly skilled engineers, technicians, and other professionals from the defense industry are members.

One paralyzed VME client is an avid small-stakes poker player. When he is ready to put his cards on the table, he twitches a muscle in his shoulder, and an EKG patch on the shoulder sends a signal that activates a tiny electric motor attached to a flexible brace on his right hand. This mechanism allows him to open and close the fingers of his hand—something he had not been able to do since a spinal cord injury in 1977. Another six-person VME team is working on a microwave probe for treatment of inoperable brain tumors that would literally "cook" a malignant tumor by microwave irradiation. In yet another project, VME volunteers taught two teenaged brothers with muscular dystrophy to do computer-aided drafting on a specially equipped terminal at home. The two are now employed turning out isometric drawings for a local firm.

The work of these professionals—*performed during their off-duty time and for no pay*—has had such an impact in the Baltimore area that VME is viewed as a prototype for similar high-tech volunteer groups nationwide. Says founder John Staehlin, "The ability to help people is here in this industry. I mean, it's here in spades. The question is not whether this effort is going to grow, but how it's going to grow."

Innovation of another kind shines through the work of Chicagoan Jesse White, Jr., a grade school physical education teacher who in 1959 created the **Jesse White Tumbling Team**. A total of 625 young men from ghetto neighborhoods have been members, abiding by rules that forbid smoking, drinking, drugs, gang membership, and skipping school.

The **Institute of Equestrian Therapy** in Simi Valley, California, provides horseback riding for mentally and physically handicapped people. Riding builds muscle strength, balance, and coordination, and increases joint mobility and perceptual skills while challenging students in a new and exciting way.

The mother of one young client writes:

> At age thirteen, my son was hit by a truck. He was in a coma for six months with the right side of his skull crushed, the optic nerve severed, and his whole right side paralyzed. For two years he went through many kinds of therapy, but he was still confined to a wheelchair. Still hoping that Jimmy could improve further I signed him up at the Institute for Equestrian Therapy. A few months later Jimmy was sitting upright and riding a horse. He then began to walk with a large quad cane. Before that he couldn't seem to build up the muscles to walk again and his balance was so bad. Now, after two years of therapeutic riding, Jimmy is walking without a cane and his right hand has started moving again.

Second Harvest is a private, nonprofit, nationwide network of food banks that has been feeding America's needy since 1979. In 1986, thousands of food companies donated 352 million pounds of food and grocery products—everything from fruit juice and fish to poultry and pasta. Because of surpluses or errors in production, this perfectly edible food would never have reached the supermarket shelves. Second Harvest lessens this waste by giving food companies a convenient, reliable way to channel surplus food to hungry people. Chapter 6, "Corporate Servant Leaders," gives fuller information about this excellent program.

Second Harvest has created a flow chart, "Who Benefits," from its work. The final element in the chart nicely illustrates a practical, economic aspect of our book's central idea: "Studies have shown that hunger and malnutrition affect our long-term health and productivity and increase the risk of serious illness. We all pay the price of hunger, as economic and social costs for treating malnutrition, chronic illness, unemployment, and low productivity, rise. Thus, we all benefit when fewer people are hungry."

Rapid and radical change is a palpable force in the twentieth-century world, where innovation has become a necessity. We must create many new ways of answering the awesome challenges we face. The independent sector is an important source of new ideas and projects of all kinds.

Safeguarding Alternative Points of View

Ours is a social culture, one that believes in and relies on the participation of individual people and their points of view. The diversity and freedom of the independent sector make it an arena where the values of widely divergent groups can find expression, grow in strength, and be preserved.

> "The extent to which, in any society, Third Sector organizations are free and healthy is probably as good a measure as any of how far that society can be called free."—*James Douglas,* Why Charity? The Case for a Third Sector

Religious freedom is one of the basic tenets of American society, and groups organized around spiritual expression constitute the largest subsector of the not-for-profit world. In addition to raising monies for religious activities, the work of a great many contemporary churches, synagogues, mosques, and other religious groups entails, to one degree or another, work in service—focused either

HOW SECOND HARVEST WORKS . . . WHO BENEFITS

Food companies have worked in partnership with the Second Harvest network to develop specific guidelines for the storage and handling of food. Second Harvest's member food banks and affiliates must meet these standards, and food companies are assured that their donations will be handled promptly and safely.

Second Harvest coordinates the nationwide distribution of donated food. From its Chicago headquarters, Second Harvest receives products from around the U.S. and distributes them to its food banks as efficiently as possible.

Second Harvest provides more than donated food to its member food banks. Conferences and workshops, training materials, computerized inventory systems, and other kinds of technical assistance are made available to food banks through the Second Harvest network.

Soup kitchens, food pantries, shelters, day-care programs, senior centers, and other groups know that food from Second Harvest member food banks has been "handled with care," and is safe for use in their feeding programs. Food from Second Harvest helps local charities stretch their limited budgets to buy equipment, expand programs, or even distribute a wider variety of food.

Children, the elderly, families, the unemployed, or the homeless: Second Harvest food is made available to people in every part of the United States, people whose only common denominator is hunger.

Studies have shown that hunger and malnutrition affect our long-term health and productivity and increase the risk of serious illness. **We all pay the price of hunger,** as economic and social costs for treating malnutrition, chronic illness, unemployment, and low productivity, rise. **Thus, we all benefit when fewer people are hungry.**

on their own membership or extended outward to other people and causes in this country and abroad. Some outreach efforts are actively missionary; others retain a spiritual flavor but do not seek to convert. Others put aside particular beliefs in favor of an ecumenical attitude, sometimes even one that ignores considerations of religion.

Another vast number of not-for-profit groups exist in advocacy of political points of view. All kinds of minority issues find sponsorship in organizations that span the spectrum from right- to left-wing politics. They take as their constituency one city block or hundreds of thousands of like-minded citizens across the country. These groups may never get candidates or issues on the ballot, but their members can send lobbyists to work on legislators, submit letters to newspaper editors, or stand on street corners and hand out leaflets. Such organizations can become potent forces in their communities, and they exist as available vehicles for expression as events shape changing menus of issues.

Feedback from organizations that exist outside the social and political mainstreams provides a valuable check on the activities of government and business. Nonprofits that safeguard the civil rights of particular groups, that work in protection of the environment, or that champion the cause of the consumer are the watchdogs of our society.

The very numbers of independent groups and their diversity have a beneficial effect on the American way of life. They spread our creative energies throughout a variety of organizations, working against excessive centralization of resources and helping to counteract the monolithic tendencies present in any society as large as ours.

At the same time that the hundreds of thousands of nonprofits encourage differentiation, they also provide a variety of mechanisms for bringing people together. Volunteers from all races and economic levels find themselves working elbow to elbow on projects of common concern. The generation gap is narrowed when the old and the young help each other with instruction, understanding, therapy. Involvement based on people helping people breaks the isolation of the suburban and urban ghettos, helping to clarify the distorted perceptions that come with unfamiliarity.

Nurturing the Creative and Historical Impulses

Works of art—painting, sculpture, music, dance, theater—provide windows into the minds of artists and stimulate new ways of thinking and feeling for all of us. They are vehicles of liberation for the human spirit. Museums and libraries preserve these expressions, as well as housing the vast amount of factual information that has been amassed since man began leaving records of himself and his thoughts and investigations.

While some art galleries and large theaters turn a profit, or at least attempt to, the majority of organizations, especially local and fledgling ones, depend on loyal contributors and volunteers to stay alive. Besides the activity of established, ongoing groups, every year hundreds of thousands of local art exhibitions, musical performances, and dance recitals are mounted, based on one-time grants and the efforts of dedicated volunteers. Some local libraries and museums are partially supported by tax dollars or by government grants, yet a great many rely on donations that range from the grass-roots $10 and $15 level to heftier gifts by the wealthy, buttressed by the cumulative hours of armies of volunteers.

Here's a quick sampler of how a few not-for-profit cultural ventures are supported:

- **The National Trust for Historic Preservation,** which has recorded 250,000 buildings in its National Register of Historic Places, received contributions in 1984 from a great variety of sources, among them the Travelers Companies, which provided $1 million in support of mortgages for rehabilitated urban housing; Yankee Publishing, Inc., which gave $300,000 to fund trust interns in New England; Marion duPont Scott, who bequeathed Montpelier, James Madison's home; and the 140,000 individual and 800 organizational members of the trust.
- **AT&T** has taken a leading role in sponsoring Hispanic art, underwriting large exhibits of contemporary work that tour many U.S. museums.
- The **Aid Association for Lutherans** has given more than $200,000 to develop a "full curriculum of high school music instruction to help high school musicians improve their artistry."
- **Business Volunteers for the Arts** (BVA), located in New York City, is a national program operating in more than twenty cities. BVA recruits

and trains corporate executives as arts management consultants and then places them on a pro bono basis with nonprofit arts organizations.

· During two years in the mid-1970s, residents of Cedar Mill township, Oregon (population 5,000), built a library that holds 28,000 books. It runs on the energy of some sixty volunteers who together give between 800 and 900 hours of service each month.

· Arizona Remembers, a series of two-minute reminiscences by old-timers, has been taped by volunteers from the **Arizona Historical Society** and the **Junior League** of Tucson.

The long and firmly established tradition of not-for-profit activity in our society means that cultural organizations can tap into the willingness of people to volunteer and can ask with hopefulness for donations of money and material. We can't imagine the lack of color and the barrenness of a world in which art had to be entirely self-supporting and in which students had to pay for access to the accumulated wisdom of our ancestors.

A Humanizing Force

Service work lets people care and be cared for in ways that allow their humanity and their individuality to be reflected and respected. We said earlier that quality is represented in the independent sector, and nowhere is that statement more true than in the ways that many service organizations humanize situations that would otherwise be merely mechanically efficient or practical.

In New York City's Harlem, Clara Hale, her daughter Lorraine, and other volunteers nurse drug-addicted infants back to health at **Hale House,** in a program with the goal of reuniting the children and their families. Since 1969, Hale House has rescued more than 600 children, whose mothers are encouraged to enter a drug rehabilitation program and visit their children at the House once a week. Only fourteen children have had to be placed in preadoptive homes instead of returning to their mother or relatives. The Hale House Cradle, for children who've tested positive for the AIDS virus, opened in the fall of 1987.

Near Richmond, Virginia, for several years a group of vets has arrived on Sunday mornings at the local Veterans Administration medical center to help patients get to the chapel and to attend services with them. In New York City, a group of Metropolitan Life retirees goes one night a week to the **Dwelling Place,** a soup kitchen and residence for homeless women, where they help to prepare and serve the meal in a quiet, dignified setting, giving the women the opportunity to rest, relax, and be served.

As part of a program at the **Seattle Public Library,** volunteers visit local nursing homes once a week and read to the residents. They get training, suggestions, and support from the library's program directors but have the freedom to choose material themselves, with an ear to the particular interests of their audience. A blind and retarded man who lives in a home run by New York's **Jewish Guild for the Blind** is joined for an outing every Saturday morning by a thirty-eight-year-old woman who works as an administrative assistant for an accounting firm. They walk, talk, eat ice cream, and write postcards to his favorite disc jockey.

In the California town of Cambria, a group called **Cambria's Anonymous Neighbors** is made up of seventy-five volunteers who do temporary light housekeeping, provide food, and respond to household crises. Their work has meant that about twenty elderly citizens have been able to remain in their homes rather than be institutionalized.

For a doctor from Venezuela, an engineer from Malaysia, or a graduate student from China, New York City can be overwhelming. The nonprofit **International Center** assists recently arrived foreigners in adjusting to the fast pace and complexity of city life. Volunteers participate in programs that include teaching English, finding housing and jobs, visiting local homes for evenings and weekends, sightseeing, and attending cultural events.

Pet-assisted Therapy is a program in which puppies, kittens, and rabbits, along with volunteers from New York's **American Society for the Prevention of Cruelty to Animals,** visit residents of nursing homes, hospitals, and other institutions. Residents hold the animals and receive personal attention from both the animals and volunteers. The unconditional love offered by an animal can help restore feelings of self-worth and alleviate boredom and depression. Withdrawn patients often come alive and communicate during pet therapy visits. Administrators have reported that the animals are the best tonic in the world.

Erase the cumulative hours given by these volunteers and you remove a meaningful measure of joy and hopefulness from the lives of not only the recipients but also the people who visit, help, or perhaps just talk.

Providing the Flexibility to Respond to Emergencies

Within the independent sector lie the resources—either already established or latent—for responding to newly emerging needs. Disasters do not keep business hours, and no one is immune from the onslaught of destructive weather, accidents, or fire. During the 1970s, the **American Red Cross** responded to an annual average of 30,000 disasters at a total cost of nearly $300 million. In the 1980s, this response average increased to 40,000 annually. While the Red Cross served at many headline disaster scenes involving major floods, hurricanes, tornadoes, volcanoes, and chemical and nuclear accidents, most relief action involved assisting victims of fires, transportation accidents, and other local events.

Special needs occur periodically, and because of our tradition of independent, private initiative, Americans have typically mounted campaigns against threats to our well-being or the well-being of others. Many of us remember the work of the **March of Dimes** in the 1930s and 1940s in helping to eliminate polio. During the early days of the AIDS epidemic, the **Gay Men's Health Crisis** was born in New York City, and it is today a major force in organizing and educating heterosexual and homosexual men and women against this disease.

The massive relief campaigns such as Live Aid, Farm Aid, Comic Relief, and others are possible because Americans have the habit of responding by joining together in common cause and giving of themselves and their resources.

Allowing Escape from Hopelessness and Alienation

Whether it's fighting a killer disease, seeking outlets for creative expression, giving and getting job training, or any other activity that carries meaning for an individual or group, the independent sector provides an arena for the positive application of energies.

Rather than turning inward in depression and self-destructiveness, people can take affirmative steps for their own self-improvement as well as bettering the lives of others.

THE NEW FUND-RAISING

On July 13, 1985, a sixteen-hour live musical marathon—the biggest single event in rock history—was seen by an estimated 1.5 billion television viewers in 169 countries, in addition to 90,000 audience members at John F. Kennedy Stadium in Philadelphia and 72,000 in Wembley Stadium in London. **Live Aid,** run by the organization called Band Aid, presented performances by 180 pop musicians, including David Bowie, Elvis Costello, Phil Collins, Bob Dylan, Mick Jagger, Lionel Richie, Sting, and Tina Turner, and testimonials from world figures such as Bishop Desmond Tutu, Coretta Scott King, and Linus Pauling.

The response was tremendous. Up to 22,000 pledge calls were attempted every five minutes during the last hours of the JFK concert, and Live Aid took in more than $110 million in donations for the Band Aid Trust and its African famine-relief efforts. By the fall of 1987, the trust had received $185 million in donations, including money generated by the concert and other projects, such as the musical collaboration "We Are the World."

Yet, from one perspective, money is secondary to the attention and momentum created by this global effort and other national campaigns, such as **Comic Relief** and **Farm Aid.** The raising of consciousnesses—of the celebrities involved and the public at large—may be more meaningful for the future of relief efforts. The problems of hunger and homelessness are ongoing, and easing them will require the sustained attention of large numbers of people. Broadcasts of such massive relief campaigns can be very helpful in making the service ethic an established part of our national culture.

Focus: HOPE is a Detroit-area civil and human rights organization founded in 1968. One of its major programs, Food for Seniors, involves 170 cooperating agencies (clinics, community action agencies, churches, and volunteer organizations) in identifying and enrolling the isolated and the most needy people. The program provides a monthly supply of U.S. Department of Agriculture commodity foods to more than 29,000 low-income seniors in three counties.

Many industries have closed or abandoned major work areas in Detroit. Since 1982, Focus: HOPE, supported by individuals, corporations, and foundations, has rehabilitated more than 600,000 square feet of industrial property, has negotiated more than $6 million in grants from the federal government, and has trained and employed more than 1,000 people. The organization runs the Machinist Training Institute, which annually trains 300 unemployed and underemployed men and women to be machinists and helps them find good jobs. People in the program receive eight months' free training in precision machining and metalwork, taught by master craftsmen.

We read recently about a forty-year-old Brooklyn man who had turned his life around. After quitting drugs and alcohol, he settled into a steady job and decided to do something he had gotten through life without: learning to read and write. "I always really wanted to learn," he said, "but I was drilled with low self-esteem all my life, the idea that I was just a misfit from the neighborhood who could never really do anything. But now, I'm a different person." After some time in a program sponsored by the local library system, he wrote the following brief composition: "Learning to read and write is a new way of life for me. Today there are people in my life that not only care about me, but I care about them."

In New York City's East Harlem, the **Youth Action Program** was founded in 1978 by Dorothy Stoneman. Here is her assessment of the people the agency serves:

> Young people are filled with good ideas, energy, and a sharp perception about the realities of their immediate environment. They care deeply about the pain their families and friends have undergone. When they are properly supported by adults, they swiftly become a powerful force for good. When they are ignored, insulted, deprived of respect and their intelligence demeaned, directly or indirectly, they drift aimlessly or react angrily. It's just about that simple.

Several Youth Action Program projects have gained widespread acclaim as unusual examples of young people and adults taking action together.

Actions that empower people and causes may be in behalf of one person or a hundred thousand. However such efforts manifest themselves, a viable independent sector is an invaluable source for the restoration of health to people and groups in need.

This aspect of service work leads us naturally to the following section—on the benefits that the independent sector brings to individual volunteers. Many Americans are sensitive in an emotional way to the hard circumstances of their fellowmen. Others object in principle to the way human and societal needs sometimes fall through the cracks of our dynamic and wealthy society. Others feel rewarded by helping in some way to make all our lives richer through the arts or more meaningful through our churches.

We like the words that John Gardner wrote in his book *The Recovery of Confidence:* "There is a well-tested way out of the dizzying atmosphere of talk and emotion, and that is to put one foot doggedly after another in some concrete, practical activity."

WHAT'S IN IT FOR YOU?

For the individual who is involved in voluntary service, *the rewards are extraordinary.* Conventional wisdom in the nonprofit world suggests that we should give until it feels good. We know that our work with Outward Bound often gives us goose bumps! It makes us laugh and it makes us cry. It makes us feel good. If you think carefully about yourself and choose an organization and activity to which you relate meaningfully, you are very likely to have a truly liberating and energizing experience, one from which you will benefit in many ways.

Because service work is a chance to give the best of yourself, most of the benefits are psychological—we call it psychic income—but working in behalf of other people or a cause can also result in visible, tangible improvements in your life.

"There is surely no single reason that Americans decide they want to become Peace Corps volunteers. There has always been a mixture of motives, fusing idealism and practicality. It seems fair to say that a good Volunteer must have this combination. It is hard to imagine a successful volunteer who is totally visionary, any more than one who is completely self-serving. In the early 1960s, idealism seemed to be the key, reflecting the mood of the Kennedy years. Recruitment emphasized service over technical skills. In fact, the Peace Corps has from the beginning been quite successful in imparting to generalists in its training programs the basic technical skills needed to provide useful service. On the whole, volunteers have responded ingeniously in adapting the skills taught in training to the needs of the communities in which they have served. Thus, from the start, the Peace Corps felt confident in adhering to the principle that a volunteer's most important attribute was commitment.

"Nonetheless, by the beginning of the 1970s, there was a shift in the design of Peace Corps programming, which led to a heavier emphasis on technical skills in the recruitment of volunteers. The Peace Corps began to think of itself as a more conventional development agency and shifted away from volunteers with capacities for improvisation to accommodate volunteers with existing technical training. This, as it turned out, was probably the least successful era in the Peace Corps' history.

"The end of the 1970s saw a shift back to an interest in generalists, and in volunteers with high levels of motivation who could be trained in the field. At the same time, the host countries of the Third World—a little older now, and with citizens of their own with advanced levels of training—were requesting volunteers with greater specialization, particularly in the areas of mathematics, science, forestry, engineering, and agriculture. The result, relative to earlier periods, has been an effort to recruit volunteers with "practical idealism," a combination of generalist background with some technical specialty, but more important, an ability to acquire the needed technical skills in the three months of training without ever losing the desire to make a difference. As it happens, the Peace Corps does not seem to have difficulty recruiting volunteers with these attributes."—from *Making a Difference: The Peace Corps at Twenty-Five*, edited by Milton Viorst (1986)

"The essence of voluntarism is not giving part of a surplus one doesn't need, but giving part of one's self. Such giving is more than a duty of the heart, but a way people help themselves by satisfying the deeper spiritual needs that represent the best in all of us."— *Kathleen Kennedy Townsend, "Americans and the Cause of Voluntarism,"* *in* The Washington Monthly, *October 1983*

The Freedom of Choice

We live in a society with an extraordinary degree of personal freedom. Nevertheless we can sometimes feel controlled, forced to respond to a bottom line that screams for attention at our job, or to the needs of our families, or to zoning laws that won't let us build the kind of addition to the house that we really want. Perhaps we feel compelled to remain in a job or profession we don't really like; maybe we socialize with people whose values we don't truly share. We find ourselves routinely making compromises and modifying our convictions.

In the independent sector, people choose the cause, the particular group, the type of activity that suits them. They opt for a structured or an ad hoc type of organization or environment. They decide whether to work one-on-one with another person or to get involved in policy-making or raising money. They can become a member of a team or work individually. They can make a variety of time commitments: once a month, two hours three times a week, intensive projects four weekends out of the year. If they like the work, they stay and perhaps become more deeply involved. If not, or if they change or the organization changes, then they leave, hopefully to try again for a better fit with another group.

We don't want to convey the impression that volunteers new to a service organization can dictate their roles and levels of responsibility. The point is that because service work is based on freely given time and energies, volunteers are given much more latitude than are paid employees in the business and public sectors. Volunteers as a rule are screened in a very general way, in terms of their basic interests, skills, and personalities. But if an accountant wants to try his hand at publicity, that's what he'll be able to do. Service work can give us an expanded view of our abilities and can lead to ideas for new careers.

Involvement in service, including the way you direct monetary contributions, is primarily controlled by you. The flip-side benefit to the organization is that it receives energies that you deliver at full throttle and out of dedication.

"The tragedy of life is not death; the tragedy is to die with commitments undefined, with convictions undeclared, and with service unfulfilled." —*Ernest L. Boyer, president of the Carnegie Foundation for the Advancement of Teaching, in a commencement address at Nazareth College, May 1987*

Generally speaking, people in not-for-profit work say what they think and act directly from their convictions. Organizationally, nonprofits must channel and persuade rather than direct or order, as is more readily done in business or the professions. It's not always easy to make decisions or achieve unanimous agreement out of diversity. However, this variety can result in a lot more personal satisfaction and can bring real vitality to an organization, provided that the group evolves ways of capturing and channeling the dynamic energy that is available.

Some people forgo group involvement to act individually on personal conviction or impulse. Working out of Hickory, North Carolina, Charles Keyes, known as the Parson of the Hills, for more than fifty years has carried on a nondenominational ministry, donating toys and clothing to needy children in five states.

Although businessman Eugene Lang is deeply involved in educational philanthropy, he acted on impulse in 1981 when, at a graduation ceremony, he spontaneously offered to pay for the college educations of sixty-one sixth-graders in New York City's East Harlem. Lang subsequently established the **I Have a Dream Foundation** to advise and support other individuals and groups around the country who want to offer college educations to disad-vantaged sixth-graders. By the spring of 1988, more than 100 programs had been created, providing scholarships for more than 5,000 students and programs to help them with their work and to keep them personally motivated. Eugene Lang speaks about his service work in his own words following this chapter.

Two investment bankers, Thomas Anderson and Denis Cole-man, after seeing the success of the Tita Dam project in the African country of Burkina Faso, pledged to raise $1.5 million over five years for long-range development projects for the village of Men-aka in Mali, where people were starving because of drought and deforestation.

Service work—whether an individual project or a group effort, whether on a project-by-project or an ongoing basis—offers the volunteer a unique freedom of choice and expression, an oppor-tunity to project ideals and privately held values that may not otherwise be called into play.

Making a Difference and Empowerment

Service and empowerment seem to exist in a dynamic interrela-tionship; they appear to feed off one another. Outward Bound courses generally include a service project, placed at a point when the students have been empowered by breaking through a series of challenges. When they feel good enough about themselves, they are further challenged with the service project to share with others some of that good feeling about themselves. The generally success-ful results confirm our belief: when empowered, people feel the impulse to serve; when they serve, they feel an empowering surge of self-confidence.

Service work is based on the deep personal values and freely given energies of the volunteer. As a result, when we perform works of service, we feel a sense of making a difference, of doing something significant. And, just as physical exercise builds bodily muscle and coordination, the exercise of our values helps us incor-porate them into our daily lives. Service can put us in touch with the extremely strong forces connected with ideals, can literally give us the power of our convictions.

A difference is often made not by money but by the simple act of people caring for other people. In the **I Have a Dream** programs, it seems that the money to be paid for education six or seven years in the future is not the kids' primary motivation. It is the involvement of an adult who cares, the process of being shepherded through junior high and high school, a mentor to keep them from dropping out by providing support for their academic efforts and their personal well-being.

As someone involved in service work on any day, you may feel you have made a difference when you've run a meeting well, when a policy has finally been hammered out to the satisfaction of all board members, when you've had a good conversation with an elderly friend, or when you've made a sick child laugh. Over a period of time, you will know that your local library can remain open two nights a week because of money you raised or that the throw-away kid you have been tutoring has decided to become a vet. Sooner than you think, the voice that asks "What does it all mean?" will have been silenced.

We get the sense that many people today don't like themselves very much. Working in the service of people or a cause can show you a previously unexercised part of yourself. It can make you see yourself more clearly, and it can make you like yourself better. In reaching out, you can gain self-respect and discover that you are a good person. Service can bring you courage, a sense of inner power that you've never experienced before.

> "The most troublesome consequence of self-preoccupation is boredom, and the cure for boredom is not diversion: it is to find some work to do, something to care about."—*John Gardner,* The Recovery of Confidence

John: *Service work is a tremendous source of renewed energy, a process in which people tap into their vitality by doing things they really enjoy or believe in. Becoming president of Outward Bound was a real turning point for me. I had been in the same corporate group for ten years and was running on four cylinders without really knowing it. When I took on the new job, I found myself tremendously energized. Involved in something I really believed in, I became much more productive, engaged for a large part of every day in substantive work resulting in action.*

In the morning, I hit the ground running, and my life is enriched by working with others who are dedicated to expanding the horizons of students served by Outward Bound. Along with hard work and a dash of frustration, which is probably inherent in nonprofit organizations, there is so much joy, satisfaction, and the chance to make a difference.

Anyone in service work—board members, committee chairs, fund-raisers, direct service providers—can tap into their most vital energies through participation in the kind of activity that is right for them.

Personal Growth

Service work can be exciting. It can mean pushing yourself to new levels of accomplishment, taking risks, meeting new people, building new bridges, stepping onto new paths, trying something that is a bit different. People often make use of volunteer work when they want to explore untried aspects of themselves.

Ellie: *The independent sector is a place where you can test and stretch your abilities. Being president of the British-American Chamber of Commerce changed my life. It taught me a lot about British culture, it provided me with a crash course on finance, I learned a tremendous amount about people, and it gave me invaluable insights into leadership. During those two heady years, I met with many of Margaret Thatcher's cabinet and with Washington officials like Secretary of Labor William Brock. I dealt with the heads of leading corporations and attended black-tie dinners where I was the only woman. I learned to be comfortable speaking in public.*

It was extremely important for me to learn when to speak up and when to keep silent. There were times when I knew I was over my head, and I just held my nose and closed my eyes and prayed that it would all go well. And there were other times when I felt very confident. In one sense, it was a risky undertaking, in which I might have failed. On balance, I think I made many positive contributions, along with some mistakes, but I most certainly walked away from the experience with a heightened sense of my capabilities.

In a similar way, my involvement with Outward Bound has enlarged my ability to take charge of my life. It showed me that I was more than I knew and taught me to dig down deep within myself. This ability has given both John and me strength in our marriage and in our work lives.

Service can illuminate a new path, a new direction for your life. It makes you less self-conscious, and in the process parts of yourself emerge that you may have unintentionally kept submerged. Consider these aspects of service:

· Service helps break rigid patterns of relating and teaches new ways of give and take with other people. Volunteers consistently report improved friendships and better relationships within their families.
· Service activities can put us in touch with parts of ourselves we may have ignored. Someone who has always had a quiet personality may find that he has qualities of leadership. A successful, high-powered entrepreneur may discover that she enjoys bringing her emotional side into play.
· A service project can help us through or out of a period of personal difficulty: losing a job, a divorce, the death of a family member or friend. It can ease transitions of all kinds: changing careers, children leaving the nest, retirement, moving to a new town.

Service is personally liberating. It helps to break the constricting cycle of self-absorption. Our friend Carol Noyes, a longtime worker for nonprofit causes, puts it this way: "It certainly is a way of getting outside of one's own selfish considerations, and the more you do it, the more you realize how lucky you are." We firmly believe that if everybody threw their problems into a pile in the middle of a room, you'd grab your own back in a minute. Working for and with others is the best way we know to put our lives and our problems into perspective.

A student volunteer from a New York City private school made the following statement after working with the homeless: "You know how you open a big refrigerator and it's filled with food, and you say, oh, there's nothing to eat here? I never do that anymore."

A Way to Help

In the 1985 Gallup poll commissioned by **Independent Sector,** 52 percent of the respondents reported that the desire to do something useful to help others was a major reason for their becoming involved in volunteering. The world of service provides endless

opportunities for people who want to "give back," to return something to society for what it has done for them. Diana Cecil, a
magazine advertising representative, is a volunteer for the **Fresh
Air Fund** in New York City. For several summers when she was a
child, that program allowed her to spend two weeks with a family
in upstate New York, where she developed a love for the outdoors
and an affinity for sports that otherwise she might never have
known. Dr. Arthur Berken, the son of a taxi driver, got through
medical school on scholarships and feels he has something to "pay
back" to society. Today he is one of seven physicians at Mid-Island
Internal Medicine in Bethpage, Long Island, who work one day a
week without pay.

Service can be a way to confront a problem you have experienced
either personally, in your family, or through a friend. Bette-Ann
Gwathmey created a foundation to endow a laboratory for medical
research after her son died of cancer. Sylvia Lawrey founded the
National Multiple Sclerosis Society when her brother was diag-
nosed with the disease. One reason Ted Yamamori works with
Food for the Hungry is that as a child in Japan at the close of the
Second World War he was close to death from extreme malnutrition. Norma Phillips, president of **Mothers Against Drunk Driving,** joined the organization when her son Dean and his girlfriend
were killed by a drunk driver.

We read an article recently by a man who was cured of Hodg-
kin's disease fifteen years ago. He didn't know what to call the
dominating urge he felt to establish an income source that would
provide money for charity. When he had successfully completed a
real estate project that would generate $25,000 a year, he men-
tioned it to a Jewish friend who had escaped the Nazis in Europe in
the 1930s. She gave his urge a name: survivor's debt.

Other people want to help, not in direct response to something
that happened to them, but because they feel they have enough
and can give something to others. They feel lucky, fortunate,
blessed—sometimes even though they have troubles in their own
lives. They make a good living, or a modest one; they are healthy,
or reasonably so; they have solid families and enriching friendships, or at least enough of these kinds of sustenance to keep them
going. They choose a cause and find the time to direct some energy
to helping others.

A STORY OF SERVICE TO A GROUP OF SPECIAL MEN

Robert Rheault, a West Point career Army officer, commanded the Special Forces in Vietnam in the late 1960s. A full colonel, he came back to the United States and resigned his commission due to policy differences with the Army high command. At that stage in his life, he decided he wanted to give something back to society.

Bob went to work as a staff member of the Hurricane Island Outward Bound School. As the years passed, he felt that a wilderness challenge experience such as Outward Bound could help Vietnam combat veterans suffering from post–traumatic stress disorder (PTSD). There were tens of thousands of those vets out there— suffering flashbacks, unable to sustain relationships, hold a job, stay married, or handle alcohol or drugs. Bob wanted to help those walking wounded.

He started a one-man crusade. Working with the doctors at the Northampton (Massachusetts) Veterans Hospital, he took the hardest cases out into the wilderness for five days at a time. Backpacking, rock-climbing, rappelling, going through rope obstacle courses high in the trees, these men confronted fear again, shared challenges, and supported each other. They began to talk about their feelings. Within a few days, this program was getting at buried emotions that years of group therapy hadn't reached.

Backed by the Northampton doctors, Bob went to Washington to seek the support of the Veterans Administration. Up to this point, Bob had been raising money to live on and delivering the program for free. He wanted to see the VA recognize and adopt the program for implementation in many VA hospitals across the country. It is estimated that 200,000 to 300,000 vets suffer from PTSD.

Over a period of several years, Bob raised money from the private sector to run the program, while continuing efforts to have the VA integrate and fund the program. The effort continues and programs are being conducted out of the Northampton and Tacoma (Washington) VA hospitals.

Bob Rheault is winning his fight to help men whom many forgot. He does it because he wants to make a difference. Once highly trained to make war, he now is helping rebuild lives shattered by battle.

Many celebrities lend their names and faces—and contribute money and often long hours of dedicated work—to nonprofit causes. Country singer Willie Nelson has said of his involvement with **Farm Aid,** "I know what it's like to feel down, and once I realized how bad the farm crisis was, I had to help."

Elizabeth Taylor's efforts on behalf of the **American Foundation for AIDS Research** have helped to make other famous people more willing to raise money to stop that disease. Helen Hayes is a spokeswoman for **Meals on Wheels.** Bill Cosby works with **Outward Bound.** Mary Tyler Moore represents the **Juvenile Diabetes Foundation.** Sally Struthers travels for the **Christian Children's Fund.** Emma Sams founded the **Starlight Foundation** to grant wishes to sick and dying children. Victoria Principal speaks for the **Arthritis Foundation.** Paul Newman created a food company, Newman's Own, that makes and sells popcorn, salad dressing, and spaghetti sauce, with all profits going to charity.

Sports figures are among the celebrities most active in the cause of service. Outfielder Dave Winfield established a foundation that for years has sponsored health clinics in the New York area, as well as awarding scholarships to needy students in the health field. Hockey great Wayne Gretzky works in behalf of the blind, the mentally retarded, and people with juvenile diabetes. Tennis star Pam Shriver organized a tournament to benefit cystic fibrosis research. Golfer Patty Sheehan is the benefactor for a group home for troubled adolescent girls. Defensive end George Martin has visited about 2,000 children in hospital wards.

When he was asked why he works for the **Muscular Dystrophy Foundation,** Jerry Lewis responded, "I love the way I feel when I'm working for my kids."

Some people have been brought up with service as a family ideal or tradition. Others just spontaneously come up with the notion of getting involved because "it's the right thing to do." There's no denying that altruism, humanitarianism, and the unadorned desire to help others remain extremely strong forces in our society. As our friend Bill Grant, chairman of New York Life International Investment, Inc., put it, "It is in the classic Judeo-Christian ethic that you must serve your fellowman. It is not sufficient to write a check. You have to be hands on in giving back to the system in which you have earned your achievements."

We've come across many examples of people whose lives and careers bubble with an enthusiasm that spills over into a desire to share their skills with others. Every other Saturday, a retired veterinarian provides free care to the pets of people living in the skid row area of Seattle. In Denver, "Daddy" Bruce Randolph, owner of Daddy Bruce's barbecue restaurant, each year delivers free Thanksgiving dinners to thousands of people. Tucson nurseryman Bill Garber has inspired more than 1,500 schoolchildren to grow vegetable gardens at their schools and to be more aware of nutrition.

Service to others can spring from the anger we feel about the exploitation of people. Arthur Hamm, vice president of a major bank, made these comments when we talked with him about his work with **Covenant House,** the youth rescue organization that operates near New York City's Times Square:

> On the one hand, there are feelings of happiness and euphoria when you see the incredible work that an operation like that actually does and the dedication of the people involved. On the other hand, there are just the opposite feelings when you see the tremendous depravity of the people who pick these kids up in the bus terminal and introduce them to drugs and prostitution. You want to rid the world of these people, and on the other hand you want to cuddle and love.
>
> I've worked with other places that are not quite like that. There's a home for the elderly across the street from where I live. There's a lot of pathos there as well, but you don't experience the anger that is generated by seeing people preying on other people.

We were very moved by the comment of Don Looney of Anderson, South Carolina, who recently returned from an **Outward Bound** alumni expedition to Mexico:

> I came for the volcanoes and left with a heart full of memories about the children in an overcrowded orphanage run by Mother Teresa. The thing I will never forget is holding little David (a severely handicapped boy) in my arms, tears streaming down both our faces in a moment of recognition and unexplainable joy. I intend to return there after I prepare myself to serve in a long-term way.

All of these self-created impulses—some rooted in happiness and enthusiasm, others in deep sadness—find expression when we reach out to other people. In this impulse to share, everyone gives and everyone gets.

Participation in the Community

However small or local the effort, when you perform a work of service, you not only get in touch with your own best instincts, you also find your good works reflected in the lives of those around you. In fact, it's easy to argue that service work is virtually synonymous with community involvement, whether that community is a geographic entity or a religious or artistic community of the spirit.

A great number of people come to service work out of a desire to become more involved in their communities. They are responding to what we believe is a basic human instinct to belong to a larger group, to participate in a cause greater than one's own. We're convinced that identification with other people and participation in their lives are vital to personal happiness.

> "I think most of us are looking for a calling, not a job. Most of us. . . have jobs that are too small for our spirit. Jobs are not big enough for people."—*From an interview in* Working, *by Studs Terkel*

One reason people sometimes give for why they do service work is "insurance," an idea that's related to the "giving back" ethic: people donate time to a hospital or nursing home because they feel that they may need such institutions at some future time. Even if they don't have children in school, they man a cafeteria serving station to help educate the next generation of adults, who will run the community when they retire.

Our friend Carol Noyes reflected on her service work in this way: "Being involved in the nonprofit area has been extremely fulfilling, and as time goes on, it gets more so, because the causes of population and environment, which are the two that I'm involved in, seem to be more vital to the future of the world and my grand-children than they ever were before."

The impulse for community service isn't limited to individuals. Large corporations as well as small commercial enterprises are becoming increasingly involved in community projects. We've devoted chapter 6 to showing ways in which business interacts with the not-for-profit sector, and many of these relationships are both innovative and promising. We especially like the programs of large companies that can regularly mobilize sizable groups of employees and retirees to fan out into the community for special projects, and the growing tendency for companies to "adopt" schools or classes, with employees taking active, personal roles in helping the students learn.

Involvement in community affairs helps the volunteer feel rooted and connected. In our society, people frequently relocate for career and family reasons, and volunteering is a ready-made opportunity for becoming involved with the people and important concerns of a new town.

Service gives us a sense, if not exactly of control, at least of responsible participation in the affairs of the surrounding world. And, again, it is a way to get out of ourselves, to escape the petty or weighty concerns that tend to bog us down.

One of the most pleasurable aspects of service work is the people you meet. As we've pointed out, nonprofit service organizations are driven from within by the values they espouse, rather than by a more external profit motive or public policy. Value-driven organizations attract a certain kind of person, and people at all levels of an organization share this value orientation. When you join with others in service work, you tend to enter a network of like-minded people, individuals who share your priorities. This phenomenon is a constant theme of the people we talked to for this book. It's simply true that *people find some of their best friends and most long-lasting relationships in their service work.*

Service introduces you to a new circle of people, and this can be a broadening and valuable experience, since our particular professions, jobs, and vocations can limit the kinds of people we associate with. Opening our horizons by cooperating in service work with other community leaders, people who are dedicated, people with different life experiences, can be extremely enriching, especially for a younger person coming up the ladder and building his or her life.

Deborah Swailes Caldwell, director of marketing for Westwood Pharmaceuticals of Buffalo, New York, has joined **Western New York United Against Drug & Alcohol Abuse** (WNY United), a grass-roots community effort to stamp out the growing problem of drug use. She got involved because, "I wanted to do something to help my community. This was an opportunity for me to take my professional skills and turn them into a community service." As a member of the executive and media committees of WNY United, Debbie has helped plan and promote an initial awareness campaign, called Face the Facts, and an anti-drug rally attended by more than 1,500 people.

New Contacts, Greater Expertise

Service work can lead to new contacts, greater expertise, added skills, even a new job or career. In the service setting, we can apply our professional skills, perhaps experimenting with new approaches not open to us in our jobs. Or we can try out talents we suspect we have or would like to develop.

We had a conversation with Whitney MacMillan, chairman and CEO of Cargill, the largest privately owned business in the United States. At a very young age, he was advised by a mentor in the corporation to become involved in county and state politics as a way to broaden his experience. Whitney says that dealing with older power brokers became one of the most important learning experiences of his career. The scope of the tasks he was assigned gave him more responsibility at a much younger age than he could have hoped to achieve at Cargill, and working with senior people on a peer level gave him the confidence to apply what he learned to his business career. He calls this early volunteering experience a major factor in his success in becoming chairman of the company.

Betty Ballard, a literacy volunteer, says that she has never liked working as a secretary, although she has done it for twenty-eight years. She was brainstorming about other career possibilities when someone posed the question, "What is it in your life that you like doing so much that you would do it for nothing?" The answer was easy: her volunteer work helping adults learn to read and write. Betty is now investigating how she can translate her skills as a tutor into a setting where she can teach basic office skills and attitudes for success to young people who, in many cases, are trying to enter the work force without adequate training. She tells her experiences in her own words following chapter 5.

John: *Contacts you make in service work can definitely help you in your present business. When as a young man I was involved with the Red Cross, the Salinas Rescue Mission, and the local Junior Chamber of Commerce, it was good business as well, because I was a merchant. I was creating business for my automobile dealership in meeting people I wouldn't otherwise have known.*

Ellie: *My work with service organizations—as volunteer president and board member—has given me insight into the way things work at the higher levels of nonprofit groups and thus an ability, in my professional life, to be very effective in searching for people to fill executive positions in that area. I've become aware of the requirements for success in the running of a non-profit, and of the sometimes undefined personal and professional qualities that organizations look for. My volunteer involvements have most definitely added to my repertoire of skills.*

Expanded relationships lead to expanded possibilities of all kinds. When you sit with other people on a board of directors or work side by side with them in a training workshop, you observe and are observed. Ideas of all kinds flow back and forth among people in these settings, including information about jobs and careers. Anything can happen: you may hear about positions that are open, you may see someone who would be right for your company or firm, someone may spot you as a good candidate for a job. We know of many cases in which important jobs were landed or deals closed because of a relationship born in a service setting. We feel that service work is networking of the highest order, because it is not the superficial banter of the cocktail party but a real experience of sharing the best in yourself with other people.

EVERYONE BENEFITS

People of all ages and all types can take enormous benefits from service work.

Young People

Teenagers are poised for involvement in the affairs of the world. As they formulate their identities and their ways of relating, they examine cultural values and try out social skills. Generally open to commitment, they tend to be idealistic and have energy and time to invest. Because they are thinking about going to college or entering the work force, they are usually eager to try out different roles. Tapping into the basic human predilection to be of service to others helps them with their self-confidence, it helps with their self-motivation, and it helps to ease some of the problems of teenage alienation.

When she was at prep school in Troy, New York, our daughter, Jennifer Kuhn, took great pleasure in her role as a big sister in a local program, and many of our friends report that their children are most enthusiastic about service roles they have undertaken.

Kurt Hahn, the founder of Outward Bound, believed that young people *want* to serve—that they only need to be shown how. He said:

> There are three ways of trying to win the young. There is persuasion, there is compulsion and there is attraction. You can preach to them, that is a hook without a worm; you can say, "You must volunteer," that is of the devil; and you can tell them, "You are needed," that appeal hardly ever fails.

Britain's Prince Philip agrees. Speaking at a benefit dinner celebrating the completion of Outward Bound's first twenty-five years of service in October 1987, he said:

> [Hahn] saw that the way to overcome the effects of puberty was to face the young with progressively more challenging and more adult

demands. He always had them reaching for things which were only just within their capacities to grasp. He wanted greater responsibility and wider opportunities to drag them through the uncertainties and ignorance of adolescence. He wanted them to discover their potential as whole people through challenge and achievement.

The Hahn philosophy makes performing service to others an essential part of the process of growing to a responsible adulthood, and we see it proved true time and time again.

Career and Family Builders

In our early adulthood, the nonprofit sides of both our lives produced more personal growth than the business sides. We were dealing with more substantive people, people who were running things.

John: *In 1955, I left Stanford Business School to start a Volkswagen dealership in Salinas, California. My mentor in that town was Carl Voss, a cousin who was a generation older and a former General Motors executive. Carl convinced the Monterey chapter of the American Red Cross to take me—a twenty-six-year-old newcomer—as its president. Not knowing the players or the politics of the group, I took a deep breath and waded in. Making some recommended personnel changes was not easy, but after taking the hard step of informing a long-serving and obstructionist committee chair that she would not be reappointed, I gained confidence. In the chapter, we later went on to raise funds to build the first blood bank in Monterey County.*

This volunteer job was a watershed experience for me and went a long way toward establishing me in the community. I was in a responsible position outside of my business, dealing in bigger numbers, bigger assets, and more people. I certainly grew because of it.

Ellie: *When I was twenty-six, a good friend asked me to take over the running of a large theater benefit for the Multiple Sclerosis Society in San Francisco. Although I had never run an event of this size before, I dove in. With time, effort, and much energy, as well as the support of numerous friends, the event took off and became a huge success. While I learned about persuasion, team-building, time allocation, and leadership skills, the biggest lesson was in fund-raising, which I've been doing, on and off, ever since.*

71

For single people, volunteer work can be the healthy diversion that keeps work from becoming a narrow, all-consuming pursuit.

When children are small, family demands can sometimes leave little time for service work. There are times in your life when perhaps you are so consumed with raising the family and getting the household squared away that it may be difficult to carve out time for other projects. We urge you not to be discouraged if for a period there just isn't enough time for service, because there will be more time later.

One method that parents of young children sometimes find workable is to be involved, either in an ongoing way or for intermittent projects, with activities centered around their children: PTA (either the organization or its projects), scouting, sports, school fairs, and church and Sunday school programs.

It is most important, however, for people in their twenties and thirties to strike a balance among work, family, and service involvement. Many of today's two-career families are painfully aware of the toll taken on family life by career demands. What we tend to ignore are the personal costs of not making time in our lives for the pleasures and benefits of service.

John: *Peter McColough, recently retired chairman of Xerox, said to me recently, as we discussed the tragedies of Wall Street investors who had killed themselves in the aftermath of the market crash in October 1987, "The tragedy lies not so much in that they took their lives, but that they had lived so totally for business that when the money was gone, there was nothing left."*

Middle-aged People

People who have faced and survived their fortieth birthday are all too familiar with the many challenges the middle years bring, challenges of a different order from those faced by people starting families and careers. Here, in short form, is a list of ways that service can help the over-forty set cope:

· For parents of children who have flown the nest, service can provide stimulating interpersonal activity including, if you want it, contact with young people.

- When a career goes stale, service can help open new horizons.
- If you don't want to leave your career but are looking for "something more," service can provide another kind of challenge and new responsibility.
- Service can make you richer of mind and spirit, rounding out your repertory of accomplishments and enjoyments.
- Friendships sometimes dry up or change at mid-life. In the service world, meeting new people is easy and often most rewarding.
- When you need a way to reconnect to the sources of your best energy, try service.

"No matter how much or how little we have accomplished in the first part of our lives, it is never too late for unprecedented experiences. The second half of our lives can actually be a time of greater risk-taking for those of us whose responsibilities may have left little room for taking chances before—not foolish or pointless risks, but risks that offer the hope of both real adventure and real reward, for ourselves and others. While some of our physical powers may be diminished, we have survival skills younger people may not have learned, a different kind of endurance that comes with the passage of time.—*Jimmy and Rosalynn Carter,* Everything to Gain: Making the Most of the Rest of Your Life

---

Older People

More people are living longer, healthier lives, with full vitality into their seventies and eighties. After retirement, service provides involvement and interaction, plus an inevitable sense of personal value and the worth of a lifetime of experience, knowledge, and wisdom about people.

Retired people are needed and wanted, in a variety of programs specifically designed to use their age and experience (the **International Executive Service Corps,** the **Older Women's League,** the **Retired Senior Volunteers Program**) as well as throughout the service world, where their experience enriches countless boards and committees and their knowledge of people brings warmth and comfort to direct service situations.

Octogenarian Finis Mitchell, naturalist, veteran mountaineer, and author, is known as the grand old man of the Wind River Range in Wyoming. We love his comment: "Men don't stop climbing mountains because they get old; they get old because they stop climbing mountains." For a retired person, service can be the new mountain to climb.

In the following chapters, we'll go into detail about activities and organizations, and give you our best advice about getting involved. In the final chapter, "Service and Your Life," we'll return to the benefits we've discussed here and describe, among other topics:

- How service work can relate to your career;
- The dilemma that women sometimes feel about service work and why it's not really a problem;
- Service and family values, with suggestions for how to successfully volunteer together.

Meanwhile, please keep in mind this not so elegant but very true phrase, which summarizes the message of this chapter: *Service gives you more than you give it.*

IN THEIR OWN WORDS

"Things must be done, people must do them. They must do them right, they must serve the intended purpose and serve it well and efficiently. If all of those things are true, then you see it on the bottom line—whether the bottom line is earnings per share or kids staying in school."

—Eugene Lang

"My father made his home, food, whatever he had, available to people who had a need. He never asked them questions or thought about being repaid in any way, and that's the same thing that my grandmothers did. As I said, I didn't realize the influence that had on me until I was a fully grown adult with kids of my own and understood better how I came to think and believe in this area."

—Rochelle Evans

"This work had a tremendous impact on my life. Because of my recovering situation, the volunteer service at St. Luke's and the Outward Bound program changed my whole life. They helped me in keeping my sobriety, in keeping the family together, and just about everything. If I hadn't gone into the volunteer services, this story about Ruth Brown might have had a different and more tragic ending."

—Ruth Brown

Eugene Lang: *In 1981, at the sixth-grade graduation at P.S. 121 in New York City's East Harlem, a school he had attended some fifty years earlier, businessman Eugene Lang offered to finance the college educations of the sixty-one graduating students. His help was not restricted to the financial gift. He soon instituted a program to help the students academically and motivationally, so that they would finish high school with the grades and the motivation to go on to college. He subsequently founded the* **I Have a Dream Foundation,** *which serves as an expanding support group that now exceeds 100 individually sponsored projects nationwide and that includes more than 5,000 students.*

I limit myself to serving on boards where I feel I have the time and ability to participate constructively in serving the institution. I don't just sit on boards. My philosophy in joining anything is a personal feeling that I can be of use, that I have something to offer that's useful. That usefulness has to go beyond money, because I don't contribute to organizations to any substantial degree unless it permits the personal involvement, the personal protoplasm of either myself or a member of my family.

I think I bring ideas to organizations, I think I bring experience. I have been involved in organizational work for many years. In many respects the problems and issues that you have to deal with in nonprofit organizations of any kind tend to run in the same general grooves. Likewise, my entire experience, my entire career has been associated with entrepreneurial ventures where I work with ideas, to try to give them economic expression, and I guess I've enjoyed considerable success in doing that. I find myself reacting to institutional problems as entrepreneurial opportunities.

I think that whether you're dealing with a profit-making or a nonprofit objective, you're dealing substantially with the same general kinds of conditions. It's only that what you expect to get out of it or expect to accomplish are quite different. The objectives and their dividends are of different characters. Nevertheless the process of realizing those objectives and their dividends is essentially the same sort of thing. Things must be done, people must do them. They must do them right, they must serve the intended purpose and serve it well and efficiently. If all of those things are true, then you see it on the bottom line—whether the bottom line is earnings per share or kids staying in school.

To talk about the dividends or rewards that one gets exposes one to the risk of seeming corny or excessively sentimental. However, recognition that comes with success is appealing to the ego. But more than that, one gets an inner sense of satisfaction and fulfillment, a warmth. I guess when you feel that warmth, ego becomes less important. Ego satisfaction is a relationship between you and the world, whereas fulfillment is essentially a relationship between yourself and your personal values and conscience.

I like both of those avenues of satisfaction. I enjoy the recognition that I get. I enjoy the kind of people and friends that one makes. I always feel that when I am committed to a certain purpose, those who join me and share that purpose become kindred; we empathize, and there's nothing like sharing a common purpose to build human relationships. Such relationships are also tremendously rewarding.

I feel that I have made deeper friendships in the course of pursuing my extracurricular interests than I have in business. Maybe it's because as time has gone by I feel much more interest in my extracurricular activities than I do in business. I no longer have the same objectives in being in business or share the same purposes with others who are in business that I do when I am involved with education or other nonprofit projects.

My commitments are largely educational . . . as a matter of fact, overwhelmingly so. However, my wife is very interested in hospitals and health care. That is her full-time avocation, and I actively support that as something that also is important to me. My children each have their particular avocations and interests. They obviously must devote much more of their time in gainful employment, in their respective careers, and with their growing families. Each of them, though, still has time to do other things, with their educational institutions or professionally in some pro bono activity. My daughter is a lawyer, and she does a lot of work pro bono for tenant groups and their problems. She's very active in dealing with housing issues and housing problems in the minority areas.

My son, who is an actor and has a more peripatetic existence, nevertheless is very active in getting support for the George School, where he went, and also for various projects associated with his profession, the Actors' Fund and so on. My oldest son, who is an investment analyst, shares a lot of my interest in education, but he is particularly active in working with Tecnion in Israel and in Symphony Space in New York. So altogether each family member has some commitment to serving society.

My wife is a trustee of Booth Memorial Hospital and a trustee of Rockefeller University, and she chairs the visiting committee for New York City hospitals. She's been in hospital work since I've known her, since she was a candy striper during the Second World War, when she was working for me as my secretary. I have a foundation where I have much of my resources, and all of my family members are trustees. We use the resources of the foundation in conjunction with our individual social commitments.

The foundation began to support the academic work and personal situations of students in the I Have a Dream program—my Dreamers—when I realized that just to promise youngsters financial support so that they could go to college would be meaningless if they didn't graduate from high school with sufficient literacy to qualify for college. The prognosis was that most of those kids would be dropping out and that those who didn't drop out would be so undereducated that they couldn't begin to think of going on to college. I recognized that the integrity of the scholarship commitment I made meant that I had to do something to ensure that as many of those kids as possible would go through secondary education successfully and be able to take advantage of the college opportunity.

I got to know a number of the parents and most of the students. The relationships vary in intensity. To some I feel very, very close and know they feel close to me. There are others who I think are close to me, but it's really hard to know exactly how I rate or how the I Have a Dream program rates with them. And then there are some with whom I have very little personal contact, but who nevertheless are part of the program and who function with the program. They are presumed to draw strength just, say, from the *éminence grise* who has his office on Forty-second Street, as well as from the support they get from the peer relationships within the group.

When I was growing up in that particular East Harlem area, it was a poor neighborhood. The ethnic makeup was quite different. When I was there, it was largely Jewish, Italian, and Puerto Rican. Today it's mostly Hispanic and, to a lesser degree, black. It was poor then, and it is poor now. In fact, the living environment, the living conditions in terms of amenities, when I grew up there were a lot poorer than they are now. Remember, I grew up in an age when one didn't have private bathrooms or hot water or electricity in tenement railroad flats. My memory of a bath is sitting in a washtub that was filled with warm water that was heated on the kitchen coal stove. Going to the toilet was going out to a cubicle in the hall. At the time, I didn't regard it as being tragic or feel I was underprivileged. That was just the way it was. Today such conditions would be unacceptable by our social standards.

On the other hand, we didn't have to contend with drugs, we didn't have to contend with the license that the Pill has given many kids, or the mores that make things a lot more open in relationships than applied in my youth. Personally, I think that the conditions under which these kids are growing up today are a lot worse than those that prevailed in my time. At least I had a family, a full family that encouraged me. They instilled in me a desire, indeed a lust for education that's still with me. Any time that I wasn't playing in the street, I spent with a book—not television. I don't think that you find that such circumstances are now a general characteristic of the East Harlem area.

It's not because the kids are not just as smart, the parents not just as loving. It's just that things are different. I realize that today most young people would not consider it civilized or acceptable to grow up without a television or a VCR. Nevertheless, most of my generation did survive, and we probably read more books and studied a little harder.

As Jack Kennedy said, the voyage of a thousand miles begins with a single step. That first step I took without premeditation back in 1981 has extended itself already beyond expectations and against all of the odds. And we will go much farther. I certainly hope so. I've been spending much of my time trying to make that possible.

I travel around the country speaking to different groups, conventions of all sorts, to educators, businessmen, citizens, special interest groups, telling them about the program. When I tell them of my experience with the program, the rewards I get, its impact on the community, its impact on children, I don't have to tell them very much more. They do respond. That's quite clear from the nationwide reaction that has developed and continues to grow. There are thousands and thousands of people who continue to contact me by mail and telephone, one way or another, even by stopping me on the street, to express their feelings about the program and, in many cases, happily, their desire to make some contribution toward its extension. That's how we get most of our new sponsors.

If someone wants to volunteer, there certainly is no end of opportunities to indulge the desire. I think it's a very good thing for people to want to do. Many people probably feel discouraged from volunteering because whatever one individual does may seem minuscule in trying to cope with a problem that's bigger than all of us. In this sense—misguided, I think—the easiest way to respond to the call of social conscience is to send a check for $10 or $20, or $100, or even $1,000, to some deductible cause. That sort of does it, doesn't it?

It's unfortunate when people feel that way, because I have always been impressed by the deep truth of Thoreau's comment that when you give, spend yourself with it. And I think that people will do that.

When, associated with giving, one finds a path to dealing at a genuinely personal level with other human beings, and associating yourself in a sensitive way with their problems, one learns the rich reward, the very, very rich rewards of giving. In so many experiences in life, the more you put into it, the greater the fulfillment. The investment of one's self is a breeder reactor of fulfillment. Just find in yourself the special niche where you can let the best that's in you express itself in ways that answer the human needs of others.

Rochelle Evans: *Director of administration and human resources for the Eastern Region of the Times Mirror Company, Rochelle Evans has two daughters, ages sixteen and twenty. She has received the Distinguished Black Woman in Industry Award from the National Council of Negro Women and has been invited to the White House to meet with President Reagan and his staff as a member of the Conference of Key Black Women in the United States. A national business and professional women's organization named her an Outstanding Young Woman in America, and the International Association of Personnel Women selected her as an Outstanding Leader and as Personnel Professional of the Year.*

I grew up in New York, in the Harlem area, attended public school in New York, graduated from City College, and have taken graduate courses both at City and at Pace University. I have always been an active person in terms of community work. I currently serve on the advisory board of **Pace University's** Masters in Publishing program, which was started about three years ago and entails helping to develop and comment on curriculum, recruiting students, providing information about the program, and so on. The program takes people who are currently employed in publishing and helps them gain skills so that they can move beyond lower-level supervisory positions into more significant roles.

I am also on the board of directors of the **Children's Orchestra Society,** which provides musical training to youth under the age of sixteen. The primary group of participants here in the city are Asians. I am on the board of directors of the **New York Employment Center for Women** and have been involved with that group for about nine years. It services all kinds of women in the city, with a primary focus on training, development, and information for women who want to upgrade their skills or change jobs from one area to another. Many of the women are in transition in one way or another, and the group provides a lot of services to women in need.

I am on the board of directors for **Camp Courant,** which is a camp in Hartford, Connecticut, that one of the Times Mirror newspapers, the Hartford *Courant,* has run for several generations. It is free to all children in the city of Hartford. They can elect to go to camp every single day, if they wish, by simply standing on the corner and waiting for the bus to pick them up. The bus picks them up for camp for the day and brings them back home. There is no charge to the camper or the camper's family. It has been a wonderful opportunity for the kids to get away, and it's a great relief to parents who have to work. They can know that their children are in a good and safe place.

I am also a member of the board of directors of the **East Manhattan Counseling Service,** which provides counseling services to the members of the church that I attend, as well as others.

I'm on the board of the **New York City Outward Bound Center,** which is exciting and extremely rewarding. It's exciting from the standpoint of the adventures that I've experienced going on one of the weekend courses, but it's also exciting from the perspective of meeting young people who never get exposed to some of the people we have going on the weekend courses. These young people need guidance and direction from older people, and they also need to know that there are other things in life beyond the communities in which they live, and that they can aspire to those things and have a better life for themselves.

From a personal perspective, I guess I've been raised with the notion that we all need to help our fellowman. No matter what kind of situation we might find ourselves in, someone else always needs help. That's just how we were raised in our household, and therefore I have that kind of bent and find a great deal of satisfaction in doing that. It makes me feel that I am doing what I think is important and making a difference, no matter how small it might be, in someone's life somewhere.

I also like the fact that I can do these things without any personal motive in terms of my own enhancement. I think what I find the most gratifying is knowing that I'm not doing this because I'm looking to get something out of it. I do it because I feel good about the fact that I can help someone else.

I didn't really think about how much of an impact my family had on me until my father died eight years ago. So many people came to his funeral and wrote to us and called us later to just talk about what a tremendous influence my father was on their lives. I realized that the model we had was my father and his family, and also my mother's mother, in terms of their ability to open up their homes.

My father made his home, food, whatever he had, available to people who had a need. He never asked them questions or thought about being repaid in any way, and that's the same thing that my grandmothers did. As I said, I didn't realize the influence that had on me until I was a fully grown adult with kids of my own and understood better how I came to think and believe in this area.

I talk about service work with my daughters more than my father did with me. My father taught more by example than by conversation. I do encourage them to do similar things—to be more giving and to be sensitive to the needs of others—and I definitely think that has had an effect on them. I include them in the things that I do so that they are not only hearing me talk about things but seeing firsthand what goes on in the lives of a whole lot of other people. They practice these things, too, and have become helpmates to a lot of people in some difficult situations.

One of my daughter Meredith's friends was apparently having a very difficult time at home and had actually, at age eleven, developed a drinking problem. It was Meredith who came to her aid and counseled with her and gave her some good advice—to see if she could move in with her father. When this girl later ran away from home, it was Meredith the mother called and it was Meredith the girl talked with to get help. Meredith has always taken on that kind of role with her teachers and people in the community.

My daughter Monique does it in a different way. She does it in her writing and volunteer work—probably a lot more like I do it. But they have both participated in school in organizations that reach out to the hungry, the poor, youth in trouble, those kinds of things.

In terms of the area I work in, human resources, service work has helped me to be able to see the needs of people in the organization and to help the organization to meet those needs. In the end, if we are doing things that are good for our employees, we're generally going to end up with better employees and we will be a better company for it.

I chose to work at Times Mirror because I really liked the value system, the corporate culture. The people I met were people who had values and standards and views that were similar to mine, and I felt comfortable with them. For me, it has been a good place to work. There have been other places that I have worked where that was not the case, and it definitely did affect my ability to perform to the fullest.

The service aspect of my life also has been helpful in the sense that people know something about you and where you are and where you've come from, and they know whether or not they'd like to have someone like that on their team. I think that it is helpful in making you perform better and in opening career doors. Service has been a very good thing for me to do, both personally and professionally.

In one nonprofit involvement, I had more responsibility than I had on my job at that time. I was head of my church's education department, which was in charge of all the educational programs, including Sunday school, adult education, Bible study, after-school programs, and summer programs. I had that position in the late seventies, early eighties, and it was a significant challenge to pull all that together, to go out and get funding for it, as well as to plan it and make sure it ran well. We had to hire staff, recruit people, and find kids to participate in the classes and programs.

It ended up that we had to service the families as well, because the neighborhood in which the church was located had a number of poor people and families on welfare, and they had all the problems that come with that—unwed mothers, children who were doing drugs, parents on drugs, poor housing, you name it. It was a bad scene for a lot of those kids, and even for the parents it was a challenge to be able to come to a Bible-study class once a week. Running that program was a very big challenge.

I think that my way of doing things is to try to do something in which I know I will have an impact, as opposed to doing something where "well, maybe . . ." I have found that the one-on-one situation or very small group allows you to have the greatest impact. If you have a board role, I think it is critical that you become familiar with the clientele the group is servicing and that you try to get to know the people it is involved with. In this way, the role will have a greater meaning for you, and you will definitely do better by the people you are serving.

Ruth Brown: *Wife, mother, board member, and philanthropist, Ruth Brown was a founding trustee of the* **Colorado Outward Bound School** *and has made volunteer service a central part of her life.*

Years ago my family were sort of pioneers to Colorado, and I grew up in that environment. I went away to boarding school in the East, to Miss Porter's in Farmington, Connecticut, and to two years of junior college in New York City. Then back to Colorado.

When the war came along, I had been doing Bundles for Britain—knitting socks, if you know what I mean. That became dull, and I thought I could do something that would mean a little more. That's when the WASPS [Women's Air Force Service Pilots] program came up, and I went into the service with the WASPS.

My family had done a lot of flying. We had one of the first private airplanes in the country, and so I had been brought up "air-minded." I was in the Bomber Training Command, where we flew

AT11s, and then in the gunnery school, where I flew B26s. I was in the WASPS just under two years.

After that, I was on several school boards, country day school board and that sort of thing. We were starting to raise a family in Carbondale, Colorado, outside of Marble and Aspen, and there wasn't too much available in the way of volunteer service in the Roaring Fork Valley until Outward Bound came along in 1961.

I became a founding trustee of the Colorado Outward Bound School partly because of the location—we lived right in the valley below Marble, where the school started. With Chuck Froelicher, then headmaster of Colorado Academy, Bill Coors of Coors Brewery, and Charles Gates of Gates Rubber Company—we all decided to get in it together and get it going. We said, we will give you a certain amount of start-up money so you can get this thing going—it sounds like a great idea.

Besides school boards, I had been involved in hospital boards, but nothing that I had really zeroed in on. I think Outward Bound was the first cause I really spent a lot of time with and was really active with, other than giving financial help.

Eventually there was another one. I'm a recovering alcoholic. I went into treatment in 1977. I was with Alcoholics Anonymous and was actively involved with the alcohol program at St. Luke's Hospital in Denver. In addition to starting the volunteer services for recovering alcoholics with St. Luke's, I organized the health service department of Outward Bound to work with alcoholics. [Outward Bound conducts short courses for alcohol and drug abusers in connection with hospital treatment. The courses help to increase self-respect and improve the patient's self-concept after the hospital stay.]

This work had a tremendous impact on my life. Because of my recovering situation, the volunteer service at St. Luke's and the Outward Bound program changed my whole life. They helped me in keeping my sobriety, in keeping the family together, and just about everything. If I hadn't gone into the volunteer services, this story about Ruth Brown might have had a different and more tragic ending.

At St. Luke's, we had a motto for recovering alcoholics—"You come first" as far as any volunteer work is concerned. St. Luke's is just a center, but it's your own self and your own sobriety that count. If anyone volunteers and they don't do it for themselves, they're not doing good volunteer work.

I would say that my most important contribution as a volunteer was in starting the Colorado Outward Bound School, helping it get off the ground. Living right there, I became deeply involved, even worrying about whether the cook was going to stay the next day and that sort of thing.

In handling the time demands of volunteer work, I think that your top priority obviously is your family life—that should be number one. Your volunteer life should be secondary. If you're really interested in doing something, you can always work it in. But it's got to take a priority in your life. If you're doing something in name only, it doesn't mean anything. You won't do well in it.

I certainly have met a lot of wonderful people. I work with a lot of people at St. Luke's that I wouldn't have come in contact with otherwise. And the same is true of Outward Bound. I think volunteer work certainly broadens your scope of acquaintances.

I could very well have been sitting and doing nothing but going to luncheons—but that is something I never took the time to do. I was too busy with the real stuff, and I just wasn't going to bother with it. Thank goodness I didn't.

It's possible to get involved in volunteer service that isn't right for you. I didn't feel that I was giving anything to a couple of hospital boards that I was on, and that they weren't really giving anything to me. So I just got off of them. I'm sure that the only reason they wanted me on the board was for financial reasons, and if I couldn't contribute other than that, I wasn't going to stick with it. Obviously a board member of such institutions is there for a variety of reasons, and one of them usually is how much he or she can contribute financially. That is a high priority in terms of board service, but I think you've got to consider the help you can give other than just the money.

A volunteer has to be very interested in what he or she is doing. You ought to be willing to spend a certain amount of time, beyond whatever financial help you can give.

I don't think you want to get involved with anything that you're not too excited about. If you feel that everybody else is working for an organization and so you had probably better do something, too—if you get into service with that idea and you're not truly interested in the cause—you're not going to give anything to it.

CHAPTER THREE

A SERVICE SAMPLER: FROM AARP TO ZOOS

WITHIN the not-for-profit world, hundreds of thousands of national and local organizations address specific issues and needs, using millions of volunteers. In this chapter, we offer what we hope will be an eye-opening sampler of a few of those groups. All the organizations listed below are private nonprofits, but not all directly provide services to people in need. Some are volunteer-staffed associations that work in behalf of a group of people or advocate for a cause.

We've organized our service sampler into nine categories:

Umbrella Groups
Social Services
Education
Culture
Health
Environment/Animals
International Organizations
Groups of Interest to Children and Youth
Groups of Interest to Senior Citizens and Retired People

Because the nonprofit world is so vast and because so many thousands of groups exist, we begin each section with a general description of the types of organizations within that category. After the generic discussion, we describe several specific groups. *We are not promoting these organizations nor are we attempting to provide a directory.* The descriptions are offered as parts of a sampler for your perusal, to give you an idea, grounded in facts and descriptions, of some of the groups that make up the independent sector and the ways they use volunteers. (Chapter 5, "Putting Service in Your Life," will explain in detail how to find a service organization that is right for you.)

Most of the groups we've listed are national in scope, although we have included a few local organizations where noted, whose programs could be adapted for other local situations. We hope that by examining this sampler of nonprofits and by following our "how-to" advice in chapter 5, you will be both inspired and prepared to join or start a group that suits your interests and talents.

UMBRELLA GROUPS

Listed below are six important national organizations that service, support, monitor, and represent individual organizations in the private nonprofit sector. Across the country, more than 2,300 local **United Ways** and 380 **Volunteer Centers** (sometimes called Voluntary Centers or Volunteer Bureaus) operate as local umbrella groups and clearinghouses. Local **chambers of commerce, civic groups,** and **women's associations** are often excellent sources of information about not-for-profit groups and programs.

Independent Sector
1828 L Street, N.W.
Washington, D.C. 20036
(202) 223-8100

Independent Sector is a nonprofit coalition of 650 corporate, foundation, and voluntary organization members with national interest and impact in philanthropy and voluntary action. The organization's mission is to create a forum to encourage the giving, volunteering, and not-for-profit initiatives that help to better serve people, communities, and causes. The group's current programs and activities include Daring Goals for a Caring Society, to stimulate measurable growth in support of the sector through increased giving and volunteering (the "Give Five" campaign); public information and education, to promote active citizenship and community service; government relations, to develop and maintain effective relationships with government; research, to understand the sector and the ways it can be of greatest service to society; effective sector leadership and management; and communications, to provide a meeting ground for cooperation and learning among the organizations of the sector.

InterAction

American Council for Voluntary International Action
200 Park Avenue South
New York, New York 10003
(212) 777-8210

InterAction, a membership association of U.S. private voluntary organizations, exists to enhance the capacities of its members engaged in international humanitarian efforts. Standing committees include the Development Assistance Committee, which promotes information-sharing, professional development, and joint action; the Development Education Committee, which supports education on issues relating to Third World development and global interdependence; the Migration and Refugee Affairs Committee, the most directly operational committee; the Resources Committee, especially active through its African Emergency Subcommittee; the Public Policy Committee; and the Private Funding Committee. InterAction publishes *InterAction Member Profiles*, a 135-page compilation of essential information on 106 InterAction members, including descriptions of personnel, programs, geographic areas of activity, financial data, and telecommunications capabilities ($18; $8 to members).

National Charities Information Bureau

19 Union Square West
New York, New York 10003-3395
(212) 929-6300

The National Charities Information Bureau (NCIB) provides information about organizations that solicit funds nationally, and evaluates national agencies in the light of its eight Standards in Philanthropy. NCIB provides in-depth reports on more than 300 nonprofit organizations; the *Wise Giving Guide*, a six-times-a-year summary of its evaluations of all organizations on which it reports; *The Volunteer Board Member in Philanthropy*, a handbook for volunteer board members; *NCIB Standards in Philanthropy*, a guide for donors and agencies; and *A Grantmaker's Guide*, a manual on how to use Form 990, filed by most nonprofit organizations and available to the public, to learn more about almost any charity. Three individual reports and single copies of the *Wise Giving Guide* are available free, and contributors to the NCIB receive the *Guide* for a year. Other publications are available at cost.

Philanthropic Advisory Service
Council of Better Business Bureaus
1515 Wilson Boulevard
Arlington, Virginia 22209
(703) 276-0133

The Philanthropic Advisory Service (PAS) of the Council of Better Business Bureaus (CBBB) exists primarily to educate donors. While PAS never recommends one charity over another, it offers valuable information to help donors make their giving decisions. PAS collects and distributes information on thousands of nonprofit organizations that solicit nationally or have national or international service programs. PAS provides one- to four-page summaries of individual organizations (three reports available free of charge) and issues on a bimonthly basis *Give But Give Wisely,* a concise summary of who meets and does not meet CBBB standards ($1 per issue). PAS publishes the following brochures, available without cost with a stamped, self-addressed business envelope: *CBBB Standards for Charitable Solicitations, Tips on Charitable Giving,* and *Tips on Tax Deductions for Charitable Contributions.*

United Way of America
701 North Fairfax Street
Alexandria, Virginia 22314-2045
(703) 836-7100

The national association for 2,300 **United Way** organizations throughout the United States, United Way of America provides tools and resources for local United Way use, assisting in fund-raising, community problem-solving, fund distribution, and volunteer development and training. Local United Ways are autonomous and locally governed by a volunteer board of directors. In addition to serving as board members, volunteers for United Ways are involved in fund-raising, allocations, decision-making, planning for community health and human services, management assistance and consultation to not-for-profit organizations, and training. Many United Ways serve as clearinghouses to match individuals with volunteer opportunities. United Ways collectively raised $2.44 billion in 1986 from individuals, businesses, and foundations. These funds support approximately 37,000 charities, helping tens of millions of people. Approximately 90 percent of all funds raised go directly to needed services in the community.

VOLUNTEER—The National Center
1111 North 19th Street, Suite 500
Arlington, Virginia 22209
(703) 276-0542

VOLUNTEER—The National Center works to strengthen the volunteer sector in the United States, existing for the sole purpose of stimulating and supporting more effective volunteering by citizens to help solve local problems. The organization acts as the primary information resource for nonprofit organizations, business, government, and the media on the nature, scope, and techniques of volunteering in America. It is a national consulting resource for corporations that seek to encourage and assist their employees in becoming involved in their communities as volunteers. VOLUNTEER supports and helps strengthen the development of the more than 380 local Volunteer Centers across the United States; assistance is also provided to those communities starting new Volunteer Centers. The organization sponsors and promotes National Volunteer Week and, with ACTION (the federal domestic volunteer agency), sponsors the President's Volunteer Action Awards.

SOCIAL SERVICES

Limited space permits us to describe only a very few specific groups. Thousands of national and local organizations exist to provide social services: giving inner-city kids a summer vacation in the country, promoting cooperation and understanding among all sectors of society, welcoming foreign people to our country, providing disaster relief, providing assistance to the disabled and training for the unemployed, rescuing "throwaway" kids, to name only a few. Such services and thousands of others aim to improve the lives of people.

Soup kitchens provide meals and **homeless shelters** offer daytime or overnight accommodation. Some have programs to reintegrate the people they serve into independent living, through housing placement, literacy and job training, and personal counseling. **Food reclamation programs** collect surplus fresh and packaged food and distribute it to feeding programs. **Meal delivery programs** take warm or packaged food to homebound people.

Community centers and **settlement houses** offer a range of personal and family services, from recreation and education to job training, homework and mentoring programs for youth, crisis intervention for families, senior services, aid for the disabled, community mental health programs, and day care.

Some **crisis centers** and **family support centers** exist specifically to provide respite and shelter for battered wives, abused children, and families with immediate financial emergencies; others offer counseling for drug and alcohol addiction and for youth at risk. Many educate and advocate for the prevention of family abuse.

Hotlines of all kinds are channels for help for runaways, people with sexually transmitted disease, people with AIDS, battered wives, pregnant teenagers, abused children, potential suicides, drug and alcohol abusers, and others. **Telephone reassurance programs** provide daily contact with homebound or retarded people.

Halfway houses work with troubled youth, ex-offenders, mentally retarded people, and others, providing them with the personal, educational, and occupational support that will establish them as successful independent members of society.

Senior citizens centers offer fellowship and services to older people, from escorting, social outings, and nutritional advice to help with health insurance, legal advice, and tax counsel.

Many **civic groups** (such as Kiwanis, Rotary, Lions Club, and others), **women's clubs,** and **youth groups** offer a wide variety of social service programs in their local communities, including mentoring for young people, help for the disabled, environmental programs, and assistance to the elderly. Some participate as partners with community social service agencies.

Churches, synagogues, and mosques conduct programs of all kinds, both for their own members and for people beyond their congregations—educational programs, personal counseling, fellowship and support groups, soup kitchens and homeless shelters, services for needy children, and programs for senior citizens.

Public agencies and **local and state governments** operate all kinds of social service programs, from help for troubled youth and battered children to job training.

For people charged with or convicted of crimes and for parolees and ex-offenders, the **court systems** and **jails and prisons** provide programs of support and rehabilitation. Many communities use volunteers to provide personalized help for the victims of crime and for children within the foster parent system, among others.

Police departments often run programs for local youth. Especially in smaller communities, **fire departments** and **emergency medical services** are frequently staffed by volunteers.

Political and other advocacy groups (for human and civil rights, and environmental and consumer protection, among others) operate programs with a local, regional, or national focus.

Listed below are some specific national organizations, plus a few local ones, to give you a detailed idea of the kinds of groups and programs that exist.

American Red Cross
17th and D Streets, N.W.
Washington, D.C. 20006
(202) 737-8300

The American Red Cross is a federally chartered not-for-profit corporation which engages in human service activities throughout the United States and on U.S. military installations in foreign countries. It has thousands of employees and millions of volunteers who help provide its services. Volunteers are found in community health clinics, child care centers, and hospitals. They work in disaster situations, collect and distribute blood, drive Red Cross vehicles, visit the elderly, teach community service courses in health maintenance and accident prevention, and perform a myriad of other services. Leadership volunteers are also needed for administrative and policy positions, such as the chapter board and committees.

Association for Retarded Citizens
2501 Avenue J
Arlington, Texas 76006
(817) 640-0204

The Association for Retarded Citizens of the United States is devoted to helping to meet the needs of more than 6 million children and adults with mental retardation, through services that include employment, training, education, independent living, and the opportunity to reach their greatest level of personal fulfillment and potential. Some 160,000 members work through 1,300 state and local chapters. Volunteers serve as citizen advocates, respite care providers, assistants at special events, speakers before civic groups, committee workers, and in other roles needed by a local chapter.

The Association of Junior Leagues
660 First Avenue
New York, New York 10016-3241
(212) 683-1515

The Association of Junior Leagues is an international organization of women committed to promoting voluntarism and to improving the community through the effective action and leadership of trained volunteers. The 270 Junior Leagues throughout the United States, Canada, Mexico, and Great Britain have a collective membership of more than 172,000 women. In 1986, more than 13,800 women were admitted for training as members; half were employed, 42 percent of them full-time. During the same year, Junior League members volunteered more than 8 million hours to advocacy and work on projects dealing with substance abuse, child abuse and neglect, education, cultural enrichment, health, family services, the arts, criminal justice, historic preservation, urban revitalization, and recreation.

Covenant House
460 West 41st Street
New York, New York 10036
(212) 613-0300
(Chapters in several cities)

Covenant House, a twenty-four-hour crisis center serving homeless and runaway youth under age twenty-one, provides food, shelter, clothing, medical care, legal assistance, educational and vocational guidance, and counseling. The Rights of Passage Program gives young people an opportunity to pursue longer-range educational and career goals by providing a supportive living environment for up to eighteen months. An integral part of the operation, volunteers participate in two kinds of work: non–child care (clerical work, food service, housekeeping) and direct child care, in which people assist counselors, serve meals and snacks, offer recreation in the gym, staff the lounge, tutor, provide escorts, and perform other tasks. Covenant House has sites in New York, Houston, Fort Lauderdale, Toronto, New Orleans, and Central America.

Family Service America
11700 West Lake Park Drive
Park Place
Milwaukee, Wisconsin 53224
(414) 359-2111

Family Service America (FSA) is the headquarters organization of a voluntary movement dedicated to helping families. Founded in 1911, FSA has a network of 290 local member agencies throughout the United States and Canada. During 1986, in the entire network, 7,000 professional staff supported by 10,000 volunteers served more than 3 million people. FSA headquarters is happy to refer individuals to the local agency nearest them. Volunteers are involved as board members and in fund-raising, public relations, and governance. Direct service opportunities include volunteer companionship, crisis intervention, parental support, community education, transportation services for the elderly and disabled, and respite care.

Focus: HOPE
1355 Oakman Boulevard
Detroit, Michigan 48238
(313) 883-7440
(A local organization)

Focus: HOPE is a metropolitan Detroit civil and human rights organization founded in 1968. Each year, the organization spends more than $25 million to feed 70,000 babies, small children, and elderly people who live in poverty. Annually, Focus: HOPE trains 300 jobless men and women to be machinists and helps them find good jobs. They employ and train 200 others in a variety of manufacturing companies developed at Focus: HOPE's Industry Mall. Almost completed in fall 1987 was Focus: HOPE's Center for Children, a nursery, day-care, Montessori school for 220 children of parents with new jobs or in training. Retired people and other volunteers contribute their skills in industrial technology, education, science, engineering, and computers, among other areas.

The Fortune Society
39 West 19th Street
New York, New York 10011
(212) 206-7070
(A local organization)

Based on the idea that the way to reduce crime is to maximize opportunities for those who have been in trouble in the past, The Fortune Society widens options for ex-offenders and juveniles, through one-to-one counseling, one-to-one tutoring, and vocational training. In addition to direct service to offenders and ex-offenders, the society works on the local and national levels in community education—sending speakers and panelists to schools and community groups, government investigations, and radio and television broadcasts—and in advocating changes in the criminal justice system. The organization uses hundreds of volunteers throughout its operation and needs tutors to teach reading and math to ex-offenders and adolescents, at their offices. Training is provided.

The Fresh Air Fund
1040 Avenue of the Americas
New York, New York 10018
(212) 221-0900
(A local organization)

Each summer, through The Fresh Air Fund, 8,500 New York City young-sters visit volunteer host families who live in rural and suburban commu-nities across thirteen northeastern states. In addition, 2,500 boys and girls attend four Fresh Air camps located in Upstate New York; Camp Hidden Valley serves both able-bodied and disabled children. The Friendly Town program is overseen on a local level by volunteers respon-sible for publicizing the program and recruiting new host families; boys and girls from ages six to sixteen visit for two weeks or more, and families enjoy their young guests so much that 60 percent of the children are invited to visit the same host families year after year. In New York City, the organization uses volunteers for evening telephoning and work with children in the summers.

Habitat for Humanity
Habitat and Church Streets
Americus, Georgia 31709
(912) 924-6935

Habitat for Humanity, an ecumenical Christian housing ministry, works with families unable to afford a commercial home loan. Together they build low-cost housing at no profit and with no interest, using donations and no government funds. Volunteers serve at headquarters, at more than 250 North American projects, and at more than fifty projects in twenty-five developing countries, and are used in many areas, including accounting, administration, bookkeeping, child care, construction, clerical, graphic arts, maintenance, photography and darkroom, public relations, shipping and handling, and word processing. By far, most volunteer work takes place at the local project sites. Contact headquarters for information on how to get in touch with these sites or on how to start a project.

The Holiday Project
1388 Sutter Street, Suite 500
San Francisco, California 94109
(415) 474-7285

The Holiday Project began in 1971, when eight people in San Francisco joined together on Christmas Day to visit patients and share Christmas dinner in a local hospital. Over the years, the project grew to include Chanukah as well as Christmas, and visits to prison, nursing homes, psychiatric facilities, and shelters for battered wives and children. The Holiday Project has expanded to more than 200 communities. During the 1986 holiday season, 19,606 participants visited nearly 172,000 people in 1,829 institutions, an accomplishment made possible by a corps of 2,700 management volunteers. In addition to visiting and serving on a management team, volunteers make gifts, attend gift-wrap parties, provide entertainment, and serve on committees that raise funds and attend to legal, accounting, and public relations matters.

The International Center in New York
119 West 40th Street
New York, New York 10018
(212) 921-8205
(A local organization)

The International Center in New York offers a variety of programs designed to help recently arrived foreigners adjust to American life. The center aids students, foreign emissaries and trainees, refugees, and immigrants—all foreigners legally in the United States, except tourists. During 1986, more than 1,000 volunteers at the center served about 2,200 foreigners, providing English lessons, arranging appointments, helping with personal problems and the need for jobs and housing, setting up dinner and weekend visits in local homes, holding orientation programs and seminars, conducting sight-seeing tours, and organizing cultural activities.

League of Women Voters Education Fund
1730 M Street, N.W.
Washington, D.C. 20036
(202) 429-1965

The League of Women Voters Education Fund (LWVEF) was established in 1957 as a charitable trust to increase public understanding of major public policy issues and to promote involvement of citizens in government decision-making. Consisting of a body of 250,000 members and supporters, the LWVEF provides a variety of services: research, education, litigation, publications, and conferences on current policy issues and on techniques to help citizens take part more effectively in the democratic process. Local leagues exist in more than 1,200 communities nationwide.

Mothers Against Drunk Driving
669 Airport Freeway, Suite 310
Hurst, Texas 76053
(817) 268-MADD

Mothers Against Drunk Driving (MADD) mobilizes victims and their allies to establish the public conviction that drunk driving is unacceptable and criminal, in order to promote corresponding public policies, programs, and personal accountability. When thirteen-year-old Cari Lightner died at the hands of a repeat-offender drunk driver in Fair Oaks, California, in 1980, Mothers Against Drunk Driving was born. In less than five years, MADD grew from a one-woman organization to a nationwide nonprofit corporation with over a half million supporters and members. Thousands of MADD volunteers are active in more than 375 chapters in forty-eight states.

National Association on Volunteers in Criminal Justice

University of Wisconsin-Milwaukee Criminal Justice Institute
P.O. Box 786
Milwaukee, Wisconsin 53201
(414) 229-5630

Nationwide, 300,000 volunteers are actively engaged in justice volunteerism. Founded in 1970, the National Association on Volunteers in Criminal Justice (NAVCJ) serves the needs of justice volunteers, volunteer managers, and other justice personnel. Committed to the improvement of the juvenile and criminal justice systems through citizen participation, the organization seeks to enhance the image of justice volunteerism by serving as an advocate for citizen volunteers and building the efforts of local programs into a national constituency. A quarterly newsletter, *NAVCJ in Action*, reports on justice volunteer activities throughout the nation and Canada.

National Committee for Prevention of Child Abuse

332 South Michigan Avenue, Suite 950
Chicago, Illinois 60604-4357
(312) 663-3520

The National Committee for Prevention of Child Abuse (NCPCA) works to stop child abuse before it occurs—specifically, to reduce child abuse in the United States by 20 percent by 1990. A network of NCPCA chapters in all fifty states works for prevention through public awareness and education, a variety of community-based prevention services, research and evaluation, and advocacy. NCPCA's nationwide effort is implemented locally in the grass roots of America. Some people become involved as chapter board members; some help with fund-raising and others with direct services. Thousands of individuals are involved at the national and local levels in hundreds of programs that offer prevention services.

The National Urban League
500 East 62nd Street
New York, New York 10021
(212) 310-9000

The National Urban League (NUL) is a nonpartisan interracial community service organization that works to secure equal opportunities in all sectors of society for black Americans and other minorities. The NUL works through direct service, in which well over a million individuals each year are assisted in such areas as job placement and training, housing, and health care; research into social and economic issues, to provide information essential to the formulation of policy decisions at the national and local levels; advocacy for blacks, other minorities, and the poor; and bridge building, to create firm understanding between white and black America. The NUL has 113 local affiliates and embraces more than 30,000 volunteers of all races.

Planned Parenthood Federation of America
810 Seventh Avenue
New York, New York 10019
(212) 541-7800

The Planned Parenthood Federation has 183 affiliates across the United States, an office in Washington, and three regional offices. Each Planned Parenthood affiliate provides medical services, education, counseling, and advocacy for reproductive rights. In 1986, medical services were provided to 2.3 million women and men, and education programs, materials, and curricula are used by many people in affiliate communities. In 1986 and 1987, adolescent pregnancy prevention, international family planning, and threats to reproductive rights were of particular concern. Volunteers serve on the affiliate and regional boards of directors, and work in fund-raising, educational programs, counseling, advocacy, and medical services.

Runaway Hotline
P.O. Box 12428
Austin, Texas 78711
(512) 463-1980 and (800) 231-6946

The Runaway Hotline is a toll-free hotline for runaway youth. It is operated by volunteers twenty-four hours a day, every day of the year. The Runaway Hotline serves as a nationwide information and referral center for runaways needing food, shelter, counseling, medical assistance, and related services. The hotline also allows a runaway to relay a personal and confidential message to his or her parents. The Runaway Hotline receives approximately 200 calls a day, from runaways, parents of runaways, children who are thinking about running away, and persons wanting information. The hotline has a staff of more than 125 dedicated volunteers.

Spence-Chapin Services to Families and Children
6 East 94th Street
New York, New York 10128
(212) 369-0300
(A local organization)

Spence-Chapin Services to Families and Children is a voluntary, nonsectarian social service agency that provides services to families and children. In addition to sponsoring adoption and foster parent programs, the agency reaches out to families in stress, women who face unintended pregnancies, mothers whose difficulties interfere with their parenting ability, and emotionally disturbed and developmentally delayed children two and a half to five years old. During the afternoon hours, this last program uses the volunteer services of therapeutic companions, college students, and community members who agree to spend a minimum of one afternoon a week for a year with the child.

Volunteers in Service to America (VISTA)
ACTION
806 Connecticut Avenue, N.W., Room 1000
Washington, D.C. 20525
(202) 634-9424 and (800) 424-8867

VISTA is a full-time, year-long volunteer program run by ACTION, the federal domestic volunteer agency. Men and women of all ages and backgrounds commit themselves to increasing the capability of low-income people to improve the conditions of their lives. Volunteers are assigned to local sponsors, which may be state or local public agencies or private, nonprofit organizations. Volunteers live and work among the poor, serving in urban and rural areas and on Indian reservations. They share their skills and experience in fields such as literacy, employment training, food distribution, shelter for the homeless, and neighborhood revitalization. A VISTA volunteer must be a citizen or permanent resident of the United States and at least eighteen years old. There is no upper age limit.

Women in Community Service
1900 North Beauregard Street
Alexandria, Virginia 22311
(703) 671-0500 and (800) 562-2677

Women in Community Service (WICS) is an independent coalition of five major national groups: American GI Forum Women, Church Women United, National Council of Catholic Women, National Council of Jewish Women, and National Council of Negro Women. WICS works in communities to improve the quality of life for women and youth in poverty by providing opportunities in education, vocational training, employment, and dependent care. Since its founding in 1964, WICS has helped more than 300,000 young people through Job Corps referral and support. WICS uses more than 3,000 volunteers to implement its programs. Volunteer activities include interviewing, counseling, group leadership, office management, public relations, letter-writing, and community outreach.

EDUCATION

Elementary and secondary public and private schools offer many programs—run by volunteers—that go beyond their basic curricula, including special classes in nonacademic subjects, remedial tutoring, work with gifted students, after-school activities and clubs, sports programs, and day care. Other volunteers work as street-crossing guards, vocational and personal counselors, and aides in playgrounds and in classrooms, cafeterias, and libraries. Public schools are directed by elected boards of education and private schools by voluntary boards of directors. Parent-teacher organizations often form an important channel for community contribution to schools. For private schools, fund-raising programs are critically important.

Colleges and universities rely on the participation of able and interested people who serve as directors and advisers. Institutions of higher education offer many supplemental educational programs, including remedial tutoring, and special help for foreign and handicapped students. Alumni form the core of volunteer groups at many schools.

In addition to the schools themselves, many groups address educational issues and problems, offering a variety of approaches.

Adopt-A-School
Los Angeles Unified School District
450 North Grand Avenue, Room H-237
Los Angeles, California 90012
(213) 625-6989
(A local organization)

The Los Angeles Adopt-A-School Program began in 1979 with one company and one school. As a result of that success, the program has expanded to the point where hundreds of schools have been adopted by local businesses. There are numerous ways in which a company's resources may enrich a school's educational program: one-on-one or group tutoring, mini-course lectures, sharing of hobbies, career counseling and awareness, club sponsorship, parent workshops, teacher workshops, student employment, etc. Because each school has a different set of needs and companies have different resources, each adoption is unique. Both schools and companies report that this is one of the best programs in which they have participated.

American Museum of Natural History
Central Park West at 79th Street
New York, New York 10024-5192
(212) 769-5000
(A local organization)

The American Museum of Natural History has a volunteer staff of more than 500 people who represent 10 percent of the labor force. Museum volunteer employees work both with the public and in departments. Some of the tasks performed by volunteers who work with the public include staffing information desks, acting as facilitators at museum functions, conducting guided tours, teaching children, and demonstrating origami paper folding at holiday time. Volunteers who work in departments make use of their clerical or technical skills; their work includes cataloging and numbering artifacts and specimens, casting fossil bones, and working on museum research projects and animal behavior studies.

Council for Adult and Experiential Learning
10840 Little Patuxent Parkway, Suite 203
Columbia, Maryland 21044
(301) 997-3535

The Council for Adult and Experiential Learning (CAEL) is an association of colleges, universities, and educational professionals devoted to three causes: the recognition of college-level learning wherever achieved; the expansion and sophisticated use of hands-on experience in college studies; and increased responsiveness of higher education providers to the needs of adult learners. CAEL's regional staff consists largely of volunteers, and at local institutions most CAEL activity is done by college or university staff members whose work is voluntary. CAEL is a clearing-house for information on experiential learning and on new developments in achieving improved responsiveness to adult learner needs by colleges and universities.

Goodwill Industries of America
9200 Wisconsin Avenue
Bethesda, Maryland 20814-3896
(301) 530-6500

Goodwill Industries, through 176 authorized agencies throughout the United States and Canada, provides vocational services for people with disabilities and special needs. Local Goodwill Industries organizations provide vocational evaluation, work training, and employment and job placement services. The collection, processing, and sale of donated materials, which provide training and employment opportunities, furnish nearly 51 percent of the revenue needed to sustain these services. Volunteers serve on the local boards of directors. Other activities on the local level may include fund-raising, direct client services and aid, and assistance with sorting books and pricing antiques.

The Great Books Foundation
40 East Huron Street
Chicago, Illinois 60611
(312) 332-5870 and (800) 222-5870

Established in 1947, The Great Books Foundation provides people of all ages with a lifelong program of liberal education through the reading and discussion of great works of literature. It derives its income from the sale of its books, from fees for training, and from educational grants. The foundation publishes paperback sets of readings for discussion and administers training courses that prepare volunteers, teachers, and librarians to conduct Junior and Adult Great Books groups. More than 18,000 leaders are trained in these courses each year. The Junior Great Books program is available for every grade from second through twelfth, and most are part of school programs. Adult Great Books groups meet in libraries, offices, homes, churches, and community centers across the nation.

I Have a Dream Foundation
31 West 34th Street
New York, New York 10001
(212) 736-1730

The I Have a Dream Foundation acts as a clearinghouse of ideas and programs for individual I Have a Dream projects, with the basic goal of helping each sponsored student ("dreamer") graduate from high school and then complete college or find a fulfilling job. The foundation conducts seminars, training programs, and orientations for all new sponsors and project coordinators, and for the community-based organizations and volunteers through which they work. Throughout the educational process, dreamers become involved in relationships with adults and peers within a very personalized and committed environment. At the end of 1987, approximately 4,000 dreamers were sponsored in programs in sixteen cities across the country.

Literacy Volunteers of America
5795 Widewaters Parkway
Syracuse, New York 13214-1846
(315) 445-8000

Literacy Volunteers of America (LVA) was founded in 1962 to combat the problem of adult illiteracy in the United States. Its primary premise is that well-trained and carefully supported volunteers can be effective tutors of adults and that, with the enlistment of this huge pool of talent, a significant impact can be made on the problem. Since 1962, LVA has grown to include more than 250 programs in thirty-three states. In that time, approximately 100,000 LVA volunteers have tutored more than 120,000 students in basic reading and English as a second language. Currently, more than 50,000 tutors and students are involved in LVA's programs.

The National PTA
700 North Rush Street
Chicago, Illinois 60611-2571
(312) 787-0977

The National PTA is a nonprofit volunteer association devoted to acting as an advocate for children and teenagers. More than 6.1 million parents, teachers, students, grandparents, and others with an interest in children belong to the PTA. They participate in 26,100 local PTA units in every state. Ongoing National PTA programs include the Drug and Alcohol

Abuse Prevention Project, Reflections Cultural Arts Award Program, Child Safety and Protection Month, School Is What WE Make It!, and Teacher Appreciation Week. The Office of Governmental Relations in Washington, D.C., monitors legislative activity related to children and teenagers. Activities on the local level include parent education meetings, fund-raising, providing school volunteers, and special education programs for parents and students.

National School Volunteer Program
701 North Fairfax Street, Suite 320
Alexandria, Virginia 22314
(703) 836-4880

The National School Volunteer Program (NSVP) provides leadership for school volunteers. NSVP members—parents, retirees, college students, businesspeople, and educators—build partnerships between public education and the community. More than 4.3 million school volunteers provide administrative advice; serve on advisory committees; tutor students; provide one-to-one attention to gifted pupils; assist in special projects such as home construction, marketing, finance, science, and math; help in health, sex, and drug education programs; assist with career guidance; and arrange and supervise special holiday and assembly programs and field trips. Contact the NSVP to find out what types of volunteer programs are available nationwide or for information on how to set up a volunteer program.

Outward Bound USA
384 Field Point Road
Greenwich, Connecticut 06830
(203) 661-0797 and (800) 243-8520
(Schools in several states)

Seeking to help young people and adults develop leadership qualities, self-esteem, a sense of service and compassion, and sensitivity to the environment, Outward Bound offers its programs to a broad spectrum of society and provides financial aid to that end. By confronting a series of increasingly difficult physical and mental tasks, participants call on previously unrecognized reserves of strength and perseverance. More than 3,000 schools and many social agencies have developed similar programs, and several states have used Outward Bound concepts for rehabilitative programs. Serving 18,000 people annually, Outward Bound is guided nationally and in its five independently chartered schools by 240 trustees and 300 volunteer members of advisory boards.

Reading Is Fundamental
Smithsonian Institution, Suite 500
600 Maryland Avenue, S.W.
Washington, D.C. 20560
(202) 287-3371

Reading Is Fundamental (RIF) is a national organization that works for a literate America by inspiring young people to read and to aspire through reading. With the help of more than 85,000 volunteers, RIF conducts imaginative activities that bring books to life and make reading a meaningful experience for children. RIF works through a grass-roots network of local projects—10,000 locations nationwide in 1986—that makes it possible for millions of children to choose and to own books that interest them—without cost to them or their families. In 1986 alone, more than 2 million youngsters chose nearly 7 million books to call their own.

Recording for the Blind
20 Roszel Road
Princeton, New Jersey 08540
(609) 452-0606

Recording for the Blind (RFB) provides recorded educational books free on loan to blind and other print-handicapped people, operating twenty-nine recording studios across the country, in addition to the national headquarters and Master Tape Library in Princeton, Founded in 1948, RFB now provides more than 125,000 recorded books to 20,000 people each year. Volunteers have recorded each of the 70,000 texts now in the Master Tape Library, and they add more than 3,000 new titles each year. Volunteers must have completed two years of college (or the equivalent) and be able to donate two hours of their time each week. Increasingly, RFB needs volunteers in specialized areas such as computer science, law, medicine, engineering, mathematics, and the physical sciences.

CULTURE

Libraries are often staffed partially or totally by volunteers. While some are supported by government money, many owe their existence to the efforts of fund-raisers and the creativity of volunteer trustees. Some publicly and privately funded libraries use volunteers in on-site programs in which children hear books read aloud, young people and adults get instruction in reading and writing, and the visually handicapped are assisted with special materials. Others send volunteers out in programs of visitation to hospitals and nursing homes, where books are read aloud and discussions held.

Museums and historical societies train volunteer docents (people who conduct groups through galleries or exhibits) to guide the public to a full appreciation of their holdings. Many integrate volunteers into their newsletters and other educational activities, as well as labeling and cataloging work.

Dance, theater, opera, and musical organizations are often supported by actively involved boards of directors and fund-raisers. Financial and legal professionals sometimes contribute their expertise on a pro bono basis. These cultural groups call on other volunteers to assist with functions from ticket-taking and ushering to constructing scenery, administration, advertising and promotion, and office work.

Public television and radio stations are supported by funds raised from corporations, foundations, and individuals, and by the efforts of volunteers who donate their professional expertise in publicity and programming, assist in administration, and perform clerical tasks.

Community and neighborhood newspapers are often designed, written, and produced on a voluntary, nonprofit basis.

American Association of Museums
1225 Eye Street, N.W.
Washington, D.C. 20005
(202) 289-1818

The American Association of Museums has the major objective of advancing the welfare of the nation's museums in service to the public. The association actively advocates on the national political scene on behalf of cultural and educational organizations. The role that volunteers play in the life of museums is phenomenal. Some smaller museums are staffed solely by volunteers, while even the largest urban institutions rely heavily on volunteers as docents (guides), catalogers, fund-raisers, and trustees. Volunteers of all ages can participate in their local museums in a large variety of ways, among them multilingual programs, junior- and senior-citizen docent programs, lending and on-the-road exhibit programs, special education programs, and video presentations.

American Symphony Orchestra League
777 14th Street, N.W., Suite 500
Washington, D.C. 20005
(202) 628-0099

The American Symphony Orchestra League was founded in 1942 as a national service and educational association, chartered by Congress, for the nation's symphony orchestras. The Volunteer Council of the league was founded in 1964 to guide the development of services to orchestra volunteers. The league's membership encompasses all levels of orchestra activity: management and staff, trustees, volunteers, conductors, and musicians. Trustees and volunteers participate not only in board leadership roles but also in fund-raising projects, ticket sales campaigns, educational projects, and community relations. They are an important part of an orchestra's strength and vitality within the community.

Business Volunteers for the Arts
Arts & Business Council, Inc.
130 East 40th Street
New York, New York 10016
(212) 683-5555
(Chapters in several cities)

Business Volunteers for the Arts (BVA) operates in more than twenty cities, training corporate executives as arts management consultants and placing them on a pro bono basis with nonprofit arts organizations. Volunteers must commit to one year of service and complete a ten-hour training course. More than 1,700 professionals have helped more than 1,600 cultural organizations, and the program has generated more than $15 million in volunteer time, in-kind services, and grants. Affiliate offices are in Albuquerque; Atlanta; Baltimore; Boston; Chicago; Fort Worth; Houston; Los Angeles; Madison, New Jersey; Miami; New Brunswick, New Jersey; New Haven; Oakland; Philadelphia; Red Bank, New Jersey; Richmond; Sacramento; San Francisco; San Jose; Seattle; Washington, D.C.; and West Palm Beach.

The Metropolitan Museum of Art
Fifth Avenue at 82nd Street
New York, New York 10028
(212) 879-5500
(A local organization)

The Metropolitan Museum of Art has an active staff of 600 volunteers: 300 working in libraries, offices, and curatorial departments, and 300 conducting tours, eighteen of which are available each day to the public on a walk-in basis. Among the museum's numerous touring programs are Volunteers for Elementary and Junior High School Students, Volunteers for Seniors, Volunteers for Disabled Visitors. Training programs, run by members of the museum staff, are demanding and require independent research on the part of the volunteer. Lectures on various aspects of the museum, its collections, and temporary exhibitions are provided for volunteers throughout the year.

National Public Radio
2025 M Street, N.W.
Washington, D.C. 20036
(202) 822-2000

Incorporated in 1970 with ninety public radio stations, National Public Radio (NPR) is a private, not-for-profit membership organization that now has 350 member stations. In addition to programming, NPR provides member stations with various support services. Volunteers are essential in the operation of the Audience Services Unit of NPR's Public Information Department. During 1987, they donated more than 5,000 hours as they responded to listener phone and mail inquiries, researched informational requests, provided tours of NPR facilities, and fulfilled orders for customized cassettes of NPR programming. Individual member stations are likely to use volunteers to supplement their staffs.

National Trust for Historic Preservation
1785 Massachusetts Avenue, N.W.
Washington, D.C. 20036
(202) 673-4000

Chartered by Congress with responsibility for encouraging public participation in the preservation of sites, buildings, and objects significant in American history and culture, the National Trust for Historic Preservation fights to save our historic and architectural heritage from destruction. Through programs such as the National Main Street Center, the National Trust is at work in more than 325 towns in twenty-six states, helping to retain the special historic quality of each Main Street while revitalizing it. Members help to give new life to historic districts, older neighborhoods, urban waterfronts, buildings, and famous homes. They also help protect more than seventy-five historic properties across the country.

Oregon Shakespearean Festival Association
15 South Pioneer Street
P.O. Box 158
Ashland, Oregon 97520-9901
(503) 482-2111
(A local organization)

During an eight-month season in 1988, the Oregon Shakespearean Festival Association (OSFA) presented plays by Shakespeare, Ibsen, O'Neill, Pirandello, and Durang, among others. The festival attracts more than 300,000 visitors annually. Fourteen groups of more than 800 volunteers are involved in every aspect of the operation, which includes a garden club; a festival exhibit center; hostesses; the board of directors and emeritus board; endowment trustees; a welcome team for new company members; Red Coats, who assist patrons; the Tudor Guild, which provides financial assistance to company members and studies Shakespearean literature; and OSFA relief volunteers, who help during overload times in the offices, costume shop, box office, scene shop, and other areas.

Volunteer Lawyers for the Arts
1285 Avenue of the Americas, 3rd Floor
New York, New York 10019
(212) 977-9270

Volunteer Lawyers for the Arts (VLA) was founded in 1969 to provide the arts community with free legal assistance and education. Artists and arts organizations that have arts-related legal problems and cannot afford private counsel are eligible for VLA's services. VLA works with all creative fields, including literature, dance, theater, music, film, and the visual arts. In New York, more than 900 attorneys donate time, providing counseling and representation on such matters as libel; copyright, patent, and trademark; contracts; insurance; labor relations; housing, loft, and performing space; and nonprofit incorporation and tax exemption. Thirty-seven other VLAs nationwide provide similar services.

Young Audiences
115 East 92nd Street
New York, New York 10128
(212) 831-8110

Young Audiences (YA), the nation's largest performing arts education organization, reaches 4.7 million public school children annually with specially designed participatory music, dance, and theater programs. A network of thirty-seven chapters selects and trains more than 2,000 professional performers who present more than 28,000 in-school programs, 90 percent of them in elementary schools. YA chapters serve big cities and small towns, and an increasing number of community programs involving adults and children are presented in libraries, museums, parks, and other public places. Hundreds of volunteers are part of this energetic network that brings the arts to children.

HEALTH

Hospitals integrate volunteers into a wide range of programs dealing with patients, including admissions, friendly visiting, language translation, help in feeding and other care, assistance in occupational and speech therapy, escorting to and from X-ray and therapy departments, reassurance in emergency rooms and waiting rooms, as well as for clerical assistance, reception, gift shop sales, and other functions.

Hospices and in-home hospice programs match terminally ill patients with volunteers who form a relationship of reassurance and caring for the practical and emotional needs of the dying person and his or her family.

Friendly visitors in **nursing homes** bring warmth and a continuity of human caring to people who might otherwise be isolated or ignored.

Many **clinics** use volunteers to receive, prepare, and comfort patients. **Public health programs,** such as flu immunization campaigns and public education projects, use volunteers in administration and publicity. **Blood banks** are often partially staffed by volunteers. **Visiting nurse services** use volunteers in preparing materials, friendly visiting, and telephone reassurance.

AIDS groups have responded to the epidemic by raising money, forming buddy systems to support people with AIDS, advocating for their rights, working to provide them with quality health care and housing, manning hotlines, and lobbying for aggressive efforts to stop the disease.

Health organizations of all kinds work for the cure of and public education about specific diseases and for the support of the victims of those illnesses.

Alzheimer's Disease and Related Disorders Association
70 East Lake Street, Suite 600
Chicago, Illinois 60601
(312) 853-3060 and (800) 621-0379 [in Illinois: (800) 572-6037]

Alzheimer's Disease and Related Disorders Association (ADRDA) is dedicated to easing the burden of and finding the cure for Alzheimer's disease and related disorders. This mission is carried out through supporting research, education, chapter formation, advocacy, and patient and family service. Since its inception in 1980, ADRDA has grown to more than 170 chapters, which are staffed largely by volunteers and which offer ongoing family support, sponsor seminars, pursue advocacy, and distribute books, brochures, and quarterly newsletters.

American Cancer Society
90 Park Avenue
New York, New York 10016
(212) 599-3600

The American Cancer Society is dedicated to eliminating cancer as a major health problem by preventing cancer, saving lives from cancer, and diminishing suffering from cancer through research, education, and service. At every level of the organization, volunteers and staff share in the management and implementation of cancer control programs and the operation of the society. Volunteers plan for and implement programs, raise funds, formulate policy, and make governance decisions. People interested in exploring volunteer activities should contact their local unit or their division office.

American Diabetes Association
1660 Duke Street
Alexandria, Virginia 22314
(703) 549-1500 and (800) ADA-DISC

The American Diabetes Association (ADA) exists to inform people that diabetes is serious and to involve them in its mission: to promote the search for a preventive and cure for diabetes and to improve the well-being of all people with diabetes and their families. The ADA focuses on three major areas—research, service (through patient, professional, and public education programs), and fund-raising—and relies on the assistance of thousands of volunteers in more than 800 chapters and 58 affiliates.

American Foundation for the Blind
15 West 16th Street
New York, New York 10011
(212) 620-2000

The American Foundation for the Blind (AFB) serves the needs of visually disabled people through public education, social and technological research, recorded books and periodicals, consultation and referrals, consumer products, publications, and advocacy programs. AFB works in partnership with more than 700 schools, senior centers, corporations, consumer groups, and professional organizations, and has a wide range of opportunities for volunteers, among them board membership, reading and recording for the blind, consulting, and assisting in the library.

American Heart Association
7320 Greenville Avenue
Dallas, Texas 75231
(214) 373-6300

Studies conducted in New York City and Boston in the early 1900s on whether heart disease patients could return to work led to the development of the American Heart Association. Now a worldwide voluntary organization with more than 2 million volunteers, the American Heart Association spends about $129 million each year on scientific research, public and professional education, and community service programs to reduce premature death and disability from heart disease, stroke, and other cardiovascular diseases.

American Lung Association
1740 Broadway
New York, New York 10019-4374
(212) 315-8700

Founded in 1904 to combat tuberculosis, today the American Lung Association (ALA), its 135 affiliated associations throughout the country, and its medical section, the American Thoracic Society, are dedicated to the control and prevention of all lung diseases and some of their related causes, including smoking, air pollution, and occupational lung hazards. ALA's public health education and research programs are supported by donations to Christmas Seals® and by other voluntary contributions. Volunteers serve as officers and members of boards of directors, help plan and conduct program activities, and assist with fund-raising.

Arthritis Foundation

1314 Spring Street, N.W.
Atlanta, Georgia 30309
(404) 872-7100

The Arthritis Foundation is a national association committed to finding the causes, cures, and prevention for arthritis in its many forms. The foundation, which consists of seventy-one chapters and divisions throughout the country, strongly supports direct research and the training of research scientists, and funds clinical research centers, patient services programs, and other educational and advocacy activities.

Leukemia Society of America

733 Third Avenue
New York, New York 10017
(212) 573-8484

The Leukemia Society of America is dedicated to finding the causes and cures for leukemia and related diseases. The society has fifty-seven chapters in thirty-one states and Washington, D.C., and supports programs of research, patient assistance, public and professional education, and community service. The society's chapters always welcome volunteers to help coordinate fund-raising events and public education programs. Medical professionals can assist with family support groups, professional education, and patient assistance.

National AIDS Network

1012 14th Street, N.W., Suite 601
Washington, D.C. 20005
(202) 347-0390

A national advocate for community-based institutions, the National AIDS Network (NAN) attempts to meet the needs of AIDS education and service providers, supplying resources and working with members in the search for effective programs. Members are AIDS organizations, public health departments, businesses, and individuals. NAN maintains a storehouse of readily available data for use by its members. A clearinghouse solicits materials and information, and answers inquiries, directing those seeking materials to the most current and helpful resources. NAN has expertise on the topic of minorities and AIDS. The network sponsors training programs and conferences, and administrates the NAN Fund, which provides grants in support of food distribution services, direct financial aid programs, housing, and comparable services.

National Down Syndrome Society
141 Fifth Avenue
New York, New York 10010
(212) 460-9330 and (800) 221-4602

The National Down Syndrome Society (NDSS) was established to promote public awareness about Down syndrome, to support research into its causes and amelioration, and to develop programs for families and individuals that can be replicated throughout the country. An 800 hotline enables NDSS to answer the questions and concerns of families, relatives, physicians, helping professionals, and other interested individuals, and to provide referral to parent support groups and other resources. The society has produced an informational packet that it mails out free of charge to the general public. The dedication of volunteers in a variety of capacities enables the NDSS to carry out its work.

National Easter Seal Society
2023 West Ogden Avenue
Chicago, Illinois 60612
(312) 243-8400

The National Easter Seal Society's mission is to promote the highest level of independence for people with disabilities. The society is a nationwide network of 200 state and local societies operating 400 program sites. Easter Seals provides physical, occupational, and speech/language therapies; vocational evaluation and training; camping and recreation; and psychological counseling, to meet specific community needs. More than a million people of all ages and with every kind of disability are served annually. Easter Seals also refers people with disabilities to appropriate resources. Volunteers participate through local service, board membership, fund-raising, and direct contributions.

National Fund for Medical Education
35 Kneeland Street
Boston, Massachusetts 02111
(617) 482-5501

Dedicated to the concept that medical education is an instrument that can be used to improve health care delivery for all Americans, since 1950 the National Fund for Medical Education (NFME) has functioned uniquely to raise funds and provide grants for this purpose. Leaders from business and medicine collaborate on the fund's board of directors to identify key issues the health system faces in meeting society's needs; to raise venture capital from corporations, foundations, and individuals; and to fund grantees across the country. The money entrusted to NFME by American industry is invested in people and projects that have the potential to change our health care system for the better.

National Multiple Sclerosis Society
205 East 42nd Street
New York, New York 10017
(212) 986-3240

The National Multiple Sclerosis Society serves persons with multiple sclerosis, their families, health professionals, and the interested public. The society supports research, education, advocacy, and the design of programs. Direct services are provided by 140 local chapters, which also offer counseling and referral services. Eighty-two treatment centers are supported by chapters in thirty states. Volunteers are involved in direct service (transportation, support groups, friendly visiting, telephone reassurance), fund-raising, awareness campaigns, and general problem-solving.

National Society to Prevent Blindness
500 East Remington Road
Schaumburg, Illinois 60173-4557
(312) 843-2020

Founded in 1908, the National Society to Prevent Blindness works to preserve sight and prevent blindness through community service programs, public and professional education, and research. Volunteers perform glaucoma screening and preschool vision testing, help in affiliate offices, and serve on boards and committees of the national organization and local organizations across the country.

STD National Hotline
American Social Health Association
260 Sheridan Avenue, Suite B-40
Palo Alto, California 94306
(415) 327-6465

Volunteer operators speak to individuals concerned about sexually transmissible diseases (STDs), taking calls from all over the country from 8:00 A.M. to 8:00 P.M., Monday through Friday. They are committed to encouraging action and giving callers the tools for action, through referrals to community health care resources for diagnosis, treatment, and follow-up.

The program is open to anyone with an interest in human service and a sincere desire to help other people work out problems. The hotline supports the efforts of volunteers to get academic, internship, and work-experience credit for their participation.

Volunteers for Medical Engineering
3 East 329
The Good Samaritan Hospital
5601 Loch Raven Boulevard
Baltimore, Maryland 21239
(301) 532-4360
(A local organization)

Begun in 1981, Volunteers for Medical Engineering (VME) aids the handicapped and furthers medical science in general through technology transfer. Today more than 200 skilled engineers, technicians, and defense industry professionals are members. Motivated by concern for the disabled and an interest in biomedical technology, they spend much of their off-duty time working without pay on medical engineering projects: among them, a hip orthosis, an apparatus that could enable handicapped people to walk; a computer program to help aphasia sufferers relearn verbal skills; special stainless-steel clamps to hold sections of a defective spinal column in place; a mobile standing frame, similar to a wheelchair except that it allows the user to stand rather than sit. Plans are being made for establishment of VME chapters in other cities.

ENVIRONMENT/ANIMALS

Environmental groups work for the protection of the natural world, advocating against air and water pollution, the thoughtless "development" of unspoiled landscapes, and cruelty to animals. Many support educational and advocacy programs on the local, state, and national levels. Some conduct environmental research projects, run cleanup campaigns, operate educational centers, and rescue injured animals. **Neighborhood cleanup groups** and **recycling centers** are grass-roots efforts for a healthy environment.

Parks—municipal, state, and national—often use squads of volunteers as monitoring and cleanup personnel, and as trail guides. Some conduct sports and recreation programs.

Zoos are sources of education and enjoyment for children and adults. In many large and small zoos, volunteers play roles that range from selling in the gift shop to guiding tours to helping care for the animals. Volunteers in **botanical gardens** conduct tours and assist in greenhouse and grounds-keeping work.

Societies for the Prevention of Cruelty to Animals throughout the country work for the care and protection of animals.

Cincinnati Zoo
3400 Vine Street
Cincinnati, Ohio 45220
(513) 281-4701
(A local organization)

The Cincinnati Zoo has been a forerunner among zoos in the use of volunteers as an integral part of its total operation. In 1986, volunteers clocked an extraordinary total of 86,363 hours. A few of the many jobs they perform are giving tours of the zoo to schoolchildren; adding a personal touch as ZVIs (Zoo Volunteer Interpreters); sharing information about the zoo with the community through the Speakers' Bureau; working in the Media Center; assisting with the A.D.O.P.T. (Animals Depend on People Too) program, a fund-raising effort; performing as Zoosters, a group that hand-makes and sells items at special events, to help cover the costs of signs and graphics around the zoo; managing the Zoo Shop and the Kids' Shop. A special summer program uses Volunteens, who, in addition to answering visitors' questions, assist with the care of the Children's Zoo animals.

Earthwatch
680 Mount Auburn Street
P.O. Box 403
Watertown, Massachusetts 02272
(617) 926-8200

Earthwatch supports the efforts of scholars to preserve the world's endangered habitats and species, explore the heritage of its peoples, and promote world health and international cooperation. Its members sponsor research expeditions, sharing both the costs and the labors of fieldwork. Earthwatch strives to increase public understanding of science and to expand our knowledge of the earth and its inhabitants. Founded in 1971, it has mobilized 950 projects in seventy-five countries, providing researchers with 15,100 volunteers and more than $8.5 million in funds and equipment. Earthwatch is committed to providing opportunities for teachers and students to participate in research expeditions. Sponsors underwrite fellowships for teachers (K–12) and scholarships for high school students.

The Humane Society of the United States
2100 L Street, N.W.
Washington, D.C. 20037
(202) 452-1100

The Humane Society of the United States (HSUS) works to improve the lives of wild and domestic animals. With an active constituency of more than 500,000 persons, the HSUS operates several programs. Foremost among them are continuing efforts to eliminate the surplus of homeless cats and dogs and the attendant suffering these animals experience, including Professional Education Training Seminars to ensure quality care for companion animals. HSUS works to stop the use of live animals for testing and research, to protect marine animals, and to improve conditions for food animals. The legislative staff monitors national policies and promotes the welfare of animals. One legislative priority is protection of endangered species, fur-bearing animals, and wild horses.

The Izaak Walton League of America
1701 North Fort Myer Drive, Suite 1100
Arlington, Virginia 22209
(703) 528-1818 and (800) IKE-LINE

The Izaak Walton League is a conservation organization with 50,000 members working to protect natural resources on the local, state, and national levels. League members are hunters, fishermen, and others who share a commitment to the conservation and wise use of the nation's soil, air, waters, woods, and wildlife. The league has approximately 400 local chapters, many with property, that provide focal points for such conservation activities as clinics on fishing and wildlife habitat, programs for young people, tree-planting, hunter safety instruction, environmental education, and issues advocacy. Volunteers are involved in every phase of league efforts from boards to fund-raising, conservation projects, and advocacy.

Keep America Beautiful
9 West Broad Street
Stamford, Connecticut 06902
(203) 323-8987

Keep America Beautiful (KAB), formed in 1953, is dedicated to building a national cleanliness ethic through improved waste-handling practices at the community level. The Keep America Beautiful System, introduced in 1976, is designed to improve community solid-waste-handling practices and has been adopted by more than 400 communities in forty states. Litter reductions in KAB System communities average 32 percent in the first year and up to 80 percent within five years. In one community, volunteer participation—ranging from educational workshops, special events, litter prevention programs, and executive planning meetings—totaled 129,557 hours and was worth $434,037, calculated at minimum wage.

National Audubon Society
950 Third Avenue
New York, New York 10022
(212) 546-9100

The National Audubon Society is a conservation organization of more than 550,000 members working at international, national, regional, state, and local levels toward the preservation and wise use of America's natural heritage. Programs focus on scientific research, wildlife protection, conservation education, and environmental action. A nationwide sanctuary system protects more than 250,000 acres of unique natural habitat for birds, wildlife, and plants. The organization runs education centers, workshops, and camps, supported by more than 500 chapters throughout the country. Within local chapters, activities include field trips, films and lectures, and work on current issues.

The Nature Conservancy
1800 North Kent Street
Arlington, Virginia 22209
(703) 841-5300

The Nature Conservancy is an international membership organization whose resources are devoted to the protection of ecologically significant areas and the diversity of life they support. Highest priority is placed on the preservation of rare and endangered species through the systematic identification, protection, and management of critical habitats. The national headquarters are located in metropolitan Washington, D.C., with four regional offices, field offices in forty-seven states, and an International Program office in Washington, D.C. Volunteers are appreciated in any capacity, from pro bono public relations work to preserve maintenance. Interested persons should contact the field office nearest them for more information.

Sierra Club
730 Polk Street
San Francisco, California 94109
(415) 776-2211

The Sierra Club promotes conservation of the natural environment by influencing public policy decisions. Its purposes are to explore, enjoy, and protect the wild places of the earth; to practice and promote the responsible use of the earth's ecosystems and resources; to educate and enlist humanity to protect and restore the quality of the natural and human environment; and to use all lawful means to carry out those objectives. In addition to specific issues selected as national conservation campaigns, two major ongoing club programs are the International Program, with its focus on the environmental impact of international development aid and lending, and the Population Growth and Policy Program, with its emphasis on family planning in the U.S. foreign assistance budget.

Take Pride in America
P.O. Box 1339
Jessup, Maryland 20794

The public and private agencies that sponsor the Take Pride in America campaign include the Department of the Interior, ACTION (the federal domestic volunteer agency), the U.S. Chamber of Commerce, Keep America Beautiful, and VOLUNTEER—The National Center. With public awareness efforts centering on television, radio, and print media, thousands of projects to help reduce abuse and promote wise use of public lands are being supported by individuals, businesses, educational institutions, and civic organizations. Information packets, including *50 Ways Every Citizen Can Participate* and a list of contacts by state, can be obtained by writing to the address above.

INTERNATIONAL ORGANIZATIONS

Secular and religious **development and relief agencies** send emergency food and nutritional and agricultural advisers to developing countries throughout the world. Others provide short- and long-term medical and other technical aid, in the form of supplies and personnel. Through **sponsorship programs,** Americans can send money for the care of a child in a foreign country. **Exchange programs** promote international understanding.

Americares Foundation
51 Locust Avenue
New Canaan, Connecticut 06840
(203) 966-5195 and (800) 648-FAST

Based on the idea that items we produce in abundance in our fortunate society can be lifesavers elsewhere, the Americares Foundation works with the corporate world, researching needs and putting donations swiftly into the right hands. Americares is proud of their consistently low overhead (less than 1 percent), which allows a $1 contribution to deliver a minimum of $25 worth of aid. In 1985, the foundation sent $44 million worth of medicines and relief to nineteen countries—with a budget of $200,000. Across the country and around the world, Americares joins forces with like-minded individuals, agencies, and corporations.

Amnesty International USA
322 Eighth Avenue
New York, New York 10001
(212) 807-8400

Amnesty International is an independent worldwide movement working impartially for the release of all prisoners of conscience, fair and prompt trials for political prisoners, and an end to torture and executions. More than 500,000 members and supporters in 150 countries participate in a variety of programs, among them community- and campus-based groups who write letters, publicize, and organize actions in behalf of individual prisoners; Freedom Writers, a network of people who write in behalf of prisoners (each month, Amnesty International USA sends them information on three cases, along with letters addressed to the appropriate officials); and programs that use the expertise of health and legal professionals.

Food for the Hungry
P.O. Box E
Scottsdale, Arizona 85252-9987
(602) 998-3100

Food for the Hungry is a Christian nondenominational international relief and development agency that has ongoing programs in twelve countries. Trained Hunger Corps volunteers, who raise their own support, serve for two years in Third World projects such as food distribution, horticulture, small animal husbandry, and water development. A volunteer may participate in the construction of a building, dam, or well, or conduct nutritional surveys. The Everychild program channels donations from individuals to the support of children. Monthly contributions help provide food, seed, tools, and other self-help items, such as solar cookers, trays for soilless growing, and much more, for a child and his or her family.

International Christian Youth Exchange
134 West 26th Street
New York, New York 10001
(212) 206-7307

Established as a German-American program in 1949, International Christian Youth Exchange (ICYE) today is a federation of national committees in twenty-eight countries in Europe, North America, Latin America, Africa, and Asia and the Pacific. A network of staff and volunteers in each country is committed to working toward peace and justice through international exchange. ICYE is endorsed by major Protestant and Catholic denominations. High school students ages sixteen through eighteen live with a host family and attend high school in a host country's community. People eighteen through twenty-four serve as volunteers with community projects. Other opportunities for volunteer participation are to join one of the regional teams in the United States that coordinate programs for exchange participants; to act as a host family or host voluntary service agency; and to form a sponsoring committee in the community to support participation in the ICYE program.

Interplast
378-J Cambridge Avenue
Palo Alto, California 94306
(415) 329-0670

Interplast is an organization of volunteer surgeons, pediatricians, anesthesiologists, and nurses from leading medical institutions in the United States and Canada who provide free reconstructive plastic surgery for children in developing nations who have been physically and socially scarred by birth defects or injuries. Before an Interplast visit, these children are often ostracized by their peers, living a painful and isolated existence. After the Interplast team has come, scores of youngsters find a new life and are accepted not only by other people but by themselves as well. In the fiscal year ending March 1987, 215 volunteer medical people made twenty trips to developing countries, performing 1,394 free operations.

Meals for Millions/
Freedom from Hunger Foundation
1644 DaVinci Court
P.O. Box 2000
Davis, California 95617
(916) 758-6200

Through its Applied Nutrition programs and self-help approach, Meals for Millions/Freedom from Hunger Foundation works against malnutrition around the world, including poor areas of the United States, and toward the goal of a hunger-free world. The organization's objectives are to improve the nutritional status of children and pregnant and nursing women, and to create opportunities for the hungry and poor to become part of the permanent solution to world hunger, by establishing an ongoing development process that is self-sustaining in the community. The organization's president has written, "We can help turn the victims of poverty into victors, by helping people help themselves and take control of their own lives' possibilities."

Northwest Medical Teams
P.O. Box 17075
Salem, Oregon 97305
(503) 399-8326

Northwest Medical Teams (NMT) is a Christian relief agency dedicated to providing medical care, equipment, and supplies to the needy of the world, relying on the active involvement of committed men and women who will serve as physicians, nurses, and medical technicians in countries with desperate needs. While the primary focus of NMT is to meet emergency needs, their program falls into three categories: acute emergency care when natural or man-made disaster strikes; intermediate care to displaced persons or refugees of famine or politics; and long-term care in clinics for the treatment of acute and infectious diseases and for the training of local doctors and personnel.

OEF International
1815 H Street, N.W., 11th Floor
Washington, D.C. 20006
(202) 466-3430

Formerly known as the Overseas Education Fund, OEF International designs and delivers training and technical assistance programs that address the economic and social needs of low-income women in developing countries. OEF's efforts have enabled tens of thousands of women in more than fifty countries to work together to manage profitable enterprises, increase local food production, overcome legal inequities, and organize for community development. In the United States, OEF works to increase public awareness about the critical roles of Third World women in development. OEF's U.S. membership is made up of women in business, corporate executives, and entrepreneurs, who are valuable sources for fund-raising and are committed to strengthening the role of women in developing countries.

Oxfam America
115 Broadway
Boston, Massachusetts 02116
(617) 482-1211

Oxfam America is an international agency that funds self-help development projects and disaster relief in poor countries in Africa, Asia, Latin America, and the Caribbean, and also prepares and distributes educational materials on issues of development and hunger for people in the United States. Overseas, the organization's grants support small projects that reach into villages and rural areas where local groups are working to increase their own food production or for economic self-reliance. In the United States, it conducts educational campaigns and speaks out about public policies that hinder its grass-roots development work abroad.

Peace Corps
806 Connecticut Avenue, N.W.
Washington, D.C. 20526
(202) 254-9814 and (800) 424-8580, ext. 93

The Peace Corps, now in its third decade, continues to rely on the dedication and commitment of Americans of all ages who volunteer to spend two years helping the people of developing countries to meet their basic needs for health care, food, shelter, and education. The goals of the Peace Corps as originally set out by Congress remain unchanged: to help promote world peace and friendship; to help developing countries to meet their needs for skilled men and women; to help promote mutual understanding between the people of the United States and those of developing nations. There are now more than 6,000 volunteers and trainees in sixty-two nations in Latin America, Africa, Asia, and the Pacific. They offer skills in a wide variety of programs: maternal and child health, family nutrition, freshwater fisheries, agriculture extension, teacher training, math and science education, vocational training, small business consulting, public administration, natural resource development, forestry, conservation, energy, engineering, special education, and industrial arts.

Sister Cities International
120 South Payne Street
Alexandria, Virginia 22314
(703) 836-3535

The Sister City program as a national concept was launched at the White House in 1956 when President Dwight Eisenhower called for massive exchanges between Americans and the peoples of other lands. Hundreds of American cities responded and today are carrying out meaningful exchanges with their affiliates in eighty-six nations. The ideal affiliation involves a large number of citizens and organizations in both communities, engaged in continuing projects of mutual interest. Cities and their citizens exchange people, ideas, and culture in a variety of educational, institutional, municipal, professional, technical, and youth projects.

Volunteers in Technical Assistance
1815 North Lynn Street, Suite 200
Arlington, Virginia 22209-2079
(703) 276-1800

Volunteers in Technical Assistance (VITA) is an international development organization. It makes available to individuals and groups in developing countries a variety of information and technical resources aimed at fostering self-sufficiency: needs assessment and program development support; consulting services; information systems training; and management of long-term field projects. VITA places special emphasis on agriculture and food processing, renewable energy applications, water supply and sanitation, housing and construction, and small business development. VITA's activities are facilitated by the active involvement of thousands of volunteer technical experts from around the world.

Youth for Understanding International Exchange
3501 Newark Street, N.W.
Washington, D.C. 20016-3167
(202) 966-6800

Youth for Understanding International Exchange (YFU) is dedicated to improving international and intercultural understanding through exchange programs for high school students. Founded in 1951, YFU operates exchange programs with more than two dozen countries, and more than 125,000 students have participated in the program. The organization operates from an International Center in Washington, D.C., and thirteen regional offices across the United States. More than 2,500 volunteers work with the YFU program in their home communities, helping in the recruitment, selection, and orientation of students and host parents. Volunteers also assist in counseling and support services, in training of other volunteers, and in fund-raising and public affairs.

GROUPS OF INTEREST TO CHILDREN AND YOUTH

While young people can become involved in many of the organizations described above, there are many groups that are designed for the primary participation of the young. Here's a small sample.

Boy Scouts of America
1325 Walnut Hill Lane
Irving, Texas 75038-3096
(214) 580-2000

The purpose of Boy Scouts of America is to provide an educational program for boys and young adults: to build character, to train in the responsibilities of participatory citizenship, and to develop personal fitness. Community organizations that are granted charters use scouting programs as part of their youth programs. They select adult leaders, provide resources and facilities, and recruit participants. More than 400 Boy Scout Councils administer programs locally. Adult volunteer leaders, assisted by a few full-time staff members, help chartered organizations to use scouting programs, train leaders, develop and maintain camping opportunities, recruit new members, and organize activities.

Camp Fire
4601 Madison Avenue
Kansas City, Missouri 64112-1278
(816) 756-1950

Camp Fire is a youth agency serving both boys and girls, with programs in the four major areas of clubs, camping, self-reliance courses, and child care. The purpose of Camp Fire is to provide, through a program of informal education, opportunities for youth to realize their potential and to function effectively as caring, self-directed individuals, responsible to themselves and others. As an organization, Camp Fire seeks to improve those conditions in society that affect young people. Youth membership is nearly 400,000, and more than 60,000 adult members serve in a volunteer capacity. Volunteers may be program leaders, board members, or office staff in the nearly 300 local councils nationwide.

Campus Compact: The Project for Public and Community Service
Box 1975, Brown University
Providence, Rhode Island 02912
(401) 863-1119

Campus Compact, a national coalition of college and university presidents, works with university staff, students, service organizations, and community, state, and national leaders to promote public service. The group provides information and technical assistance to campus public service programs, develops public policy that encourages student public service, strengthens links between the campuses and off-campus service organizations, places the issue of public service on the national agenda, and identifies sources of financial support for campus public service programs and for students involved in service work. Campus Compact is developing a public service network that will assist college and university service programs in matching students seeking service opportunities with local and regional agencies.

Campus Outreach Opportunity League
810 18th Street, N.W., Suite 705
Washington, D.C. 20006
(202) 783-8855

Campus Outreach Opportunity League (COOL) is a national network that promotes and supports student involvement in addressing community needs. In addition to direct, on-campus outreach work, COOL has developed resources to help build stronger student community service organizations, including on-site peer consulting and technical assistance (in COOL's first three years, the staff visited more than 200 campuses); a newsletter and a resource book, a 200-page manual of practical advice on how to start and run a campus community service organization, as well as ideas on programming, recruitment, promotion, fund-raising, and available resources; state and regional workshops and an annual national conference; and special projects, such as Campus Green, designed to increase student involvement in environmental issues.

City Volunteer Corps
842 Broadway
New York, New York 10003
(212) 475-6444
(A local organization)

The City Volunteer Corps (CVC), funded by the City of New York, each year recruits, trains, and fields 1,000 New Yorkers, aged seventeen to twenty, to provide full- and part-time community service. Working in teams, City Volunteers (CVs) provide a broad range of needed services to city agencies and not-for-profit organizations: tutoring elementary school children, rehabilitating abandoned housing for the homeless, teaching daily living skills to the disabled, caring for the elderly and homebound, and beautifying parks and beaches. CVs attend college credit, college preparation, high school equivalency, adult literacy, and English as a second language courses. They receive a weekly expense stipend and after a year of service are awarded scholarships or cash.

Future Homemakers of America
1910 Association Drive
Reston, Virginia 22091
(703) 476-4900

Future Homemakers of America is a national vocational student organization whose 300,000 male and female members are involved in home economics education in junior and senior high schools. Its mission is to help youth assume active roles in society through education in personal growth, family life, vocational preparation, and community involvement. There are fifty-three state associations and 11,000 local chapters. Programs include the development of skills in money management and financial planning; the encouragement of leadership skills for advancement in food service careers; community service projects; a peer education program that addresses personal self-awareness, nutrition, and fitness; and local projects on AIDS education, teen pregnancy, substance abuse, and family communication.

Girl Scouts of the U.S.A.
830 Third Avenue
New York, New York 10022
(212) 940-7500

Girl Scouts of the U.S.A. is open to all girls aged five to seventeen and to adults, both men and women. Its purpose is to help each girl realize her individual potential through activities such as career exploration and community service. Girls are introduced to science, the arts, the out-of-doors, and people. They grow in skill and self-confidence, have fun, make new friends, and earn meaningful recognition. More than 2,200,000 girls participate, and there are 669,000 adult members. Adults volunteer as board members, consultants, and troop leaders. Troops—174,000, including troops overseas in sixty-two countries—are organized by 335 local Girl Scout councils.

Junior Achievement
45 Clubhouse Drive
Colorado Springs, Colorado 80906
(303) 540-8000

Junior Achievement (JA) provides economic education for youth. In partnership with the business and educational communities, JA serves students of all races in 237 of the nation's inner cities, suburbs, and rural areas. With volunteer business executives and teachers working in tandem, programs reach three age levels: fifth and sixth grades, eighth and ninth grades, and high school. Economics are brought to life for one million students each year, in three in-school programs (Applied Economics, Project Business, and Business Basics), as well as after school in the original JA Company program, in which, during the 1986–87 school year, more than 104,000 high school students learned how to run a business by going into business.

YMCA of the USA
101 North Wacker Drive
Chicago, Illinois 60606-7386
(312) 977-0031

The YMCA is dedicated to building health of body, mind, and spirit. Part of a worldwide movement, it puts Christian principles into practice through programs that promote good health, strong families, youth leadership, community development, and international understanding. YMCAs are open to men, women, and children of all ages, incomes, abilities, races, and religions, at more than 2,000 locations in fifty states. In 1986, the YMCA served 13 million people, making it one of the largest community service organizations in the country. More than 360,000 hometown volunteers take part in all aspects of the YMCA, from being on boards to teaching classes to working at front desks. The organization depends on its volunteers to come up with new programs, help run them, and raise money.

YWCA of the U.S.A.
726 Broadway
New York, New York 10003
(212) 614-2851

The YWCA of the U.S.A. is made up of some 400 community and student associations operating at more than 3,000 locations throughout the nation. More than 1.5 million women, girls, and their families participate in YWCA activities. YWCAs offer vocational, educational, and personal development programs, as well as special programs for infants, children, and teens, and for seniors, the handicapped, and other groups with special needs. The YWCA advocates for women and the issues that affect them nationally and locally. More than 120,000 volunteers representing every walk of life, economic group, and ethnic, racial, and religious background donate their time, energy, and talent, working in partnership with staff.

GROUPS OF INTEREST TO SENIOR CITIZENS AND RETIRED PEOPLE

Older people are actively involved throughout the independent sector and are valued for their wealth of experience and expertise. Many organizations have been formed to specifically focus on the talents of senior citizens.

American Association of Retired Persons
1909 K Street, N.W.
Washington, D.C. 20049
(202) 872-4700

More than 28 million people aged fifty and over are members of the American Association of Retired Persons (AARP). Members are active in community, state, and national affairs. Through approximately 3,500 AARP chapters and 2,600 Retired Teachers Association units across the country, members can become involved in volunteer service and fellowship activities. To assist local groups, AARP maintains a volunteer network of more than 6,000 officials in ten geographic regions. An additional 30,000 volunteers serve in such programs as Tax-Aide, Medicare assistance, and driver improvement. Others participate in state and local legislative activities. AARP's Volunteer Talent Bank gives interested members and other older people access to AARP volunteer opportunities as well as positions in other volunteer organizations; to register, contact AARP.

Foster Grandparent Program
ACTION
806 Connecticut Avenue, N.W., Room 1006
Washington, D.C. 20525
(202) 634-9349 and (800) 424-8867

Through the Foster Grandparent Program (FGP)—run by ACTION, the federal domestic volunteer agency—low-income Americans aged sixty and older provide person-to-person service to children. In 1986, through 249 FGP projects, some 19,000 volunteers gave close to 20 million hours to children suffering from various disabilities—abuse and neglect, handicaps, drug and alcohol abuse, mental retardation, illiteracy, and delinquency. Foster grandparents serve four hours a day, five days a week, through nonprofit agencies such as schools, hospitals, juvenile detention centers, Head Start, shelters, state schools, and drug rehabilitation centers. The program allows volunteers a stipend of $2.20 per hour, transportation and meal assistance, and insurance.

Gray Panthers
311 South Juniper Street, Suite 601
Philadelphia, Pennsylvania 19107
(215) 545-6555

The Gray Panthers, founded in 1970, seek to promote an intergenerational philosophy and positive attitudes toward aging and to oppose age discrimination. The group works for the greater collective empowerment of all people, including the dependent, and encourages a greater appreciation of the racial, ethnic, and cultural diversity of American society. Specific areas of interest include Social Security, access to health care, a national health service, peace, nursing home reform, the rights of the disabled, and housing. The Gray Panthers have 70,000 national members-at-large plus an active local chapter membership of about 10,000. The nearly 100 local chapters in almost thirty states have a high degree of autonomy on issue emphasis and tactical decisions.

International Executive Service Corps
8 Stamford Forum
P.O. Box 10005
Stamford, Connecticut 60904-2005
(203) 967-6000

International Executive Service Corps (IESC) recruits retired, highly skilled U.S. executives and technical advisers to share their years of experience with businesses in the developing nations. The men and women selected by IESC work as volunteers. They serve as advisers on short-term assignments, implement improvements, and develop guidelines that the client can follow in the future. IESC has answered requests to help businesses ranging from the manufacture of handbags to steel mills. Working in eighty-four different nations since advisers were first sent abroad in 1965, IESC has completed more than 11,000 projects and has some 9,000 experienced men and women ready to supply their expertise.

National Executive Service Corps
257 Park Avenue South
New York, New York 10003
(212) 867-5010

The National Executive Service Corps (NESC) is a management consulting organization dedicated to improving the effectiveness of organizations that exist for the betterment of society. NESC provides management improvement services that utilize the experience of retired senior-level businesspeople. These seasoned consultants contribute their time to achieve solutions to operational problems for a broad spectrum of educational, health, social service, cultural, and religious organizations. Consulting assignments average six months and conclude with written analyses and recommendations for future action. NESC serves clients in all regions of the country and has helped organize thirty independent Executive Service Corps throughout the United States.

Older Women's League
730 11th Street, N.W., Suite 300
Washington, D.C. 20001
(202) 783-6686

The Older Women's League (OWL) is a national membership organization addressing the special concerns of midlife and older women. OWL's purpose is to propose solutions to the difficult problems women face as they age and to educate and support women as they pursue these solutions. OWL's agenda currently is focused on such issues as Social Security reform, pension rights, health care in retirement, job opportunities, and care-giver support services. OWL chapters are located in 100 communities in thirty-five states, with a membership of 17,000. With the exception of a small, Washington-based staff, OWL is an all-volunteer organization. Volunteers work on the board of directors, do fund-raising and other support activities, and are involved with issues advocacy.

Retired Senior Volunteer Program
ACTION
806 Connecticut Avenue, N.W., Room 1006
Washington, D.C. 20525
(202) 634-9353 and (800) 424-8867

In 1986, the Retired Senior Volunteer Program (RSVP)—run by ACTION, the federal domestic volunteer agency—celebrated its fifteenth anniversary. Through 750 projects, 365,000 volunteers aged sixty or older were assigned to 51,000 community agencies nationwide. RSVP volunteers serve in courts, schools, museums, libraries, hospices, hospitals, nursing homes, and other service centers. They may be reimbursed for transportation expenses. Current RSVP projects emphasize services to youth, literacy, drug abuse, in-home care, consumer education, crime prevention, and management assistance to private nonprofit and public agencies.

SCORE
1129 20th Street, N.W., Suite 410
Washington, D.C. 20036
(202) 653-6279 and (800) 368-5855

SCORE is the acronym for the Service Corps of Retired Executives, a 12,500-member association of volunteers who work out of 592 locations in every state of the Union. SCORE is sponsored by the U.S. Small Business Administration and funded with $2.1 million annually. Members counsel people wanting to go into business or to expand existing businesses, and helps those in financial trouble. Counseling is always free, though a small charge is made for workshops. SCORE was established in 1964 and handles about 620,000 clients annually.

Senior Companion Program
ACTION
806 Connecticut Avenue, N.W., Room 1006
Washington, D.C. 20525
(202) 634-9351 and (800) 424-8867

In the Senior Companion Program (SCP)—run by ACTION, the federal domestic volunteer agency—low-income Americans aged sixty and older provide personalized assistance to older adults in need of care and companionship. In 1986, approximately 5,300 Companions helped 18,600 clients achieve their highest level of independent living. Through ninety-seven SCP projects, volunteers gave more than 5.6 million hours to clients who are homebound and at risk of being institutionalized. Senior Companions, who work twenty hours per week, receive a stipend of $2.20 per hour, meals, transportation assistance, and insurance.

IN THEIR OWN WORDS

"The volunteer is like an angel who appears and gives these people an outlet, someone they can 'conspire' with against family, friends, or staff. So just listening to a patient can be a tremendous thing."

—Michael Lutin

"The most moving experience I have had in the nonprofit world was in attending my first President's Volunteer Action Awards luncheon, where President Reagan personally gave the awards. I had helped select the winners, and seeing those people receive awards from the president for such outstanding service was indeed a humbling experience."

—Betty James

"I think that if we're going to attract good people and hope to expand volunteerism, it should be talked about, because the working world has to be educated to the fact that you can't have it both ways. If you really want that job to be done, you have to respect the volunteer who takes the time to get the task accomplished."

—Debbie Scott

Michael Lutin: *Michael Lutin is an astrologer, counselor, and writer who has built a multifaceted career. In addition to a private practice in which he provides individual counseling, he is well known in professional astrological circles as a writer and lecturer. He gained popular fame in the mid-1980s with his witty column in* Vanity Fair *magazine. Three mornings a week, he volunteers at the Spellman Unit, set up to deal with AIDS patients, at St. Clare's Hospital, a Roman Catholic medical-surgical hospital in Manhattan.*

You can volunteer at St. Clare's on any basis you want. There are hotline people, who work mainly with telephones, the AIDS hotline connected with the hospital. People call in and say, where can I be tested, where is the nearest center to me, etc. Some of the problems are serious medical problems, and some of the calls are from scared people—they're called the worried well—and some are just cranks. But it serves a definite function in helping to educate the public, because if you have a certain symptom, you want to talk to someone about it.

Suppose a person really hates hospitals but wants to do something for AIDS. I know one guy who goes around to all the businesses, getting them to contribute various items, to either AIDS patients or the hospital, whatever equipment the hospital may need. But that person is not interested in working either on the hotline or the floor. Someone else may be into fund-raising. There's one person who wants to offer his beach home to AIDS patients.

Then you have floor people. Floor people for AIDS patients are different from the others. For one thing, the commitment is different, because you're working on a ward where many people are normally afraid to go. So immediately you're in a much more intense and passionate environment.

I don't want to pass over that lightly, because the volunteer has a very special position in a patient's life. The volunteer is not a staff member—staff members are sometimes looked upon by the patients as authority figures, you know, nurses and doctors. Volunteers are not family, either. So a volunteer can often get a patient to do things or talk about things that they would normally not do with the staff or their family. In that sense, they're like angels.

There was a guy yesterday when I went in, he was about thirty years old, and I could see that he might have been a pain in the ass to his family. I said to him, what would you like? And he said, well, nothing, really. I said, what would you like, if there were no limitations in the world, what would you like? He said, I'd like a vanilla milkshake. So I went out and got him a vanilla milkshake, and he loved it.

The volunteer is like an angel who appears and gives these people an outlet, someone they can "conspire" with against family, friends, or staff. So just listening to a patient can be a tremendous thing.

There are other valuable services that are done on the floor, with patients. For example, if you are into it, within the bounds of the law—because the law doesn't permit you to do certain things— you can help the staff with making beds, feeding patients. I myself am very much into that, I got into it maybe more than many people would in terms of the medical stuff.

There are many AIDS patients who are no longer able to care for themselves or feed themselves. Family members are often not there three meals a day, and staff members simply cannot do it, there just aren't enough hands to go around.

Volunteers provide various services on holidays. They decorate the place, they have parties, Christmas, Halloween, they make the decorations. I believe it was Norma Kamali who donated little live Christmas trees for all the rooms this past year.

Volunteers are preparing a visitor brochure, in which visitors will be told what the dangers are and are not—to help them to not be afraid. So many of the patients say their parents come and stand on the other side of the room, won't come near them and don't want to have anything to do with them.

There's another project, which I have been doing informally and would like very much to get done on a formal basis. When patients get discharged from the hospital, often they live alone, and they couldn't drag a cat across the room, they're so weak. What I've done, at least when I'm aware of the discharge, is I go out and buy a picnic basket of food—peanut butter, tuna fish, a loaf of bread, bananas, stuff they don't have to cook, because they can barely spread peanut butter on bread. I would like to get a program going of picnic baskets so that when these people go home, they'll at least get a start for a while.

Many donations are made for the lounges and the various

rooms, so that the decor can become less clinical and more home-like. That's a project that's run by volunteers.

We have a clothing room—because many of our people are very poor and don't have any clothes to go home in. This one guy was so afraid to ask for anything when he was going to be discharged. So I said, wouldn't you like some clothes? He said, well, yeah. I said, I'll go down and get you a shirt, what color do you want? And he said, oh, I don't care. I said, you must like some colors better than others—he was afraid to ask for a color. So he said blue. I came back and said, I only have an Yves Saint Laurent in the blue, and he said, oh, that's all right. The next time I saw him, he sent me back for socks, and the next time he sent me back for pants, and then when I came back he sent me for shoes. He was afraid to ask for everything all at once. He thought if he stretched it out over my visits, it would be okay.

We also have arts and crafts—the volunteers often take part in that. The patients who are able to go down to the lounge, and they make things or paint things, and that's a wonderful pastime. We have a library, donated books that are shelved. We have a musical library, for records and albums and stuff. That's all done and arranged by volunteers.

Sometimes a patient wants you to go out on an errand. You go out and get bananas or a newspaper, something like that. We have also envisioned a project that is not happening yet. We're calling it the Night Watchers. Many patients get very frightened during the night, and we'd like to see a system where we will rotate, so that we will sit through night shifts and be available for any patient who gets scared, or to help put the family's mind at ease.

And then there's ongoing care. This is a problem that we don't know how to deal with yet. Once AIDS patients get in the hospital, they lose their apartments—then what? They're mostly very depressed people anyway, because they've been given this terrifying diagnosis, so they don't have the same kind of goals they once had. How to deal with them, how to help them, where are they going to go afterward, who's going to take care of them, that sort of thing. Many patients are not connected with **Gay Men's Health Crisis,** which does a lot in that area. The social workers come in at this point and do what they can, and a lot of volunteers are involved in that as well. We also have a very special project of building a roof garden on top of the hospital.

The training of volunteer staff is done by staff members and volunteers. There's orientation, supervision, scheduling, various speakers come and tell you how to make a bed, how to feed a patient, the newest advances in medication, education about AIDS.

When I first got there, the director said to me, when you first come on you're going to have personal relationships and it's going to be heartbreaking. But after a while, he said, it's going to be like a bus accident. I will never forget that, because it was such a vivid image. He said, you're just going to run around and do bandaging, but the feelings will become generalized.

I had a very favorite person in Room 306. He was just the most cooperative sweet guy, and I would go in there and I'd say, Tony, how are you today, and he'd say, great, and I'd say, well, you'd never tell me if it wasn't great. He just quietly went into his coma and quietly died, never complaining. That's a good four or five weeks ago, and even now that's Tony's room. I can't quite really care for the guy in that room yet. I just sort of go in and give him his stuff and leave. So you get attached no matter what you think.

But as sad as it is for me, the enormity of it is allowing me to carry on, because the enormity of their suffering, the oddness and the weirdness of their suffering, and the bizarre nature of what happens to them—that allows me to carry on even though it's so terribly sad.

Probably my motives are mixed. Maybe I think that I won't catch it if I do this, and God will see me doing such good work, maybe part of that's true.

When I first went there, I tried to stay away from the scariest rooms. There was one guy who had one arm, and he stayed in a darkened room all the time, and I would never go in that room. I don't think I even took ice in there.

And the second or third time, the minute I arrived the nurse said to me, sit with him, he's got a high fever. And I went into this darkened room with this guy with one arm, and I was terrified. And then I realized, what am I doing? This is what I'm here for. And so I took off his gown and gave him an alcohol rub, and I continued to give him alcohol baths until his family came, and then they did it, and then his fever went away, and eventually I became friends with him. He became one of my favorite people, and we became friends outside of the hospital.

And now I make it my business to go into the rooms where the people are the worst, because that is in fact what I'm there for. So I go in there and I hold their hand, no matter what kind of horrendous shape they're in, and take care of them and change them and make their beds and give them something to drink.

I'm just thinking of one particular patient. I took care of him for so many weeks. He lived so much longer than you thought that he was going to live—they often do. And then one day you come in, and you're sure he's going to be dead, and he's out of bed and eating pancakes and asking you to go get him lasagna. They just get stronger, the life force is so tremendous. You can actually see the battle taking place between the virus and their life force. And then you'll think that they're better, and you'll come in in the morning and they will have died quietly during the night.

When I first went there on a Monday—it was supposed to be Mondays from eight to twelve—I realized that if I only did it on Mondays, it would take me five years before I learned where the ice machine was. So I decided that I was going to go Monday, Thursday, and Saturday for about two and a half hours each. I've never deviated from it, except on the few weekends when I have been on a business trip, for conferences, but except for that, I've never just gone off for the weekend.

Tomorrow I'm going to the Berkshires, but I'm not going until after the hospital. So I've never just decided, oh, forget it, and gone to the Berkshires. Some people, because it's a volunteer thing, might do that, although most take it very seriously. Monday's my day, Thursday's my day, Saturday's my day.

When I leave that hospital every day, I feel that I've been paid. It's unbelievably rewarding in several ways. One, your patients are so grateful for a glass of water. One guy was dying yesterday, he just lay there. Medication doesn't do much good at this point. He just whimpers, just whimpers. His body is already dead, you feel like you're moving a corpse. There's no life in the muscles whatsoever, but his mind is still alive.

And he's cognizant, because I said to him yesterday, can you hear me, and he said, yeah. I said, would you like a glass of water, and he just opened his eyes, and I poured water down his throat, because he's not able to do anything. And he swallowed it, and he was so happy. So you have a level of . . . you know, it's like the sponge and Christ on the cross, you actually feel that sometimes.

Working at St. Clare's Hospital has been such an amazing experience, the love that's on the floor, the special caring, because anybody who works with AIDS patients is there because they want to be. I mean, the term Holy Ghost has a whole new meaning. There's magic going on in that place. The staff, the head nurse is just, I mean, I'm happy to even just see her for a minute during the day, she's such a wonderful person. The clerical people are also so great. The orderlies, the staff, just the associations you have.

I would never have had dealings with these people, plus I never had much interest in medicine or medical things, I still don't. So not only do you feel good because you are helping somebody who is really in need, but you are associating with people who are doing something so crucial and meaningful.

Everyone volunteers for different motives. I never understood it, and you know something, I never, ever had any interest in it. My friends used to talk about their volunteering, and I used to think, gee, they're so fortunate to be able to volunteer, I'm just struggling to keep my head above water in my career. I could never spare the time. Now that I'm involved, it's been great. I don't ever intend to stop it in the foreseeable future.

Betty James: *Betty James serves on the President's Volunteer Action Advisory Council, which advises ACTION, the federal domestic volunteer agency, and, along with VOLUNTEER—The National Center, sponsors the President's Volunteer Action Awards, a privately funded national program to recognize achievement by individuals and organizations (see page 26).*

I have not worked since I was married. Before I was married, I was a technical writer and editor, and much of my volunteer work has been in the writing and editing field. I have worked on various community newspapers and magazines, and also for our church. Other than that, I've primarily been involved in volunteer fundraising activities for our local school, hospital, church, and the Republican party.

I think that anyone who volunteers his or her talent or time receives a wonderful reward; the rewards are far greater than the effort put in. There are so many benefits that come from volunteering.

My husband is very active in the Freedoms Foundation of Valley Forge, which has the goal of creating a sense of civic responsibility in young people. So many of our schools no longer teach civics, and the Foundation offers an educational program for outstanding juniors from high schools throughout the country, who are brought to the campus at Valley Forge. They are trained for a week or two in what we call the good old American spirit of civic responsibility and then sent back to their respective schools, with the hope that they will become leaders in their senior year.

Also, in the summers there is an extensive training program for high school teachers. One of the primary objectives of the Freedoms Foundation of Valley Forge is to recognize outstanding teachers throughout the country for their special efforts in teaching the values of democracy and freedom.

In terms of board membership, my primary effort has been with hospitals. I have usually started in a volunteer capacity, in raising funds, and that has led to serving on the board of trustees. I have not become involved with any board straight out, and my experience would say that it's a matter of working up through the ranks, knowing the volunteer program, and then going on to management.

The most moving experience I have had in the nonprofit world was in attending my first President's Volunteer Action Awards luncheon, where President Reagan personally gave the awards. I had helped select the winners, and seeing those people receive awards from the president for such outstanding service was indeed a humbling experience.

The interesting thing about these awards is that some are for individuals and some are for organizations; however, they are not the typical organizations found in most major cities. We try to find unusual types of volunteer activities, but ones that can be replicated anywhere in the country.

Debbie Scott: *An athlete and a pilot, in addition to being a wife and mother, Debbie Scott has been chairperson of the board of trustees of the* **Ethel Walker School** *in Simsbury, Connecticut, and of the* **Hurricane Island Outward Bound School** *in Maine. She has a wonderful sense of humor and outstanding judgment, and she gets things done with a light touch.*

I grew up in New Jersey, in Oradell and Englewood, but at 15 I went away to school. I was always fooling around and I guess they insisted I go where I would work. I went from public to private day school for one year and finally they sent me off to boarding school, which was probably the best thing that ever happened to me. I went to Ethel Walker. That was great, because they really challenged me and made me realize the great advantage of hard work, which up to then I had managed to get away without. I had three very good years at Ethel Walker.

I knew about volunteer work as a child. My mother and my grandmother did some, although I don't remember anything major. At Ethel Walker, I certainly was given a lot of understanding about what can be done—just in thinking about the world at large as a bigger place and the needs in general, the problems. In those days you had to go to chapel, but it was nondenominational and they had different speakers. So I was inspired by many people at the school and left there with the attitude that service was just a normal expectation I would have of myself.

I went on to Smith College but left halfway to get married— when I was just twenty-one, which is incredible to me, looking back. We had a child right away. I don't know who I thought was going to teach me what I was supposed to know. I certainly had no qualms about it, I just went right into it. I had three children within the first five years, but even then I was involved in volunteer work with the **Junior League.** I was eager to get involved in something other than diapers.

Even though I only had two years of college, it was enough to make me aware—and my mother, father, and grandmother had, too—that there was more to life than just staying home. My first volunteer work after I was married was at the **Stamford, Connecticut, Day Care Center,** an early day care facility. From then on, I just did various things that fit in well with my time restraints, nothing particularly amazing, no major responsibility. But mostly it involved education.

Some of it was boring and uninteresting and just duty work, and some was interesting, as I got more involved. Later I worked with a cooperative nursery school and wound up on the board there. I was also on various committees in the New Canaan, Connecticut, public schools. Eventually, my kids ended up in private school, and I was very active in the usual volunteer duties expected of you in private day schools.

Later when our last child was headed for boarding school, I decided to go back to college. I had also begun to be involved with Ethel Walker as an alumna. I got more and more involved, became a board member, and finally was offered the chair of the board of trustees. It was a very interesting time, a very scary time. I almost didn't take it because I recognized the real problems, but I decided to go for it.

I went for it because I saw an opportunity to make a difference in the school in areas that I thought could be changed and improved. I felt that there were things happening both in education for women and in education for teenagers. I became interested in adolescence, and it dovetailed beautifully with what I had learned about education through my own children.

I became chairman of the nominating committee at a time when the male chairman had been in office a long time. He had done a lot for the school. But a number of other board members, whom I agreed with, felt that certain key issues were not being addressed and that lack of resolution was causing increasing problems. Some women on the board were concerned that they weren't being used, that too many board committees were inactive at a time when there were many hot issues in education that were pertinent and important to the secondary school years. I had an opportunity to bring about a major new direction by nominating a woman as chairman. She was a terrific gal whom I admire tremendously, and she in turn made some major board changes.

The significant benefit for me, as I chaired other committees of the board, was an opportunity to get involved at a higher level in an area where I had an interest. I became involved at a level on which, had I been in the work world, I just couldn't have participated. If I had jumped into a career at that point I would have had to start at a much lower level, and it would have taken longer for me to be recognized in the general competition with my peers and within a corporate organization.

In this context, I was able to be an influence at the policy level. It was very satisfying. Although it was scary, it was an exciting opportunity. It also afforded me the chance to be with people who were stimulating, including some people that I had made assumptions about. I saw how they really operated and that my assumptions had been pretty naïve. I got to know people as people instead of by their positions.

After being on the Ethel Walker board for six or seven years, I was asked to serve as the chairman, a post I held for five years. It was while I was chairman of the board at Ethel Walker that I was invited to go on the board of the Hurricane Island Outward Bound School. Later I became chairperson of that school as well, the year that I got off the board at Walkers. That position led me to service on the executive committee of Outward Bound USA.

It was with some thought, concern, and nervousness that I took the chair at Hurricane Island, because I didn't know the board as well, and I felt very insecure when I took it. But it turned out to be a good fit, a challenging job with an outstanding group of people.

In both my major involvements, I don't think I handled the time demands terribly well. It was hard to do because your obligation to family is less clear after your children are off in college. You see a tremendous time opening up for yourself, but it's amazing how family ties and needs continue.

I was very involved in the Ethel Walker situation. For at least a five-year period, from 1975 to 1980, it was extremely time-consuming. Situations occurred that caused me many a sleepless night. I must say that I was sort of drawn into some responsibilities—because the situation required me to be—rather than choosing to be. The school was going through major challenges, from the debate on going coeducational, to some serious personnel issues. I can't say I chose to put that much time into it, but I did.

As for Hurricane Island, once I was in the position of chair, rightly or wrongly I felt the responsibility very strongly and gave probably more time than my family would tell you was a good idea.

My advice to anyone with an opportunity to get into a significant volunteer spot would be to do it. It certainly has enriched my life more than I could ever have dreamed of. With all the difficulties, it was a very, very valuable experience for me. I can't imagine not doing it again. I certainly feel positive.

I would say as a caveat: don't expect the people around you to take you as seriously as you take your work. I think people like to think that they admire people for volunteer work, and we all do—

it's like apple pie and motherhood—but it is often relegated to a position of lesser importance. I don't mean to be cynical because I clearly would do it again, but I feel it is a little like women's war work in World War II: now that we need them, let's get them out there, but let's send them home when we don't.

I feel that volunteer work has one major obstacle, and I don't know whether it will ever be possible to remove it. It is the fact that money talks, and if you are out working in a job that is bringing in money—I don't care what level it is on—you are one step above the volunteers. Volunteers are not bringing home a paycheck; therefore, their time is continually adjustable, it is something they can always put aside, they don't *have* to be there.

People think you should cancel obligations or adjust appointments in favor of other activities. You have to have a lot of moxie and a lot of courage to say, I'm sorry, I can't because this volunteer work is important.

To me the fact that volunteer time and work is not valued in the same way as paid work is a key issue for the volunteer world. It doesn't get addressed. I think that if we're going to attract good people and hope to expand volunteerism, it should be talked about, because the working world has to be educated to the fact that you can't have it both ways. If you really want that job to be done, you have to respect the volunteer who takes the time to get the task accomplished.

One of the most important personal qualities that a volunteer can have is that you have to be perceptive. Having a little talent for mediation is good—I shouldn't say a little, I should say a lot. I think you have to certainly be willing to work and put your heart and soul into it, which would be true of any job. I think openness is important, so that you can really tap into where other people are, because you meet many different people coming from different points of view and backgrounds. A certain broad interest is helpful, and certainly a good sense of humor.

One of the most challenging things about volunteer work is getting into a position where you're responsible and have to take the heat. What an opportunity to learn about yourself—what you do well and what you don't! I have learned a lot by being associated with people I could not possibly have learned from if I met them in social situations. Cocktail parties and dinners are not really when they talk about their own business affairs and their lives and what they do. And I certainly would not have known anything about marketing and finance.

I have met some people from different walks of life that I never would have met, and been able to talk to and listen to them, and to learn to have an appreciation for them. I think that's broadening, I think it's a very expansive experience as well as a humbling one. The sheer number of situations that have come across my path have certainly taught me that very few solutions are black and white. Things that I might have been much quicker to make judgments about—now I think I'm just a world apart from that attitude. Missing these experiences would have left me a much narrower person.

CHAPTER FOUR

ROLES TO PLAY: FROM WORKER BEE TO A SEAT ON THE BOARD

*A*s you think about the types of organizations presented in chapter 3, you may begin to picture yourself in a "niche," working in service with a nonprofit group. In this brief chapter, we'll bring into focus some of the tasks and responsibilities to be undertaken. The roles fall into three broad categories:

Direct service: direct work for people or a cause, and the application of skills that surround and support such work.

Work on **committees** charged with planning, publicity, education, advocacy, development (fund-raising), and other responsibilities, and on special ad hoc committees, or task forces.

Membership on the **board of directors,** as either a regular (full) board member or a member of an advisory board, and perhaps as a member of the board's executive committee.

As with organizations in the public and commercial sectors, no one category of worker can perform effectively without the others.

The people in each role depend on those in the other capacities to execute their tasks in good faith. No role is more important than another.

> "The investment of one's self is a breeder reactor of fulfillment. Just find in yourself the special niche where you can let the best that's in you express itself in ways that answer the human needs of others."
> —*Eugene Lang*

Chapter 5 will lead you through a process of thinking about yourself and help you find, evaluate, and choose an organization and a role. For now, as you consider the descriptions that follow, remember that one of the greatest pleasures of nonprofit work is the freedom to decide what you want to do. Don't be bound by your current position or even by the things you already know how to do. The independent sector is a wonderful arena for learning and expansion. Listen to your preferences and act on them.

DIRECT SERVICE

Direct service work, characterized primarily by hands-on involvement, implements the program of a service organization. Such work can be a one-time project or an ongoing commitment, can mean working with a group or be an involvement with a single individual, can regularly happen in a set location or involve moving from place to place.

The category holds tremendous variety. *Some of your most valuable skills and talents can be employed in direct service work.*

People involved in direct service are sometimes referred to as "worker bees." While many assignments consist of very basic activities (child care, answering telephones, cooking, cleanup, delivery, escorting), they are generally very badly needed by the people or causes served. Many direct service volunteers report that they find a profound sense of satisfaction in performing simple tasks in service to others.

More complicated, sophisticated, and technical knowledge and abilities can also be part of direct service work, which includes teaching everything from auto mechanics to childbirth techniques, photography, and swimming; providing counseling on taxation, mortgages, medical insurance, and running a small business; setting books in Braille and translating for someone who speaks a foreign language; providing conflict resolution; and countless other specialized talents.

To describe the possibilities and the scope of direct service, we've created a series of quick takes—concise descriptions of tasks that entail personal contact with people and the tangible aspects of programs. Here, pared down for easy skimming, are:

126 WAYS TO GIVE DIRECT SERVICE

You can:

Serve as an **ambulance aide.**

Answer telephones in a telethon.

Assist animal keepers at your local zoo.

Assist crime victims with sustained personal support.

Lead a **bicycling club** at a youth center.

Do the **bookkeeping** for your community center.

Set books in **Braille** for visually handicapped readers.

Become a **buddy** to a person with AIDS.

Provide **business counsel** to a beginning entrepreneur.

Care for a child in a day care center for retarded kids.

Provide **career counseling** in a school or community center.

Work with families to stop **child abuse.**

Teach **child care and housekeeping skills** in a community center.

Join a **cleanup project** in a neighborhood, inner-city district, or park.

Offer your **clerical skills** to a school, arts group, or social service agency.

Assist in a **clinic or blood bank.**

Coach a local sports team.

Collect food in a reclamation program.

Comfort children in a hospital.

Donate your **computer programming** skills to a nonprofit group.

Conduct tours in a museum.

Participate in **conflict resolution** for community, neighborhood, and family disputes.

Cook for a soup kitchen, shelter, or meals-on-wheels program.

"I do the cooking for **Meals on Wheels** once a month, and I fill in when they need me. For example, I always fill in on the holidays. . . . I plan and coordinate and cook the meal for between sixty-five and eighty-five homebound people.

"I do it according to the season. For example, in the summertime, for these people who can't go outside, I try to bring the outside inside. I'll pack a picnic lunch and I'll put in daisies. In the fall I will use the fall colors of leaves, that type of thing. Every season I try to add something special.

"I really get excited when the food comes out great."

—*Tessa Warschaw*

Counsel dropout or troubled youth.

Become a **court-appointed advocate** for a child in the foster-care system.

Run a **crafts class** in an after-school program.

Provide **crisis intervention** for families in conflict.

Teach **daily living skills** to retarded youth and adults.

Deliver meals or food packages to homebound people.

Distribute food to the homeless.

Join an **emergency medical service.**

Escort hospital and nursing home patients on outings.

Assist in an **exercise program** for handicapped people.

Provide **financial counseling** at a community or senior center.

Work with a local rescue group to **find homes for stray animals.**

Teach **first aid and/or water safety.**

Welcome a **foreign student** into your home.

Become a **friendly visitor** to a homebound or institutionalized person.

Supervise a **game room** in a hospital or community center.

Do **gardening and landscaping** for your community, church, library, or school.

Work with **gifted students.**

Go on outings with underprivileged children.

Do **grounds-keeping work** for a zoo or botanical garden.

Assist in **group therapy** sessions at a youth center or halfway house.

Teach in a **head-start** program.

Help a prisoner study for a high school degree.

Help a retarded person get established in an independent living situation.

Help kids with homework in a drop-in center.

Hold, feed, and care for infants who aren't with their mothers.

Give classes in **home nursing** at a community center.

Work in a **hospice program** for the terminally ill.

Host an inner-city child in your home.

Answer **hotline** calls.

Be a **hugger and helper** at a Special Olympics.

Join a program to **improve police-community relations.**

Man an **information desk** at a museum or clinic.

Instruct expectant mothers in childbirth techniques and pre- and postnatal care.

Help **integrate an immigrant family** into the community.

Interview and test applicants for job-training and literacy programs.

Provide **job-training** for youth or unemployed people.

Act as a **language interpreter** in a hospital.

Maintain the **library** at a literacy center.

Make clothing for newborn babies in hospitals.

Become a **meal companion** at a hospital.

Provide **medical or paramedical care** at a shelter for battered families.

Become a **mentor** to a young person.

Provide advice on **mortgages, property management, and insurance** at a community center.

Conduct **nature walks** at a botanical garden or park.

Provide **nutritional advice** at a community center, soup kitchen, or homeless shelter.

Become an **ombudsman** for a person in a nursing home, monitoring their care and practical affairs.

Organize the slide collection at a museum or historical society.

Provide **paralegal assistance** in a court or public agency.

Teach **parenting skills** at a community center.

Assist with **patient care** in a hospital.

> "There was a guy yesterday when I went in, he was about thirty years old, and I could see that he might have been a pain in the ass to his family. I said to him, what would you like? And he said, well, nothing, really. I said, what would you like, if there were no limitations in the world, what would you like? He said, I'd like a vanilla milkshake. So I went out and got him a vanilla milkshake, and he loved it." —*Michael Lutin*

Perform in musical or theatrical presentations in hospitals, prisons, and schools.

Work with animals and people in a **pet-assisted therapy program.**

Teach **photography** in an after-school program or at a youth center.

Play with children at a community center.

Prepare beds and meals in a homeless shelter.

Provide **pro bono services** in law, medicine, management, taxation, real estate, etc.

As a **probation aide,** work with a person recently released from jail.

Provide support and reassurance for patients and families in hospital emergency and waiting rooms.

Work in a **rape crisis center.**

Read textbooks to a blind student.

Read and discuss books and magazine articles in a nursing home.

Be a **receptionist** at a clinic or hospital.

Work in a **recycling center.**

Help to **rehabilitate housing** for the elderly and disabled.

Help **relocate families** who have lost their homes.

Do **remedial tutoring** with a college student.

Join a group that **rescues animals** endangered by pollution.

Run a card party or bingo night at a nursing home.

Become a **school volunteer,** helping out in a classroom, cafeteria, office, or playground.

Share your experiences at a drug- or alcohol-abuse program.

Socialize with the guests in a homeless shelter.

Sort and distribute mail in a hospital or nursing home.

Spend holidays with institutionalized people.

Sponsor a troop of Girl Scouts, Boy Scouts, or Camp Fire kids.

Organize a **stamp, coin, or baseball card club** at a youth or senior citizen center.

Support the families of the ill, the handicapped, the mentally retarded.

Prepare and deliver **surgical supplies** in a hospital.

Take blood pressure in a community health campaign.

Provide **tax counseling** for senior citizens.

Teach English to a recently arrived immigrant.

Teach job skills to the disabled.

Teach religion classes at your church, synagogue, or mosque.

Teach yoga, aerobics, or modern dance at a community center.

Join a **telephone reassurance** project, calling elderly or retarded people once a day.

Be an operator in a **teletype deaf hotline.**

Do administrative work in a **television or radio station.**

Organize a **theater group** at a youth center.

Assist in **physical or speech therapy** in a hospital or rehabilitation center.

Serve as a **trail guide** in a park or nature preserve.

Transport elderly or disabled people to and from hospitals and doctors' offices.

Tutor a child or an adult.

"My feeling in terms of my own personal satisfaction is that sitting on a charitable board and approving programs and raising funds is important, but I feel I can personally contribute more by getting involved directly with the kids."   —*Reuben Mark*

Usher at performances of a dance or theater company.

Visit children in a hospital or the elderly in a nursing home.

Become a **volunteer fireman.**

Participate in a **voter registration** campaign.

Join a **walkathon.**

Be a **weather watcher** for the National Weather Service.

Welcome people who have moved to your community.

Donate your **word processing skills** or **knowledge of computer software** to a nonprofit group.

Work in a summer camp for inner-city children.

With your spouse and kids, **work with a family** in a counseling program.

Write letters for people who are unable.

We've kept these ideas simple for rapid reading, but most are easy to expand. The list instantly becomes longer, the number of involvements almost infinite, when you substitute or add words. You can teach many subjects, organize and lead all kinds of clubs, provide every kind of professional advice, assist in dozens of ways in libraries and museums. The possibilities, as they say, are endless.

COMMITTEE WORK

As they take in new volunteers, many organizations offer beginning assignments that are either direct service or committee work. Committees both support the efforts of direct service volunteers and shape ways to set into action the vision and policies created by the board of directors.

Joining a committee is basically a matter of showing interest in its work and a willingness to devote the necessary time and effort. Once a member of a committee, the volunteer has a wonderful, open-ended opportunity to serve. Enthusiastic and dedicated committee members can often assume leadership positions after a relatively short time. Committee chairpersons generally sit on the board of directors, and committee membership is an excellent way to move up within an organization.

In the case of very large nonprofit groups, the structure of the national organization may be reflected on the local level; that is, there may be a national board of directors and national committees and activities, and local boards and local committees and activities. Generally, younger people first get involved on local committees and boards, where there is more hands-on work to be done.

Not every organization will have all the committees we'll discuss, and some groups will have ones we don't mention here. While most are permanent or standing committees, boards sometimes appoint ad hoc committees or task forces.

The Planning Committee

Members of planning committees are charged with developing strategies and action plans to implement the organization's mission. The programs—for example, the providing of direct service, a public education or advocacy campaign, a fund-raising effort— are often the products of close interaction between the planning committee and the board of directors.

The planning committee may be asked to give the board a proposal for improved volunteer recruitment, an evaluation of whether a larger facility is needed for direct services to clients, funding needs for the short and long terms, or a projected five-year overall plan.

Work on a planning committee requires vision, innovation, and sound managerial judgment. Effective members of planning committees are able to

- Draw up carefully considered goals and objectives;
- Construct useful calendars and budgets;
- Think in both immediate and long-range terms;
- Identify, obtain, and use resources;
- Put leaders in charge of specific tasks;
- Be aware of public relations.

The Publicity Committee

Interpreting the organization's mission and activities to the public is the responsibility of the publicity committee. Activities can range from writing publicity and news releases to editing a newsletter, public speaking, creating public service ads, organizing mailings, and participating in community fairs. Outreach efforts, such as invitations to prospective clients to join literacy programs, get family counseling, or apply for job training, are also part of the publicity effort.

Committee members should know how to structure information for interest and readability. They should be good at understanding the unusual aspects and human-interest angles of organizational news and be aware of applying basic journalistic principles in presenting facts. They should understand the print and broadcast media and how to make material easy for them to use.

An essential requirement for publicity committee members is true dedication to the organization's work and enthusiasm that shines through in the materials and programs they create.

Promoting Issues and Ideas: A Guide to Public Relations for Nonprofit Organizations provides detailed advice on planning, developing informational materials, publicity, advertising, and speaking before the public (see "For Further Reading").

The Education Committee

The work of the education committee is related to publicity, but the education committee is charged with carrying to the public not merely news about the organization but information that is part of the group's reason for being. Familiar examples are the work of the large health organizations in disseminating information about the hazards of smoking, the importance of blood pressure checkups, and the warning signs of cancer.

Two keys to the success of the education committee are development of high-quality information in an engaging and useful format, and the ability to identify and reach the people who need the information. Some of the ways the education committee can work are:

- Creating articles for publication or broadcast;
- Setting up courses or workshops given by direct service volunteers;
- Organizing lectures or seminars by experts, such as recovering addicts who speak against drug use;
- Placing advertisements that increase public awareness about a public health or environmental issue;

· Researching issues or conducting public opinion polls and publishing the results.

PUBLIC EDUCATION IN ACTION . . .

. . . in individual communities: In 1976, **Keep America Beautiful** instituted the Keep America Beautiful (KAB) System, a behavior-based approach to litter prevention and voluntary recycling. Ten years later, the KAB System was creating positive attitudes and practices about the handling of solid waste in 409 communities in forty states. In 1986, litter reduction in KAB System communities was averaging 32 percent in the first year and up to 80 percent within five years.

. . . for the public at large: The **National Committee for Prevention of Child Abuse** (NCPCA) strives to make the nation aware of child abuse and ways to prevent it. Their national media campaign in 1986 focused on physical abuse, with the tag line to parents "Take time out. Don't take it out on your kid." Since 1975, NCPCA has conducted a series of campaigns, in cooperation with the volunteer advertising agency Campbell-Ewald Company and the Advertising Council.

. . . through courses and other activities: **The National PTA** offers materials entitled *Parenting: The Underdeveloped Skill,* which show PTA leaders how to conduct activities that help parents improve their communication skills with preteens and teenagers. Among the fifteen topics covered are sexuality, smoking, careers, self-esteem, drug and alcohol abuse prevention, and decision-making.

The Advocacy Committee

An advocacy committee conducts information outreach differently from publicity or education committees—by lobbying for or against policies, legislation, and behavior. The committee might encourage businesses to create jobs for youth, the disabled, or ex-offenders. It might speak out against violations of housing discrimination laws. It could monitor instances of environmental damage or cruelty to animals, or provide court- and police-watching functions. It could promote school breakfast and lunch programs in inner-city districts.

Advocacy is the principal mission of some nonprofit organizations, such as those that work for the protection of the environment and animals. Along with education, advocacy forms an important part of the programs of many others that work for rights and opportunities for those they serve, such as people with diseases and disabilities and the homeless and hungry.

> **The Sierra Club** is involved with hundreds of conservation issues, ranging from the protection of specific natural areas to policy questions of global scope, through campaigns conducted locally, regionally, nationally, and internationally. The board of directors designates national conservation campaigns that correspond to the two-year cycle of the U.S. Congress. Six campaigns for 1987–88 (to protect clean air, Arctic wildlife, wilderness areas, and national parks, and to monitor toxic waste disposal and oil and gas leasing) were conducted alongside two major ongoing international programs. At the same time, the club cooperated with other agencies on issues relating to soil and water conservation programs, endangered species, test ban treaties, and nuclear power plants.

The Development (Fund-raising) Committee

Successful fund-raisers usually work closely with planning, publicity, education, and advocacy committees. They organize campaigns in which they clearly express the group's mission and focus on the strongest features of the program. They then center on the motivations of potential donors, that is, the person's, corporation's, or foundation's reasons for or self-interest in becoming involved. Finally, they are careful to let donors know as precisely as possible what their contributed money will buy.

Nonprofits rely on a large number of fund-raising methods, which we've grouped according to the skills involved in making them work well:

· Marketing skills come into play in organizing **membership** drives, **door-to-door** campaigns, placement of **canisters** on checkout counters, **telephone** and **direct mail** campaigns.

> **Amnesty International USA**'s primary tools—the letter and telegram—are remarkable for their power and simplicity. More than 500,000 members and supporters in more than 150 countries participate in a variety of programs to free prisoners of conscience and stop torture and executions. Freedom Writers is a network of individuals who write letters in behalf of prisoners. Each month, Amnesty International sends network members three prisoner of conscience cases, along with sample letters addressed to the appropriate officials. Members also organize public meetings, collect signatures for petitions, and arrange publicity events, such as vigils at government embassies. Last year, 150 of the prisoners adopted by groups in the United States were released.

· Sound and balanced managerial judgment must operate within nonprofits that charge **fees** for their services.
· Careful research and persistence are needed in seeking **grants** from foundations, corporations, labor unions, and governmental bodies.
· Strong organizational skills are required for planning and orchestrating the **special events** that, when successful, provide both funds and visibility. Special events can take the form of **gala extravaganzas**

A LONG-DISTANCE SPECIAL EVENT

On July 16, 1987, nearly 200 bicyclists from throughout the nation completed a forty-six-day, 3,400-mile journey across the United States in the **American Lung Association**'s first TransAmerica Bicycle Trek. The cross-country odyssey, which began in Seattle on June 1, raised more than $1.25 million for the fight against lung disease. The cyclists, who ranged in age from twelve to sixty-one, covered distances of 25 to 114 miles of blacktop per day.

They raised a minimum of $5,000 each toward an initial $1 million goal, which was exceeded when twenty-three riders raised more than $10,000 each. The lion's share of the funds raised were turned back to local lung associations represented by the participants, to help prevent, cure, and control such diseases as lung cancer, emphysema, chronic bronchitis, and asthma.

(concerts, fashion shows, dinners, parties, and balls) and **grass-roots community events** (garage sales, bake sales, raffles, bingo nights, carnivals, celebrity bowling or softball, golf tournaments, walk-athons, and many more). Special events organizers need plenty of lead time, many helping hands, and excellent publicity.

· The ability to ask for money, and to ask for the right amount of money, is the key to obtaining either living gifts or bequests from **individual large donors.**

· Entrepreneurial skills are needed to create an income-producing **business venture** and make it successful. Items produced for retail sale may include posters, calendars, T-shirts, mugs, and other memorabilia. Libraries, museums, parks, and other groups often generate income through gift shop sales.

A NIGHT TO REMEMBER

In 1968, the late philanthropist and *Reader's Digest* founder De-Witt Wallace invited the five Outward Bound school directors, along with Outward Bound founding trustee Josh Miner, to his New York apartment for a meeting to discuss Outward Bound's plans for the future.

At the meeting's end, Mr. Wallace handed Josh an envelope and said, "These school directors don't get to New York often. Here's something to help have a good night on the town."

Once in the dimly lit elevator, the school directors pressed Josh, "What's in the envelope?"

Josh opened the envelope and took out a check. "Good grief, it's ten thousand dollars!"

A school director took a closer look. "It's a hundred thousand dollars!"

Another examined the check. "You fool, it's one million dollars!"

At that point, the elevator operator chimed in, "Just let me hold it a minute!"

The $1 million personal check was destined to be permanent endowment money for Outward Bound staff training. The group had a good night on the town indeed.

The Finance Committee

Although our description here is brief, the responsibility of this committee is large and crucial. In creating and overseeing both operating and capital expenditure budgets, the finance committee is responsible for the fiscal health of the organization. With the planning and the development committees, it safeguards the ability of the group to stay alive.

The finance committee sees to it that the organization operates according to its approved budget. It ensures that there is sufficient cash flow to pay bills as they come due and usually approves any major banking initiatives. The committee reports regularly to the board on the financial health of the organization.

The Membership Committee

For advocacy and cause-related groups, a large and dynamic membership—one that is vocal and generous with money—is essential. The membership committee solicits new members and monitors and evaluates the current membership in order to maintain the strength that numbers can bring.

The Nominating Committee

Responsible for finding candidates and placing them on the board of directors, the nominating committee plays a key role in determining the quality of leadership that an organization will have. The committee ensures that the board contains the personal resources and professional skills that the group needs. "Building a board"—finding and attracting the strongest members—requires wisdom and hard work.

Task Forces

Boards of directors occasionally appoint ad hoc committees, often known as task forces, to research facts and opinions or to prepare recommendations for solutions to problems. For example, if a group does not have a standing planning committee, a task force might be created to develop a training program for volunteers or to decide whether the local youth population would benefit from a program of career counseling.

Some volunteers and nonprofit professionals favor the use of task forces as opposed to a system of standing committees that might become rigid and bureaucratic. Others argue for the benefits of the continuity provided by standing committees.

POLICY-MAKING: THE BOARD OF DIRECTORS

In most organizations, the nominating committee or executive committee puts forward candidates for the consideration of the current board, whose members then elect the new members, to either the regular, or full, board or to a larger advisory board. The executive committee is made up of a small number of members of the full board.

The Regular (Full) Board

The board of directors (also known as the board of trustees or the board of governors) makes policy and provides leadership for the nonprofit organization. Among the activities of board members are:

- Defining the group's mission and maintaining it as the foremost goal and standard of the organization;
- Providing governance to the organization—setting directions, not managing or operating;
- Setting intermediate goals to support accomplishment of the mission;
- Supporting and planning programs to implement the intermediate goals;
- Mobilizing resources—money and people—to operate the programs;
- Communicating with the people who will be served by and who will support the organization;
- Hiring, firing, and advising the executive director and other officers;

· Heading or serving on a committee;
· Providing for the training of committee members and direct service volunteers;
· Monitoring and evaluating the organization's success in meeting goals and serving the group's stated mission;
· Setting the overall style and tone of the organization.

Effective boards involve a mix of people of varying backgrounds and types of expertise and training, including lay community members and representatives of client groups. Yet within such a mix of people, the basic leadership needs of the organization must be met.

The best board is one that has been *consciously* shaped to serve the needs of the organization. Usually elected by the membership after being put forward by the nominating committee, board members are generally selected for their ability to:

· Provide leadership that is both imaginative and sound;
· Lend their professional expertise to the group's projects;
· Communicate the group's mission within their personal and professional circles;
· Donate and raise money;
· Add credibility and prestige to an organization.

Ellie: *Pat Cook, one of my copartners at Ward Howell, serves on the vestry of St. Bartholomew's Church in Manhattan, which operates community outreach programs for the hungry and homeless. She offered the following comments about the skills one uses on a nonprofit board:*

They're really much more the general management type of skills than anything else. You're involved in reviewing budgets, setting policy, doing everything that a general manager of a business would do. However, because there is no income from operations, you are put in a very different kind of conceptual situation, where you are deciding who has the greatest or most worthy need for the organization's help.

The church's work has given me a whole new slant in terms of not looking at something on a P&L basis. In this work, you look at something in terms of your heart and in terms of the human suffering that really needs to be addressed. That is the bottom line, and it is a different bottom line from any other I have dealt with before. More important than whether a company makes $100 million a year or $50 million a year is the fact that in many cases we're saving lives and giving people a reason to live, a meaning and a purpose in their lives. Which is very different from the corporate world and for me very, very satisfying—extremely so.

Board members must understand the organization's mission and goals, be willing to work, and have a skill to contribute that is related to the traditional goals of the group or to a developing program area. Organizations look for people with expertise in fiscal matters, law, education, fund-raising, marketing, public relations, personnel, management, and planning, to name a few.

Yet expertise alone is not enough. Board members must have imagination and vision, dedication and enthusiasm. Nominating committees look for people who are at the leading edge of their community or discipline.

While each board is different and some are more oriented toward financial support than others, most nonprofit organizations want their board members to help with fund-raising, starting with their own personal contributions. Most organizations feel that it is vital that they have 100 percent participation from their board members in the annual giving campaign.

The board that wants only money or an important name for their letterhead, however, is not likely to be a strong and truly effective one. Opera star and general director of the New York City Opera, Beverly Sills has been involved with the **March of Dimes** since 1971, serving through 1986 as national chairman of the annual Mothers March. We strongly sympathize with her sentiments, spoken in an interview in *USA Today* on November 19, 1987:

> I had been asked to serve on a lot of charitable boards, because a celebrity's name on a piece of stationery appears to be worth a lot. They also always assured me that they didn't want my time. And I felt that if the cause wasn't worth my time, why should I bother? The March of Dimes didn't come to me on that basis: They wanted my time. They also wanted my money. And they asked me to serve as an active member.

What board members must *not* have are aspirations for personal power that will subvert the goals of the organization. Likewise, nominating committees tend to avoid people whose extremely abrasive or confrontational personalities would make life difficult in a world that depends on an active and free flow of ideas and eventual consensus.

The size of a board and its meeting schedule relate to the needs of the organization. The board should not be so large as to be unwieldy but must be large enough to do the job—to raise money, to generate workable ideas, to provide perspective and problem-solving skills. The board of a medium-size or large organization might consist of between twenty and forty members. Some boards meet quarterly, but most meet once a month, or eight or nine times a year.

Many boards carry liability insurance to protect their members. In general, the board will meet its legal obligations if members follow—in their individual conduct as board members, in the conduct of the board as a whole, and in shaping the behavior of the organization—the standards of the Philanthropic Advisory Service (PAS) of the Council of Better Business Bureaus (CBBB) and the National Charities Information Bureau (NCIB). The PAS publishes *CBBB Standards for Charitable Solicitations,* with sections on public accountability, use of funds, informational materials, fund-raising practices, and the governance of organizations. The NCIB publishes *NCIB Standards in Philanthropy* and *The Volunteer Board Member in Philanthropy,* a handbook for volunteer board members. See chapter 3 for addresses for these two groups.

Brian O'Connell, president of Independent Sector, has written *The Board Member's Book,* a practical guide to the essential functions of voluntary boards. See "For Further Reading."

The Executive Committee

The officers and very active members of the full board often are appointed to a committee that works in advance of full board meetings to create agendas and frame issues for discussion, and to act for the full board between board meetings. The purposes of the executive committee are to channel the energies of the full board, by focusing attention on the most important projects, problems, and challenges, and to allow a smaller group to make decisions in a timely manner when it is impractical to call a full board meeting.

The Advisory Board

An advisory board is generally larger than a regular board. Sometimes honorary but often functional, it can be used to influence decisions but generally does not make policy. It sometimes functions as a training ground for later membership on the full board, and former members of the regular board often remain active as advisory board members. Celebrities and other influential people who are asked to be on a board for purposes of prestige and credibility often participate on the advisory board.

We hope that through these first four chapters, and the personal accounts in between, you've gained some basic knowledge about the independent sector—what it is, what it does for us, and the various types of organizations and roles it includes. The next chapter will help you to think about yourself and decide on the involvement that is right for you.

IN THEIR OWN WORDS

"When I look back to the women that I owned my gourmet food business with in Los Angeles, both of those relationships came out of working in Democratic politics and being involved in community activities in the Los Angeles area. I would say that most of what I do comes out of those kinds of cross connections, those kinds of roots."

—Millie Harmon-Meyers

"I feel like this, that when you contribute money to a charity or cause, instead of paying a lot of taxes, income taxes, you get a lot more satisfaction in seeing exactly where your money goes. You contribute, you save on taxes, and you have some sense of what the money that is coming out of your pocket is doing."

—Beth Kummerfeld

"The United States is becoming a land of people on the move. The statistics are something phenomenal, like that every two years, 20 percent of the population moves. So that very few people have a sense of community, but you can create it by making an effort yourself, by getting involved."

—Gretchen Lytle

Millie Harmon-Meyers: *After graduating from the University of California, Millie Harmon-Meyers became a schoolteacher and was involved in social welfare programs that reached out to families. At the inception of Common Cause, she was the organization's southern California coordinator. She was the director of a federally funded program for young people in Los Angeles and, since moving to New York in the mid-1980s, has continued her service work on the staff of OEF (formerly the Overseas Education Fund) and the board of CORO.*

My family situation had a lot to do with my commitment to a better community and to better government in people's lives. People's involvement in government can keep the government straight. My parents were fortunate enough to get out of Germany in the late thirties. Needless to say, there are many stories surrounding people who were part of our family or friends of the family who were less fortunate.

My parents came in with the Roosevelt administration and always felt a gratitude about their having made it to America, about having the good fortune to live a good life here. So I think that certainly set a tone. They were involved in their own survival and adjustment to a new country, so aside from my mother being involved in PTA and Red Cross neighborhood collection, there wasn't much beyond that. My father was just trying to make a living in a new country. There was a basic commitment to values and goals, and I think it was natural that as a first-generation American I would pursue these interests.

I really didn't begin to pursue them until I was out of college. In college, it was the pretty traditional life of the fifties. I graduated and became involved in teaching in the Bay Area—this was in the early sixties, when I was newly married. I was there for the sixties revolution and observed a lot of crazy things. At the same time, I felt a lot of the things that were being looked at within our society needed to be looked at.

I sensed the commitment of the Kennedy administration to a betterment of society, and in my own life I volunteered in a lot of Democratic political organizational work. One of my earliest jobs, once I started having children, was with Common Cause, which had just been founded by John Gardner and which basically addressed the issue of a citizens' lobby. I organized their phone bank groups within a community in southern California for a year or two.

Even in making a small contribution, you're around people who feel the way you do, and I think that energizes you. And I do feel that these things make a difference. Individual people can make a tremendous difference. I think we all feel that way otherwise we wouldn't be looking at Supreme Court or presidential candidates the way we do now.

Currently I'm involved in two organizations. In one, OEF, I'm actually on staff, and in the other, CORO, I'm a board member. Both address the issue of community betterment. CORO is a leadership training program with the idea of training young people for going into public service within their communities, with a focus on the United States. OEF provides training and support for women in Third World countries, so that they can actually become entrepreneurs in small business projects involved with agriculture and food production, and bring some income to themselves and their families.

Even when I owned my own business, I've always incorporated volunteerism as a major part of my life. You become involved in it through networking, as in so many other things. You know people who are involved, and they ask you to join in or you observe something and you become a part of it. CORO started in California and there I went to events. But when we moved to New York they were just starting a branch here, and some former Californians who were involved said, why not join us and help get this organization off the ground? With OEF, it was the same type of thing: good friends in California introduced me to people who were active in it here, and they said, why don't you become involved?

There are two parts to being involved in something. One, do you believe in the cause, does it fit you? Like a shoe, does it really feel comfortable? There may be some things that are comfortable about it and some things that really aren't, and I would stay away from something like that. Not that it has to be a 100 percent fit, but you want to feel that it pretty much represents where you really live. Some organizations may be too radical, too extreme, some not radical or extreme enough.

The other part is the kind of people that you're working with. The organization may have great values and goals, but they could be not your type. You don't want everybody to be like-minded, but you want to be around people whose opinions you respect, even if they're very different from you. Some of the best experiences are those that bring together people from different communities, so that you all have the opportunity to interact. You don't want to just clone yourself. But you will respect people when you do share certain goals—you will respect them and feel that they are bringing something to you and that you're bringing something to them. It's a very exciting experience when that happens.

As you get older, I think you are much more able to make these decisions more quickly, because you have already gone through some selection process in your life and it is easier to fall into the right opportunity. Of course, you could start something and find that it doesn't fit you, and you can also leave.

Volunteerism, as opposed to a paid job, allows you flexibility. You can get as involved or uninvolved as you want. There may be certain times in your life when you have a real ability to say, this is something I want to take some extra time for, and you'll throw yourself into it. And at other times you can pull back. Usually the organization can accept that and will welcome anything you can contribute, as long as at some point you do contribute. Whereas, if you are in the private sector, I don't think any employer would be too happy with someone who said, I'm very busy with other things in my life right now.

You meet many new people from many different sectors of society. Some of it is just interesting for your own personal growth and interest, and often it really does lead to other involvements in nonprofit or even social activities, people that you want to spend your time with. And often it results in work projects, where you get to know someone who has something that they're becoming involved in. When I look back to the women that I owned my gourmet food business with in Los Angeles, both of those relationships came out of working in Democratic politics and being involved in community activities in the Los Angeles area. I would say that most of what I do comes out of those kinds of cross-connections, those kinds of roots.

Service work makes you feel that you really matter, that you really are involved in a community. It gives you a core of people that you can relate to. A few years ago I came to New York after living in California for all of my life, and becoming involved in these organizations has given me a wonderful circle of people—some friends, some just extended acquaintances—but they make me feel that I am part of a very large, overwhelming city. It makes you feel that you belong.

Also I believe that whatever I am doing makes something of a difference, that I am not just taking from society, but that there is something that I am receiving and that I can contribute back. I think that makes you feel a lot richer.

I am not sure you actually get a return in terms of seeing the full measure of what you are doing. Usually it's much more conceptual. You are working toward certain goals, inching away at them. I am looking forward to visiting the OEF projects in some of the countries—apparently that is quite an exciting experience, to really see the women involved. But often you don't, as in Common Cause. Maybe the goal is something that never is achieved, that is more a chipping away at an idea and trying to push it through. Again, I think it is the idea of making a difference, of at least trying. There is just some sort of warmth that comes through in knowing that you really are doing something, that there is some action. I believe in action, that you can make a difference.

Beth Kummerfeld: *Beth Kummerfeld is a New York City business-woman who throughout her life has been involved in many activities within the nonprofit sector. She has been supportive in the revitalization of the Kenya Outward Bound School. She was a founder of the* **American Foundation for AIDS Research.**

It's really hard to say why I am doing what I am doing in volunteering and fund-raising, in serving on nonprofit boards and other volunteer work. My parents were like that, and their life was so rich with joy and the sharing of things that I grew up thinking the reason for my being here is that I have to serve others to make our lives better. And I see my daughter, who is now twenty-six, trying to improve our society because it's part of our life.

I was raised in several different countries. My parents are Japanese, and while they left Japan before I was born, we were in and out of Japan a lot. As a young girl, I remember giving charity money for Japanese flood victims. At the end of the war, we were in

Japan, and my mother mobilized the war widows, and they started some job-training centers. They were trained to type or sew or whatever they had the ability to do to earn money for themselves and their families. My parents were always doing that sort of thing. It was just a way of life.

Right now I am on the board of the American Foundation for AIDS Research, which I founded with some of my friends. I also serve in the New York City program of **Meals on Wheels** and on the board of the **Mercantile Library of New York.** I've also served on the board of the **Twyla Tharp Dance Foundation** and am involved with the **Panos Institute** of London and Washington, D.C. I am active in the Kenya effort of **Outward Bound.**

My husband is very proud and very supportive of my activities. He does his thing in nonprofit work in that he serves on many of the nonprofit boards, including the **Kaiser Foundation** and **Ronald McDonald House.** His activities are more directed to the well-being of New York City and urban life.

I came to found the American Foundation for AIDS Research through the invitation of a friend of mine, who is a cancer researcher and a pioneer scientist. She came to me about AIDS, saying, it doesn't look like it's going to stop, and unless we do something, this is going to spread in a serious way. Having established the AIDS Medical Foundation, she enlisted my fund-raising skills and invited me to become an AMF board member.

Two years later, we learned that Elizabeth Taylor was planning to set up an AIDS foundation. So we invited her to join us in kind of a semi-merger; we both gave up our identities to come up with a new identity, the American Foundation for AIDS Research. So far [in the fall of 1987] we've raised about $3.5 million, in less than a year.

The reason I like doing nonprofit work is that my life is enriched; my family's and daughter's lives are enriched. Society gets better through these efforts, and someday we won't have to do nearly as much.

If you want to get involved in public service or voluntary work, you are already nearly there. When you get involved, there is a fantastic reward in terms of self-satisfaction; there is a sense of well-being in making something happen. I consider that part of me made it happen, and that is an enormous satisfaction.

If you really want to participate, opportunities are everywhere.

You get mail all the time, saying give to this, give to that charity, asking you to write for more information. All you have to do is pick something that you can really relate to. For example, if you are concerned about the future of our environment and you get a flier from an environmental group, call them and tell them about yourself and then meet with some people. They are always ready to talk about what they are doing.

I feel like this, that when you contribute money to a charity or cause, instead of paying a lot of taxes, income taxes, you get a lot more satisfaction in seeing exactly where your money goes. You contribute, you save on taxes, and you have some sense of what the money that is coming out of your pocket is doing.

Sometimes through nonprofit work a business opportunity comes along. When you put time in and volunteer your opinion and expertise and function in a professional way, people have an opportunity to see you as a professional. That is when someone can understand what you can do, and that impression stays with that person. When a business opportunity happens, that person picks up the telephone and says, "Hey, by the way, you work with such and such a project, I was so impressed. Can we talk about doing this and this?"

In my business—in investment banking and management consulting work—I do almost no marketing. Those who come to me are mostly referrals. All I've ever done in marketing is to put together brochures of what my company does, and even the brochure project was on the urging of an attorney with whom I work. He simply wanted to refer my firm to a lot of his clients and friends.

Wherever I am I see opportunities for something I can do, in terms of a very modest amount of investment of energy and money. That is always happening, and sometimes I am so busy I cannot add another thing. But sometimes you squeeze it in and sometimes it turns out that a very little push is needed to get something realized.

Cecily Frazier, Lynn Meltzer, Gretchen Lytle: *Cecily Frazier and Lynn Meltzer share the presidency of the Parent Teacher Student Organization (PTSO) of the Rhinebeck [New York] Central School District, in addition to other volunteer involvements. Both work part-time. Gretchen Lytle, who is* *a weaver, administrates on a volunteer basis an after-school program of special classes operated by the PTSO. We talked with these three women about their volunteer work in the public school system.*

Cecily: I became involved because I thought it was important to contribute, but also I think you can get a lot of power that you could never get professionally. I don't know whether power is exactly the right word, but you can have a great deal of impact, if you're in the right place at the right time.

When my son went to first grade, I went to a PTSO committee meeting, and they had just raised $10,000 to put in a playground, and I thought, gee, I like this. It just appealed to me.

I think it's important for your children to see you feeling that their school is important. Another reason that I volunteer is my upbringing. My parents always volunteered. I learned that we have to become actively involved.

Lynn: The reason I became involved with the PTSO was that I really wanted to make my children's education an important part of their lives. I wanted it to be just a very natural thing. I wanted them to see how interested we were in their total education.

There are other reasons why I volunteer. It's a lot of fun. I get a lot of enjoyment from meeting different people, parents whose children will be friends with my children and part of their lives, as well as from keeping in touch with attitudes in the community.

It's not necessarily people who have a lot of time on their hands who volunteer. It's people who are very, very busy, and they manage to make the time.

Our meetings are really the least important of the things that we do. They're just to facilitate other activities. One of the projects we initiated was a teacher grant program, through which teachers request and receive money to do something specific in their classroom; last year the program granted $1,800. Other projects are the Family Fall Festival, which is held on a Saturday all day, outdoors and indoors, and a Bingo Night, where fathers are the emcees, all dressed in tuxedos—the prizes are soccer balls, gift certificates to the bookstore, things like that. We organize raffles, proceeds of which go for gifts on Staff Appreciation Day.

At the end of each year, we present quite sizable gifts to each of the three schools in our district—whatever they request: cash, a VCR, a computer. We try to be very careful that any money that comes in from membership dues and fund-raising projects gets put right back into the school.

When we do our book fair, we take no profit. When we've gotten a discount, we take that off the price of the books. We have a family volleyball night and an activities night, at which people and groups in the community that offer services for children get together, and parents can sort of shop around to see what's available.

We have a college night, when graduated seniors come back to talk—that program will be sponsored by the district next year and held during the school day— and we budget $1,000 for speakers at the school. We give money per student for field trips, to help defray costs. We have money available for students who can't afford things like eyeglasses.

Gretchen: Sometimes I'll agree to do something, to support a cause or an institution or the schools, and not realize what it involves. I'll find myself doing things that, if I had known at the outset what was required, I'd have said, oh, I can't do that. But having made the commitment, I find myself doing things and doing them fine, things I never thought I could do.

I've gotten better at dealing with lots of different kinds of people, including people I don't agree with. I've gotten to know certain people who, as long as you don't come across in a threatening, adversarial way, they're very open to you. And then there are other people with whom you have to come on a little stronger. Basically we have no power— we don't hire and fire people; we have to work with them. You've got to develop flexible interpersonal skills.

Lynn: You bring so much of yourself to it. You sign up for something, and when you see the end product you realize that you snowballed to get there. You say, I think I could do it better if I did it this way, and you bring a little more organization, a little more creativity to what you're doing. And all of a sudden you have something that the next person has to meet, and they add their contribution to it. That process can be very beneficial.

We've had a few projects that the PTSO has brought to the

school district that would never have existed otherwise. I'm thinking of the Child Safety Program, in which if your child doesn't come to school on a particular day, you are notified. Many features of our Study Skills course last year were incorporated into the middle school curriculum.

You learn organization itself. You know what has to be organized, what things are important, what details can be left. Also, as Gretchen said, you become involved with so many different people, asking them to help. You develop a style of asking for their time, asking for their money, asking them to correct something that has to be changed. I've found myself in a mediation role many times, between the administrators, the staff, and other parents.

Gretchen: I've had the school come to me and say, what's really going on, is this a major problem, what's your sense of the community on full-day kindergarten, or what if I present this this way? I feel that sometimes we're depended on as a sounding board.

I have found through various volunteer experiences that I can get overextended, it can take away from my work. Then I'll feel resentful of the commitment I've made, and if somebody asks one thing more, you know, it's over the edge. It's very important to keep a balance of feeling that I'm contributing but that I'm not getting to the point where I resent what I've decided to do.

Lynn: You get very good at organizing your time. If you have to deposit three checks, you do your own banking at the same time. It's a matter of a few minutes here, a few minutes there. When I pick up my daughter from violin lessons after school, I make sure that I check the box in the business office, things like that.

Gretchen: Volunteering is a great way, as a new person in an area, to make friends. When we moved here, I had a little baby, Mark's work was up the road, and, although I had background as a teacher, I didn't choose to go back to work. It is a wonderful way to get a feeling for the community. I volunteered at a residential school for emotionally disturbed children in town and eventually in the public schools, and it was a great way to make some friends, and to make some professional contacts, too, to find ways that I might get involved in other directions in my career.

Cecily: I think that when you work very closely with people, you get to truly know them and to appreciate their good qualities, in a really deep way that you don't when you're just friends. You appreciate the complexity of people much more.

It's a way to be a whole different person. People have certain perceptions of you, and maybe you share those perceptions of yourself, but you're free to do things as a volunteer that you can't do otherwise.

Gretchen: The United States is becoming a land of people on the move. The statistics are something phenomenal, like that every two years, 20 percent of the population moves. So that very few people have a sense of community, but you can create it by making an effort yourself, by getting involved.

Cecily: When I was in college, I was on this kind of global wavelength. But I've basically given that up. I give money to various national political organizations, but I don't give time because I don't see it as getting very far. Whereas when I give to the school, it's just like a ripple. I can see the effect.

Money is not a major focus of my life. I get a lot more out of volunteering than I could ever get from a job. If I worked for a big corporation, I'd be in charge of—I wouldn't even be in charge, I'd have my little cubicle. Whereas as a volunteer, it's like being the president of a corporation.

CHAPTER FIVE

PUTTING SERVICE IN YOUR LIFE

$\mathcal{G}$ETTING involved is an important first step, one that can set the tone for your enjoyment of and success in service work. We urge you not to just fall into the first organization or assignment that comes along, but to do some serious thinking about this special opportunity. Take a thorough look at yourself, and carefully investigate organizations and programs.

Please don't let the words "thorough" and "investigate" put you off. This search will be significantly different—mainly a lot more fun—than a job search. You will choose the personal qualities that you want to emphasize, the type of contribution you want to make, the cause, and the amount of time you will spend. You will analyze what you have to offer to the organization and why they should want you to be involved. But so many organizations need help that your options are many and, as a potential volunteer, you can be quite selective.

Because of the very personal nature of this matchmaking process, we can't lead you from Step 1, to Steps 2 and 3, on through the final Step 10, in which you discover your ideal involvement. Choosing service work is not an exact science. Rather, it is based on subjectives—the causes you like, the parts of yourself you want to bring into play, the way you want to relate to people, to name only a few.

"For someone who wants to get involved in helping other people, the big thing is they have got to begin. And to begin they need to take a break from what they are doing every day. They need to just realize their worth as a human being. They basically need to look at what really interests them. And that means any organization, from a group of people trying to save the butterflies on some hill to some traditional operation. They have got to get to the point where they feel the connection. It's got to be hands on—heart-felt and hands on. I mean, right from the heart, and from the hand, and, of course, they must use their head, too. But if they would just take that small step, acquire a little chunk, become involved in one thing—they have begun." —*Reno Taini*

We can present things to think about in defining your purposes and goals; a way to begin to formulate your service profile—who you are and what you want to contribute. We give you questions to ask yourself, lists of skills and abilities to scan and select from, advice about finding organizations, and tips on how to most fruitfully begin your involvement with an organization.

Our most important piece of advice is to work from your heart, not just your head. Try to get rid of preconceptions that can stand in the way of your strong feelings. In judging your priorities, indulge your subjectivity. Try to tune out the "shoulds" that so often influence our behavior. Instead respond to your strong passion for a cause; acknowledge the enjoyment you get from exercising a particular skill or ability; pay attention to your feelings about the type of environment you like best.

Remember: a lawyer can but doesn't have to do pro bono legal work; he or she can work in a soup kitchen. A nurse can become an environmental advocate. A marketing manager can help a nonprofit generate income, sit on a board of directors, or become a friendly visitor in a hospital. Service gives us a chance to tailor activities for ourselves in a very personal way. In the process, we bring out the best in ourselves—and not only bring out our best but share it with others.

You'll get the most from this process if you'll make notes in response to questions when perusing our checklists. A single 8½-

by-11-inch piece of paper ought to do it. After you've finished the chapter, you'll be able to refer to this sheet for a rough profile of yourself.

While some of your jottings may suggest causes to join or roles to play within the service world, most won't lead directly to those types of conclusions. However, this knowledge about yourself, considered in advance, will come in extremely handy when you're investigating organizations and activities.

BEGIN BY LOOKING INWARD

For some people, deciding on a cause or a role is easy. They know that they care deeply about one or more problems or issues, and they feel an impulse to contribute in a specific way. For others, no particular cause has emerged as an urgent demand on their attention, and they may be unsure of what their best contribution might be.

If you're in the latter group, don't be logical in trying to find the cause that is the "most important" or the "best way" to participate. Go subjective. Focus your analysis not outward but inward.

On the positive side, what are your hobbies; what do you do in your spare time? If you read nonfiction, what topics do you choose? What are your greatest pleasures? When you call your best friend for no particular reason, what do you talk about?

Then again, what gets your dander up? When you have the radio on in the kitchen, which news stories make you turn off the running water? When you're reading the newspaper, which articles make you talk to yourself? Ask your friends what topics you complain about most. What was the subject of the biggest argument you had during the past year?

Experiment with different ways of thinking. Take the obvious route, in which the sports-minded apply to the Special Olympics, Little League, or the Police Athletic League, and mothers and teachers join organizations that combat child abuse and promote family services. Then go beyond the obvious. Some athletically inclined people may want to get involved in social service groups that run sports programs. Those athletes who want to spend more time outdoors might apply to an environmental conservancy group or an outdoor adventure-based organization like Outward Bound. Some athletes may not want to contribute their athletic ability at all, choosing other skills to emphasize.

If, as you finish your self-analysis, you find that your thoughts are not taking a specific direction, we suggest that you visit a nearby Volunteer Center or United Way office. It may be that you need the active give-and-take of conversation with another person. A staff member at one of these offices not only can help you in your search for a cause and a role, but also will be able to describe local organizations and their programs.

THE ESSENTIAL YOU

Now let's get more specific, beginning with some of the interests, preferences, and goals that combine to make you who you are. The questions that follow should elicit some basic information about the essential you.

What is your motivation for wanting to do volunteer service? The answer to this question should form a general backdrop for your thinking. If your motivation is to exercise your initiative and to contribute in a very creative way, don't become involved in an intense team effort that ties your actions inextricably with those of other volunteers. If your motivation is personal growth, try to find a volunteer involvement that lets you be expansive in the way you want to be.

We must mention a specific caveat under this topic. People who have lost close friends or family members to illness sometimes feel motivated to volunteer for an organization related to that disease. However, especially when the death has occurred recently, the feelings of sadness or depression are still too close to the surface. While the volunteer may give excellent service, working for this cause may be detrimental to the volunteer. You should discuss such personal situations candidly with staff members of the organization.

What kind of energies do you have? Do you have spontaneous, quick reactions? Or are you more the methodical, thorough type? Once you've had those two cups of coffee, do you rev up for the day, working straight through without a break? Or are you some-one who likes to put your feet up and let your mind wander every couple of hours? Again, don't think of your career persona or the way you think you'd like to be, but the way you behave when you're home on the weekends.

Pondering this question obviously isn't going to tell you what to volunteer for, but being aware of your basic energies may help you in assessing how well you and a potential assignment will fit.

Do you like to create ideas or implement existing ones?   If you don't work best when you must abide by established ways of doing things, don't take an assignment within the hierarchy of a very bureaucratic organization. Try to find a situation in which your creative thinking will be a strength, not a stumbling block. On the other hand, if you're a follower and you know it, don't be talked into chairing a committee or running a workshop.

In thinking about this consideration, project your thinking into the future, since even strong leaders may begin in a lowly role. As with paid employment, entry jobs in the service world are some-times just that. It is when a volunteer becomes established and shows that he or she will make a solid contribution that personal preferences are most respected. When you interview, inquire about the jobs that will be available after you're established.

What's your best method of relating to people?   Do you prefer groups or one-on-one involvement? Do you like being with people for long periods of time, such as a day or a weekend, or for shorter periods? Are you a person who needs privacy or are you happiest when surrounded by others? Do you enjoy a nice quiet chat, or are you best in a fast exchange of thoughts and ideas?

What keeps you going when the going gets tough?   Is it approval and applause? Quiet feedback from other people? A sustaining belief in what you're doing? Do you need a lot of positive reinforce-ment on a regular basis, or can you go without it? People differ widely in the amounts and kinds of support they require. While a fund-raiser may be rewarded by a small number of dramatic suc-cesses, a direct service volunteer may find sustaining satisfaction in the smile of a child or the progress of a person he is tutoring.

"My advice would be: don't do it for the prestige, do it because you want to. Pick activities that you are really committed to and that you really want to make a contribution to. How to do it is just like anything else, like a business career: you start at the bottom. You should find out what you can do today to help—some rather lowly chore or menial activity.

"Just go to it and learn what the organization is about, how they operate. Don't feel you have to go on the board of trustees the first day. That will come along—if you show the other people involved that you are really committed and that you are effective."

—*John Whitehead*

What kind of environment is right (or wrong) for you?　If hospitals and nursing homes depress you and yet you still want to work with people who are convalescing, steer clear of institutional settings and investigate in-home visitation. Do you like to spend as much time as possible outdoors? Look into sports or backpacking programs, including those run by social service agencies, or environmental groups involved with trail maintenance. If you want to become a tutor, find out if the work is done in a school or in the student's home.

What are your particular passions or strengths?　Beyond not minding phone work, do you *love* talking on the telephone? Think about investigating hotlines. Are you a really good amateur artist? Maybe your church needs someone to design the bulletin. Do you especially like working with children? Think about the children's ward at the hospital or a day care center. Are you a great cook, or maybe an average cook who gets his or her greatest satisfaction from feeding people? Meals on Wheels could be just the group for you.

Have in mind a list of your particular strong points. Not all of them will be applicable to every situation, and in some situations some won't come into play at all. But be ready to bring them up if the situation suggests their usefulness.

Do you have any personal negatives?　Do you hate paperwork? (We're not talking about not liking it; we're talking about *hating* it.)

Do you have a real inability to cope with physical suffering? Do you faint at the sight of blood? Would you find it difficult to ask people for donations of money?

Again, there's no point in bringing up your aversions out of context, but if you suspect that a particular assignment or task may entail something that will cause you (and the organization) a significant problem, discuss it as early as possible.

YOUR TIME SCHEDULE

Many groups ask for a commitment of time up front. While this may be surprising to the first-time volunteer, such a request is to the benefit of both the volunteer and the organization. The typical nonprofit staff devotes considerable time and effort to integrating people into the organization, and the volunteer devotes an equivalent amount of energy.

Realistically evaluate the demands on your time:

· Family, allowing ample time for that revolving number of small emergencies;
· Work, including what you bring home from the office;
· School, making sure that you don't skimp on homework time;
· Travel, taking into account the occasional business trip and weekend at the shore.

One trap to watch out for is the temptation to substitute volunteer work for another area that may be less "fun" or satisfying but that is actually essential to your life. Don't try to escape from a difficult but important part of your life by volunteering.

In evaluating your schedule, go to all lengths to be realistic. Refer to your appointment book for the last month or two, and extract a record of the time you had free. As an alternative, look at your calendar for the next month, and jot down the times you will have free. We strongly encourage you to use your actual calendar, instead of making a generalized sort of judgment such as "I guess I can volunteer a couple of evenings a week since I always have at least three free" or "I never do much on the weekend." Your best bet is to check the record.

We must admit that if we had always followed this advice, we might have missed some very fine service experiences. We recognize the wisdom that says it is often the busiest people who get the most done!

Keep in mind the possibility of substituting service work for activity that isn't very meaningful or fulfilling. If you're "busy" several nights a week hanging out with friends or keeping up with your favorite nighttime soap operas, you might consider filling this time with a more satisfying activity.

Think in patterns: are weekdays best? Weekends? Which parts of the day: mornings, afternoons, evenings?

It's smartest to establish your best time availability beforehand, rather than reacting to the particular needs of a group. We're not suggesting that you be inflexible, but knowing your best schedule in advance can make it easier for you to decide most wisely among the options that may be offered.

> "One thing I would advise is not to spread yourself too thin. Don't get overcommitted. Select one or two organizations as the ones that you will devote most of your effort and time to rather than having six or seven that you give a very little time to. . . . You must be absolutely ruthless in your ability to say, I *will* undertake this, and I *won't* undertake that."   —*Arthur Levitt, Jr.*

YOUR INVENTORY OF SKILLS AND ABILITIES

The lists given below are long but not exhaustive; they are intended in part to demonstrate the scope of the skills and talents that can be applied to volunteer work, and in part to help jog your consciousness of yourself, to help you realize just how many capabilities, trained or untrained, you have.

Sometimes these skills and abilities may qualify you to contribute to an organization in a specific way. A person with skills in advertising or architecture may be particularly needed by an organization, and someone with an ability to listen may be just what another group requires at a given moment.

At other times, you may be called upon to teach or otherwise pass along certain skills and abilities. A vocational training program may need someone with bookkeeping skills or a knowledge of auto mechanics. And personal qualities become almost tangible commodities when mentors provide role models for young people or when retired executives advise fledgling businesses here and abroad.

We advise that as you inventory your skills and abilities, you consider all that you have, but select for prime attention only the ones that you really enjoy. Review the lists below, extracting the skills and abilities you have—and adding the ones we've left out. When thinking about particular organizations, review your list in light of their needs. A carefully considered personal inventory can help you and the organization discover your best usefulness and, by extension, lead to your greatest satisfaction from the service you give.

Skills

By skills, we mean trained, professional capabilities. However, you don't have to be a professional librarian to count library work as one of your skills or a CPA to list accounting. If you have had reasonable exposure to and experience in an area, you should consider it part of your repertory. The depth of knowledge and experience required will come out in discussion with an organization's representative. Meanwhile, you undoubtedly have many skills and should have them in mind as you offer your services.

Be specific in thinking about the areas listed below. Check them off or keep a list on that piece of paper we mentioned. You may be surprised when you see your accumulated expertise!

accounting	auto mechanics
administration	banking
advertising	bookkeeping
agriculture	Braille
arbitration, mediation	brochure/newsletter preparation
architecture	brokerage: financial, real estate
audiovisual	budgeting

bus driving
carpentry
cataloging
clerical
clinic work
collections
computer programming
conference/workshop planning
construction
continuing education
copywriting
cost analysis
counseling: personal, career,
    marriage, unemployment,
    retirement, family, teenage
crafts
curriculum design
dietetics
direct mail
dispatching
drafting
editing
electronics
energy conservation
engineering: chemical, environ-
    mental, mechanical
entrepreneurship
estimating
executive search
family planning
filing
film production
finance
first aid
food service
foreign languages
grant/proposal writing
graphic arts
housing development
insurance planning
interior design, decoration
interviewing

inventing
inventory control
investment planning
journalism
labor relations
laboratory work
landscaping
law
legal aid
library work
licensing, franchising
long-range planning
maintenance/janitorial work
management training
mapmaking
market research
marketing
massage
mechanical drawing
medical technology
medicine
merchandising
natural science
nursing
nutrition
office systems
operations management
paralegal services
paramedical services
payroll
performing: music, drama, dance
personnel management
photography
planning
policy-making
pricing
printing, typesetting
product display
production
program development
project coordinating
promotion

property management
psychiatry
psychology
public relations
public speaking
purchasing
real estate
reception
remedial reading
research
retail sales
sales management
sales representation
science: research, application
securities management
small business administration
social work
speech therapy
statistics
stenography, transcription

strategic planning
systems planning
tax counseling
teaching
teaching assistance
technical writing
telephone sales
therapy, physical
therapy, psychological
time management
tour guiding
truck driving
tutoring
typing
urban planning
veterinary medicine
videotape production
word processing
writing: advertising, business,
    creative, technical

Abilities

We're defining abilities as (1) skills you have developed in an amateur or instinctual way, and (2) special, valuable qualities. You may not think of some of these, such as assertiveness or a talent for bargaining, as anything special, but they function just as more specific abilities do. Not everyone has these qualities, and they can be of great benefit when a person consciously decides to put them into action in service to other people.

Each of these abilities, even the more specific ones, like appliance repair and photography, can be useful in a number of different settings. We saw no point in categorizing them, since each organization and program will dictate a special mix of talents for the people who will be involved. There is some intentional repetition of items, which we think often exist as both trained skills and amateur abilities.

As you review the list, note which ones apply to you. Either check them off or enter them into your notes.

abstract thinking
accuracy
adaptability
appliance repair
analytical skills
animal care
art appreciation
assertiveness
attention to detail
auto mechanics
awareness of the big picture
balance of idealism and realism
bargaining
bartending
bartering
brainstorming
budgeting
camp counseling
camping
carefulness
carpentry
chauffeuring and escorting
child care
child rearing
comfort with strangers
committee work
communications
community organizing
companionship
conflict management
construction
conversation
cooking
cooperation
coordination: people, schedules, events
courage
crafts
creative thinking
crisis intervention
decision-making
demonstrating

dispute settlement
doing favors for people
drawing
driving a car, van, or bus
emotional support
empathy
encouraging others
establishing rapport easily
event management
exercise and physical fitness
explaining things clearly
follow-up
foreign languages
friendliness
fund-raising
gardening
goal-setting
good memory
good with details
ham radio
handling money
handyman ability
hiking, backpacking
history
hobbies: all kinds
home repair
homemaking
hospice work
hosting, hostessing
housecleaning
housepainting
houseplant care
imagination
improvisational ability
independence
insightfulness
intuition about people
inventiveness
keeping secrets, confidences
letter writing
listening
logic

machine operation
machine repair
martial arts
mechanical ability
mediation
money management
motivation of others
natural science
neatness
numerical ability
organization of large events
originality
paperwork
party cleanup
party planning and preparation
patience
people orientation
perceptive observation of people
performing: dance, drama, music
persistence
personal brokering (matchmaking)
personal grooming
persuasiveness
photography
physical strength
planning
problem-solving
providing of reassurance and
 support
public speaking
reading aloud
record keeping
recovery from substance abuse
recycling

relaxation techniques
religious education
risk-taking
running a meeting
schedule-making
self-discipline
self-starting ability
sensitivity to feelings
sewing, dressmaking
science
scorekeeping
shopping
signing for the hearing-impaired
socializing
spontaneity
sports: coaching, refereeing
storytelling
stress management
supervision of adults
supervision of children
swimming
teaching
team-building
telephoning
theoretical thinking
thoroughness
travel
troubleshooting
tutoring
upholstery
visiting
word processing
working with figures
writing
yard maintenance

A Wish List

Here's a fun part: use the lists above to stimulate your thinking about (1) skills that you'd like to learn and (2) abilities you've never nurtured or developed but would like to, and make a wish list. Remember: while nonprofits are delighted to have you contribute a well-developed skill, they are usually quite willing to let you try out new areas.

One common way of gaining exposure is to join a committee; for example, while participating in support work, you can observe how a public education campaign is built. Another is entering a direct service situation as a buddy to a more experienced volunteer.

Don't ignore this vast potential for learning and personal growth. It's one of the great gifts that service bestows on volunteers.

Special Contributions You Can Make

Look to your personal and working or professional lives for any special benefits you might bring to an organization. Many people have professional or family contacts that can be extremely valuable to nonprofit groups: for example, no- or low-cost tax accountancy or the production of printed materials at cost.

Such special help can also come in the form of equipment. The employee of a publishing company may have access to books that can be used in reading programs. A family might occasionally donate the use of a private swimming pool or their children's pony. You might want to contribute the use of your car or van, a meeting room or office equipment, an empty lot.

A Note on Your Ability to Give Money

While people who become volunteers for organizations often give money to those groups, simply belonging to a group as anything but a board member generally entails no financial obligation, aside from a possible yearly membership fee that is usually around $20 or $30.

Almost all nonprofit boards want their members to contribute money. Because organizations need 100 percent participation from their trustees when they go to other individuals and to foundations to seek support, such participation is essential.

Some boards are major factors in the monetary support of their organizations. Others are oriented toward governance, work, and wisdom. Even on boards with a heavy fund-raising responsibility, there are members who are highly valued for their work and expertise, and who can afford only a token gift.

Most organizations are grateful for big givers and for wonderful workers alike. One thing is certain: if an organization more or less requires a large financial contribution from board members, this fact will not be kept secret from the candidate trustees or directors.

THINKING ABOUT INTERVIEWING

As you think about yourself and contemplate contacting organizations—whether you do it formally or through networking—you are in effect preparing to "position" yourself. In describing yourself and the kinds of contributions you want to make, you're creating the profile of yourself that you'll present to organizations and agencies. If you are most interested in a policy-making job, you'll emphasize skills that involve planning and creating ideas. People interested in direct service will focus on their abilities in working with people and any practical skills that apply.

Begin now to think about the questions you'll want answered in interviews, and get ready to participate in those conversations in an active, investigative way. Find out as much as you can about the organization, especially with an eye to how you might fit in. And when you see how the fit might be accomplished, share your insight. Don't be shy; organizations are most eager to find people who are right for them.

FINDING AN ORGANIZATION

You've thought about yourself and have made some notes about your preferences and abilities. With your "service profile" in mind, you can now commence your search for an organization. People learn about and become interested in service organizations through two basic routes: networking and investigating on their own.

Networking

Learning about organizations through friends, family, and business and other associates is an excellent way to investigate service organizations, because it has the important subjective element built in. When you know people, even if somewhat formally, as in business or with new acquaintances, you have a sense of what is important to them and a feeling for how to evaluate their comments and judgments.

Networking can operate in many ways. It may be that you will simply hear of an organization through a conversation with your cousin. On the other hand, a good friend at work may urge you to attend a recruitment meeting or to come along with him on a direct service assignment.

While networking often happens naturally, you can, of course, make it happen as well. If your parents are involved or were involved in the past but you're not sure how, sit down with them and find out. Ask your sisters and brothers, aunts and uncles.

We predict that you'll be surprised by what you learn from friends and acquaintances when you ask them, "Have you done any volunteer work?" We don't know why—maybe because it's special and personal, maybe because often it's fitted in as a relatively small part of a busy day—but many people go about their volunteer work without talking too much about it. Sometimes you have to dig a little to discover it.

Be sure to check whether your company has a community service program in place. Even if they don't have an official one, the public relations or human resources office may have information about groups the company sometimes works with. If you work for a company with established ties to community groups, some of your associates—and their spouses and children—are likely to be involved. You may find a mentor within your company, someone who can advise you on the groups that will best fit with your interests.

If you belong to a religious congregation, ask your minister, priest, or rabbi about other members who are involved in community service. Your church or synagogue is a ready-made network that you can convert to this other worthy purpose.

We've now reached the part of networking where you contact people you may not have met, and perhaps we should make this important point: people, even people you haven't met, *love to talk about their service work.* Because it is special to them, because in general they are devoted to that work, they welcome inquiries about it. And because organizations are always looking for new members, established volunteers are delighted to hear from someone who might consider joining their ranks.

Whether you are young and just starting your career, newly arrived in a strange city, or have lived in one place all your life, networking is an excellent way to find out about the dynamic organizations, the ones that are active, the ones that are growing, the ones that do the most good and are the most innovative. If you know someone who is a community leader or a board member of an organization that appeals to you, don't hesitate to call on that person for information and advice. He or she can be invaluable in introducing you to the organization and getting you involved.

You should be aware of one potential danger in the networking approach: that the enthusiasm of someone close to you will stand in for your own feelings for a cause or an organization. Let networking operate at full force in introducing you to groups and programs, but be sure that your evaluation of them, and of the rightness of your working with them, is your own.

Investigating on Your Own

Here are some types of organizations and other sources in your community that can provide direct or indirect help in your search for the service assignment that is right for you.

Volunteer Centers. Nationwide, more than 380 volunteer centers operate in 94 of the 100 largest metropolitan areas, serving an estimated 100,000 private organizations and public agencies. Sometimes known as a Voluntary Action Center or a Volunteer Bureau, such a center serves as an advocate and catalyst for volunteerism, provides leadership and support for volunteer efforts, and is the central clearinghouse for volunteering in the community.

Staff members have current information about the needs of local organizations and are trained in matching volunteers with possible assignments—although final decisions are made by the individual and the organization.

To locate the volunteer center in your area, look in the White Pages of your telephone directory under "Volunteer" or "Voluntary." If there is no listing, check the Yellow Pages under "Social Service" or "Community Organizations."

If you cannot locate a local volunteer center, write to VOLUNTEER—The National Center, Attn: Information Services, 1111 North 19th Street, Suite 500, Arlington, Virginia 22209.

United Way Offices. Twenty-three hundred local United Way organizations exist throughout the country. In addition to coordinating the raising and allocating of funds, many United Ways also serve as clearinghouses that match individuals with volunteer opportunities in the community.

Public Libraries. Explaining the purpose of your research, ask a librarian for local or regional directories of nonprofit or social service organizations.

Ask if the library has the *Encyclopedia of Associations,* a multivolume directory, organized by category, of associations of all types. Don't be put off by the size of this reference tool. Have the librarian show you how to use it. You can have some fun perusing the many types of groups that exist.

Municipal Offices. Contact the mayor's office, your city or town hall, or community center. They may have directories or lists of service organizations, or you may just get a few verbal leads. Attend town meetings or city council meetings. Have a chat with the city or town clerk. Stop in at your local police department. Ask questions like "What are the major problems in our community?" or "Which volunteer groups are doing the most good for our town?"

Local Court and Justice System.   More and more judicial systems are using volunteers in counseling and rehabilitation programs for young people and adults charged with and convicted of crimes.

Local Businesses.   Chambers of commerce and other business and consumer councils, as well as individual manufacturers, merchants, bankers, and other professionals, often have opinions about community problems and issues and the best existing ways to approach them.

Local Service Clubs.   Contact your local Kiwanis, Rotary, Lions, and other service clubs. Some local groups are mainly concerned with commercial good fellowship, but many others get involved in innovative social service efforts. For instance, the Lions have taken on a national project to assist the blind, and Rotarians are active in local scholarships.

Churches, Synagogues, Mosques.   Even if you're not a member of a congregation, contact a couple of ministers, priests, or rabbis— excellent sources of what's being done in the community.

Schools.   Call or visit the administrative offices of the elementary and secondary schools and the community colleges and universities in your area. Attend school board and PTA meetings. If you're particularly interested in a group that relates to the school setting, ask for a meeting with a school counselor, principal, teacher, coach, or other official.

Women's Clubs.   In many cities, women's clubs have long been energetic and effective sources of programs and voluntary effort. Contact your local Women's City Club, Junior League, League of Women Voters, or women's business groups.

Hospitals and Nursing Homes.   Institutions that care for ill and elderly people both need volunteers for their own programs and know about outpatient programs run by nonprofit groups. See the

> "If you really want to participate, opportunities are everywhere. You get mail all the time, saying give to this, give to that charity, asking you to write for more information. All you have to do is pick something that you can really relate to. For example, if you are concerned about the future of our environment and you get a flyer from an environmental group, call them and tell them about yourself and then meet with some people. They are always ready to talk about what they are doing." —*Beth Kummerfeld*

White and Yellow Pages, and ask first for the director of volunteer programs. If no such position exists, contact the director of administration.

Newspapers. Watch the local print media, including neighborhood and shopping handouts, for write-ups on organizations and their activities. Read editorials as well as news stories. If you're after something specific, you might even contact editors and reporters you think may have knowledge or information.

Television and Radio. The broadcast media carry many public service announcements and frequently feature stories about people helping other people or working for a worthy cause. Contact the station if you catch only the tail end of something that sounds interesting. They can usually send reprints of stories and editorials, or tell you how to contact advertisers.

Community Bulletin Boards. Check the notices and ads that people post at town halls, libraries, retailers, grocery stores, dry cleaners—wherever bulletin boards exist in your town.

Political Representatives. The offices of elected officials—local, state, and national—can be very helpful in pointing you toward organizations that solve problems or improve the quality of life. Consider contacting both present and past political leaders, as well as current candidates for public office. Attend local political meetings for insights into local problems and ideas for private action.

Performing Arts Groups.   Theater, dance, and musical groups love to learn about people who want to help in their endeavors, and most can quite readily put you to work. Some of these groups are active in community affairs and thus can function as a resource for knowledge of other organizations.

Local Museums or Historical Societies.   Again, consult the White and Yellow Pages. While some local historical societies may be essentially one-man or -woman operations, others will welcome offers of help.

Senior Citizens Centers or Agencies.   Churches, local government offices, and the telephone book will direct you to these groups, which may provide just socialization or actually run programs to support the lives of the members.

Social Service Agencies.   Public and private agencies of all kinds— serving children, families, the elderly, the unemployed, and many other groups—are listed in the telephone directory under "Health and Welfare Agencies," "Human Services," "Service Organizations," "Social Services," and similar headings.

Local Branches of National Organizations.   Research in the directories in your local library may tell you which groups have local branches. If you're in a big city, consult your local phone book. Using the *Encyclopedia of Associations* (mentioned above, under "Public Libraries"), you can also contact national organizations to find the closest chapter in a nearby town.

Special Avenues of Approach

The following suggestions are not for everyone, but may apply to particular groups.

For Students.   An increasing number of high schools are making service a part of their curricula. Many are offering—some are even requiring—a certain number of hours of service as a prerequisite for graduation. High school students should make their interest in volunteering known to the school administration; it may fit in very nicely with an existing or developing plan.

College students should contact their activities office or campus administration. Be persistent; sometimes volunteer offices are new and not well known throughout the bureaucracies in large universities.

Students can contact two relatively new national organizations that promote student volunteerism: the **Campus Outreach Opportunity League** (COOL) and **Campus Compact** (see chapter 3, under "Groups of Interest to Children and Youth," for addresses and telephone numbers). One or both of these groups may be newly established on campus, or interested students and faculty members might initiate such involvement.

For Older People.   Service opportunities for older and retired people are numerous. Beyond the need for experienced people in almost all nonprofit groups, several large programs exist that specifically use the talents of older people. A few examples are the **American Association of Retired Persons** (AARP); the **Retired Senior Volunteer Program,** run by ACTION, the federal domestic volunteer agency; and the **International Executive Service Corps** and the **National Executive Service Corps** (see chapter 3, under "Groups of Interest to Senior Citizens and Retired People").

Getting Informed

Narrow your search to a maximum of six organizations. Then collect printed material about these before contacting them for interviews. Almost all groups have some kind of handout that describes their work. If you telephone to have information sent to you, state that you are interested in working for the organization, so that they can send available material tailored for potential volunteers.

EVALUATING ORGANIZATIONS

If you don't have the guidance of a friend or acquaintance, you'll take a kind of "cold call" approach. First try to reach a director of recruitment or director of the volunteer program. If no such person exists, contact the office of the executive director. Say that you are interested in the organization, that you would like to learn more about the work they are doing and how you might fit in.

Again, you will "position" yourself in describing the kind of contribution you feel you can make. Bear in mind your reflections on the essential you. Know how you feel about the cause. And know which of your skills and abilities—developed or yet to be exercised—you want to emphasize. Besides the questions that come your way, be sure you make opportunities to say what you have to contribute.

Whether you make the contact through networking or your own investigating, you will eventually have an interview, whether it's an informal chat over coffee or an appointment at the offices of the organization. One part of your job in an interview is to present yourself, in whatever mode you choose. The other is to evaluate the organization. Eagerness and enthusiasm sometimes propel people into joining groups before they have found out much about them, and we strongly urge you to read and think carefully about non-profits you are considering.

Standard Information

In your reading and talking about organizations, try to learn about the following areas. Again, we're not suggesting that you insist on having answers to every one of these questions. These topics are offered as guides to your thinking.

What is the organization's mission and philosophy?   Do you agree with it? "Well, sure," you say. "Why else would I be interested?" This does seem like a funny question, but it's worth asking for a variety of reasons. You may have a preconception about a group that could prove, upon investigation, to be wrong. You may think you are interested because a friend or family member is; when you hear about the group's goals from a third party, they may not sound so great. You may agree with the general aim of the group, but not with their specific way of approaching it.

How is the organization funded?   Each person will have his or her own views on this. There are people who want to avoid organizations that are sponsored, even in part, by government or corporations. Others want to steer clear of groups with religious ties or political orientations. And some won't care at all where the money comes from.

How does the group relate to the community?   What other groups in the community does it have ties with? How are volunteers and board members recruited? Where does the paid staff come from? Is fund-raising done locally? How does the group benefit the community? If the organization has clients, who are they? What are the special characteristics of the client population, the needs or problems that bring them to the agency?

What is the structure of the organization?   What is the proportion of paid staff to volunteers? How is the organization structured? Is it well managed? Who is really in charge? How are the large decisions made? What about small decisions: are approvals needed or is there relative freedom to act?

How dynamic and innovative is the group?   One way to check on these qualities is to ask for a brief, casual history of the group's activities within the past two or three years.

What is expected of the volunteer?   What are the responsibilities? What are the personal qualities that are required for performing a particular task? If they can't tell you, it's a bad sign. How much decision-making is expected or required of volunteers?

Is there a volunteer program?   Or are volunteers used on an informal basis? The answers to these questions aren't meaningful in and of themselves, but your experience in an organization with a formalized program will be different in some ways from working in a group that uses volunteers on an ad hoc basis or that hasn't developed formal training and ways of moving them in and out of assignments.

What training is provided?   Is it formal or informal? One-on-one, in workshops, seminars, classes? Is it accomplished through lectures, case studies, role-playing? What topics are covered? How much training is offered, how much required?

Is there ongoing supervision, guidance, and support for volunteers? Some organizations provide in-person and telephone consultations, buddy systems, group meetings, periodic conferences, workshops. If there's no formalized support mechanisms, will there be open access to staff members? Be sure that you understand the line of communication that you will depend on.

What are the possibilities for taking greater responsibility? In other words, what are the possibilities for advancement within the organization? Even if you don't think you want to become a committee chair or board member, it's good to know whether the organization welcomes new blood circulating upward through its ranks.

Does the organization provide liability insurance for its volunteers? Opinions on the importance of this topic vary. Some people feel strongly that organizations have a responsibility to provide insurance to both direct service volunteers and board members. Certainly, board members need liability insurance coverage and possibly other forms of coverage, such as director and officers coverage or professional liability coverage.

Does the organization provide reimbursement for expenses? Are transportation, meals, and other out-of-pocket costs covered? Often they are not, but in some cases it may be appropriate.

Things to Do After the Interview

Time and circumstances permitting, your knowledge and ability to judge an organization will be benefited if you can take any of the following actions.

Visit the headquarters and/or the site where the work will take place. Being there in person is the best way to get a feel for the organization and the work. Seeing the physical setup of your own potential workplace can be particularly helpful. Most of us consciously or unconsciously visualize situations, and often they are somewhat more glamorous in our mind's eye than in reality.

Try to get an opportunity to observe the operation in the phase you are interested in. If you're going in for office administration, stop in to see how it's done. If you want to join the education committee, try to attend a meeting as an observer. If you want to do direct service, accompany an experienced volunteer on assignment.

Try to have conversations with some present members of the organization. This is an extremely important step. Try especially to contact people who are working with the assignment you will be likely to have. Bring up with them any questions that your initial interview left unanswered.

Check on the fiscal responsibility of the group. Apart from overall solvency, the main consideration for judging the fiscal responsibility of a nonprofit organization is the amount of money that it spends on its program, as opposed to the costs of administration and fund-raising. It's safe to say that a *minimum* of 50 percent of money spent should go toward program costs, and many groups and individuals call for an even higher standard, maintaining that 70 percent or more should be spent on programs.

You can ask large and small organizations for their annual reports for the last three years. If those publications don't contain information about expenditures, you can simply ask how their expense budget breaks down. It is a standard question and upstanding organizations should be able to readily provide you with an answer.

For a third-party report on local groups, contact the Better Business Bureau or Chamber of Commerce in your area.

For national organizations, two nonprofit watchdog groups can often be helpful:

The **National Charities Information Bureau** (19 Union Square West, New York, New York 10003-3395; telephone: [212] 929-6300) provides in-depth reports on more than 300 nonprofit organizations that solicit funds nationwide. Six times a year, it publishes the *Wise Giving Guide,* a summary of its evaluations of all the organizations on which it reports. The guide and up to three individual reports are available free on written request.

The Philanthropic Advisory Service (PAS) of the **Council of Better Business Bureaus** (CBBB) (1515 Wilson Boulevard, Arlington, Virginia 22209; telephone: [703] 276-0100) collects and distributes information on thousands of nonprofit organizations that solicit nationally or have national or international program services. Every other month, the PAS publishes *Give But Give Wisely,* a concise listing of the most-inquired-about charities and whether they meet CBBB standards. The organization also makes available one- to four-page summaries of individual organizations. The guide is available for $1, and three reports are available free of charge.

Do your own informal reference-checking.   Contact other community groups with whom the organization has dealings. Ask them what they think of this group, what it has accomplished in the community, how innovative and dynamic it is. If possible, get the opinion of some of the clients served by the group.

Your Overall Evaluation

If you've kept in mind at least some of the questions we've posed, you've probably learned a great deal about the group or groups you've become interested in. Now ask yourself a few summary questions.

You found out about them. Did they find out about you?   Are they seeing you for who you are? Do they know what aspects of yourself you want to contribute? Did they ask you questions that made you think they care?

How does the goal of the organization fit with your personal goals and, especially, your motivation for doing service work?   It's more than fair to consider whether your interests will be served, for the better the fit, the better the service that you will give.

What is the "feel" of the organization? Do you sense enthusiasm for their stated mission?   This is an absolute must. If you don't have a strong sense of enthusiasm or if something feels wrong to you, turn elsewhere.

What kind of energy did you sense in the people and in the organization collectively? Is it a kind of energy that you like, that you will be able to join in with?

Do you like the people you met? Do you share the same values? This is another absolute requirement.

How did the people you met relate to one another? Is this way of relating one that you are comfortable with?

What kind of attitude did you perceive about the clients or the program? Do you share a similar attitude?

Finally, based on what you've learned, draw up a brief list of the qualities you think a volunteer for this organization should have. Compare that list with the notes that make up your own profile. Are you and this group right for one another?

MAKING A COMMITMENT

When you feel that you want to offer a commitment to a group, don't say you'd like to be on the board or head up the publicity committee as your first assignment. Instead say, "I want to be involved in this organization. I believe in what you are doing— how can I help? I want to work." They'll find something for you to do, and once you've begun helping, further ways in which you can be of use will develop and more and more responsibility will be offered to you.

Kenneth Dayton, longtime chairman and CEO of the Dayton Hudson Corporation and board member of many nonprofit organizations, offered us the following advice:

> I think the important thing is for people to decide what they are really interested in, where they can make their contribution, and just let those organizations know. If they do that, they'll find that they will be asked. I pick the organization that I would most like to help and go to someone on that board and say, "I'm very interested in what you're doing. How could I be helpful?" They'll find all kinds of ways for you to be helpful.

Sometimes an organization will ask you to become involved, particularly if you are a leader in your community or profession. They may want you because of your expertise, your good judgment, your contacts with other influential people. Such overtures give you a wonderful opportunity to discuss fully the work you might do for the organization. Keep an open mind to all such invitations, but don't be so flattered that you fail to examine the factors that we've discussed in this chapter. Your motivations for joining should be strong whether you or the organization makes the first move.

TIPS FOR NEW VOLUNTEERS

When you begin any endeavor, your enthusiasm is probably very high. We have a few suggestions for channeling this positive energy so that you can enter service work with as much satisfaction and success as possible.

Be reasonable in making your initial time commitment. It's much better, for you and for the organization, to start with a very realistic and even conservative schedule. You can always expand the time you spend.

Get to know as many other members as possible. There's no better way to get knowledge about the continuity of the group's work and a sense of how programs operate and how things really get done.

Set some goals for your involvement with the group. Consider how you relate to the aims of the organization now and how you would like to be relating in six months or a year. Set objectives for yourself, as you might do in a job, but remain open to new opportunities as the organization changes and as you learn more about it.

Keep your ears and mind open. Leave preconceived ideas behind and get with the spirit of the group. Be conscious of how you begin to contribute. Listen and be sensitive to reactions to your ideas. Be positive. People want solution-givers, not problem-starters.

> "For me, volunteer service has brought a marvelous education in a new and fascinating field. When I started in international development and relief work, I knew nothing about the field. To work for Oxfam as a volunteer and director was for me a straight-up learning curve. And it's very exciting and stimulating to learn again with a real intensity. It's better than going back to school because you can do all of your learning out in the field." —Michael Shimkin

Work in a nondirective way. Nonprofits work less by top-down, authoritarian methods than by a consensus approach, a channeling of many ideas into a concerted way of serving the organization's mission. If you insist on a directive approach, people can feel that they are not being heard and they may lose interest. The best method for a leader—board member, committee chair, project head, or member of an ad hoc group of direct service volunteers—is to see what consensus is building in the group and then to make a move in that direction.

Taking on More Responsibility

When you first start out, you generally attend the meetings of your committee or project group, or begin to fulfill your direct service assignment. As time goes by and you are found to be an asset, other people will call on you. So although they may start with mundane sorts of activity, energetic and willing volunteers are soon asked to take on increasing responsibilities.

A rule of thumb is that in volunteer organizations, people and projects gravitate toward the able and energetic workers. Soon you will be on various committees, and eventually you can become more selective and serve on a committee that holds the most interest for you.

Being on the board is something that you earn and something that the nominating committee, which recommends people for board membership, will need to evaluate. In order to be recommended, you have to earn your stripes, and you do that by going to work.

Managing Your Time

Because volunteers handle the time demands of service work in very personal ways, attitudes toward and methods of time management vary considerably.

Some employers who are enthusiastic about nonprofit involvement may allow you as much time as you need to be on the phone or away from the office for direct service work or appointments. With others, you may be able to work out an arrangement: to use one hour of the day for your phone work, to take off at particular times for meetings, to use a couple of hours two mornings a week for a direct service assignment.

People who don't work or who don't work in an office face another kind of problem. For one thing, because other people in the organization know their situation, they may be called on with lots of small, miscellaneous details, or when emergencies arise. The other, tougher problem is that they must make for themselves the structure that the watchful supervisor provides for the office worker. Many people address this problem by structuring their day, with one part for their personal or family business, another for the professional work they may do at home, and another for their nonprofit work.

If your volunteer work entails a lot of telephoning, you may want to get an understanding with your coworkers about when you want to receive calls. You should feel free to be very specific about this, asking people not to call after 8:00 P.M., or not before 9:00 A.M., not on Saturdays at all—whatever structure you want to set up.

Other people in the service world will respect this kind of organization of your life. They are also aware that your time demands may become too great. If that happens, you lose effectiveness, your work or family life may suffer, and the organization may lose a valued member. For good volunteers, there is always a question of keeping a balance of the time you really have available and your own good nature and your willingness to serve.

"I feel that volunteer work has one major obstacle, and I don't know whether it will ever be possible to remove it. It is the fact that money talks, and if you are out working in a job that is bringing in money—I don't care what level it is on—you are one step above the volunteers. Volunteers are not bringing home a paycheck; therefore, their time is continually adjustable, it is something they can always put aside, they don't *have* to be there.

"People think you should cancel obligations or adjust appointments in favor of other activities. You have to have a lot of moxie and a lot of courage to say, I'm sorry, I can't because this volunteer work is important."

—Debbie Scott

If you become overextended and involved in too many activities, you probably will become less helpful to certain of them. You are in danger of becoming a member in name only, and for most people that is not a satisfying role. It is not a winning situation for you or the organization. And it may gain you a reputation you don't want.

WHAT TO DO IF IT'S NOT WORKING OUT

Even with the best efforts and intentions on your part, it's possible that a particular volunteer assignment or organization may not be to your liking. You and the organization may have misjudged your ability to cope with the assignment. You may want to work with battered children but find that your emotions overpower your ability to function well. You may realize that the time commitment you made in good faith is in fact unworkable. You may discover that the organization functions in a way you're not comfortable with.

If your problem is not with the organization but with the assignment or the particular people you are working with, you could try a different job within the same organization. If you're still enthusiastic about the general field but have gone sour on one organization, try a group that takes a different approach. Or change gears entirely, choosing another field or cause. You'll know more about yourself this time and will have a better chance at making a good match.

If you want to withdraw from an organization, don't just stop showing up. You should resign, showing as much consideration as possible. If it would be helpful, try to give a little advance notice, as you would in a paid job, or try to complete a project in process. One of the most considerate things you can do is to find someone to replace you within the organization.

FINANCIAL AND LEGAL CONSIDERATIONS

Anyone who makes sizable contributions to nonprofit organizations is advised to consult a tax accountant, and we likewise suggest that each volunteer discuss the issue of liability and insurance with the prospective organization. We'll give some general guidelines here, but these two important areas must be carefully considered by each individual.

You must itemize deductions in order to take advantage of the tax deductibility of your contributions. You can call the Internal Revenue Service and have them send you, at no cost, their booklet *Publication 526: Charitable Contributions,* which explains and gives examples of the tax law.

Tax deduction is allowed for contributions to qualified organizations, that is, those that are organized and operated only for charitable, religious, educational, scientific, or literary purposes, or for the prevention of cruelty to children or animals. Certain organizations that foster national or international amateur sports competition are also included. Check with the individual organization about the tax deductibility of contributions to it.

Volunteers can deduct unreimbursed out-of-pocket expenses directly related to the services given to a charitable organization. Contributions that are tax deductible are:

· Direct monetary gifts;
· Nonmonetary contributions of property: for example, clothing, automobiles, office equipment, works of art, securities, real estate (discuss the issue of fair market value with your tax consultant);

- Transportation expenses: bus, subway, and cab fares, automobile mileage (at an estimated 12 cents per mile or the actual expense), gas and oil, parking fees and tolls;
- The expense of maintaining special uniforms;
- Telephone bills;
- Dues, fees, and assessments;
- For tickets to benefits (dinners, concerts, theater events), the difference between the normal price (that is, the fair market value of the meal or admission) and the actual amount paid.

Not deductible are:

- The value of your volunteer time or services;
- The rental value of property you lend to a nonprofit organization;
- Dependent-care expenses (that is, baby-sitting or elder care);
- Gifts to individuals;
- Most meals and entertainment, and vacations that may involve some charitable work (discuss these issues with your tax consultant);
- Automobile repair and maintenance expenses.

It is most important to keep precise records of the names of organizations and descriptions and amounts of contributions. When making monetary contributions, write checks, don't give cash. In the case of large gifts, get a receipt or statement of donation from the organization.

In the fall of 1987, bills were introduced in both houses of the United States Congress for the passage of a Volunteer Protection Act that addresses the concern about liability that is felt by many board members and direct service volunteers. The proposed legislation would withhold 1 percent of Social Services Block Grant money from any state that fails to extend liability protection to volunteers who act in good faith within the scope of their official duties.

Individuals could still be sued for willful and wanton misconduct, and lawsuits could still be brought against organizations. More than twenty states have enacted similar legislation.

To find out about the situation in your state and to learn whether an organization provides insurance coverage for volunteers, discuss these issues with the organization.

You're about to embark on an exciting new chapter in your life. We hope our advice will be of some help. You have our sincere wishes for an enjoyable, rewarding experience!

IN THEIR OWN WORDS

"I know I can solve a problem—at least if anyone can, I can. I have a chance here . . . to use all of my talents, I mean *all* of my talents. Not only my formal training in school, but also a lot of my experiential training that I got on expeditions."

—Reno Taini

"For me, finding the right involvement was trial and error. I was always looking for something to do that would give me a sense of making a contribution. I floundered around and looked at several organizations, and they didn't work out for one reason or another. It's a good idea to research, but you absolutely must care about the cause."

—Betty Ballard

"My children and I talk a lot about the fact that not everybody is as fortunate as we are and about what we can do from a personal and political viewpoint to make a difference. At the holiday season we always pick presents with the children to wrap for other children, and when there are events and opportunities—as at WNYC—for my children to join me, I always take them and talk to them about an organization and what it does, because I really want them to take their own roles in service as soon as they can."

—Susie Fisher

Reno Taini: *Named teacher of the year in California in 1982, Reno Taini created and for the past twenty-one years has run Jefferson High School's Community Environmental Education Program, an alternative educational program often referred to as the Wilderness Class, in Daly City, California. His students are the troubled ones, borderline kids, real toughs, rebels, and punk rockers who are not making it in school and who will otherwise slip through the cracks. He uses Outward Bound methods service projects, and career exploration, and works through challenge and motivation to help them find self-esteem and a sense of true responsibility and commitment. Beyond bringing to his professional role an extra dimension of service to others, Reno is a committed board member and volunteer with several organizations. He is an inspiring speaker and addresses educators' groups around the country.*

Basically I am a first-generation Italian kid who was born in San Francisco and raised in an inner-city environment. All my life I've been in a city. The big quest I had in the early days was the out-of-doors.

I became very ingrained with the work ethic early in life, and I thought everyone else was. I really didn't ꓽo well in school, I didn't care about school. It didn't make sense. I always wanted to work. Because of a couple of inspirational teachers, I was able to adjust and, with that, get the feeling of belonging, and then actually do well in school—all the way to going to a local college.

In college I took up biological science and got involved in exploration, mostly fieldwork in the forests and mountains. Again, because of a couple of very important teachers, I got to see the world.

What I did is basically turn toward humanity as I worked in Third World countries. I realized that I really had a feeling for people who weren't like everyone else around me in San Francisco. I did well at teaching biology for a couple of years, but then gravitated toward the kids that weren't as fortunate, the inner-city kids that had problems with school. I guess I've devoted most of my life since then to those punks and quiet casualties in the public school system, designing a program that really celebrates them in such a way that it gives them the energy and power to make it in the world—like I made it.

I kind of did it my way. I've done it my way all my life, against all kinds of odds. That's why I teach a "life" survival course for kids in school. The ethic of Outward Bound came to the U.S. in the early sixties when Josh Miner [the first president of Outward Bound] brought it over here from the U.K. Right from the start I was very interested in it. It was applied to the Peace Corps training. I wasn't in the Peace Corps, but I have been very, very familiar with it all my life and almost joined it. I've been teaching a sort of Outward Bound/Peace Corps kind of program for twenty years.

I got out of college and went right into teaching and coaching. I had many jobs and did different things in summer jobs, etc. I never really was excited about teaching as my life-career job. I just did what felt right. I went where I was needed, which leads into this whole volunteer thing. Basically I was good at whatever I did. I was always needed wherever I showed up, whatever the job was. I've had many, many jobs. One way or another that volunteer attitude has allowed me to continue through some very tough times, especially in the teaching profession, because somehow I decided, well, I am doing okay here, I'm making something happen, that's not for nothing. I'm effective with people's lives.

I know I can solve a problem—at least if anyone can, I can. I have a chance here in Daly City to use all of my talents, I mean *all* of my talents. Not only my formal training in school, but also a lot of my experiential training that I got on expeditions. Teaching stimulates me; my job is fairly open-ended. It's challenging, it's rigorous, it's adventurous. There are a lot of wonderful discoveries that just happen. It's exciting, it's very intense, very inspirational.

The more I try to avoid looking at the excitement of making a difference, the more it just hits me right in the face. I see people that I taught twenty years ago, fifteen years ago—they come up to me on the street and say how important what I offered was. And sometimes I hear this: it's energizing, it's motivating, it's stretching me. The key was just that "raw stuff," that "glue" that keeps a person together—I don't even think about it that much—but it keeps me going.

I learned how to pace myself. I'm not afraid to be in a goldfish bowl, so to speak, and take a couple of harpoons sometimes when people misinterpret what is going on, because I know these kids are getting something out of this. I am not overprotective of them, I know that I've got it set up where I can help them help themselves. It's kind of a blend of my skills and a lot of my compassion. Also I know what it is like to be one of those kids, I mean, I went through it all. I came from a real rough childhood environment. I was an underdog.

What turned me to serve others were the school conditions. In my early days of teaching, the whole school was in a turmoil, in the early sixties. We had a lot of racial problems—I'm talking riots on campus. It's a tough school. I remember my first week of student teaching. I could see what was going on, and I actually helped control really tense situations just by confronting a couple of gang leaders at the right time. I wasn't afraid to do that because I was so close to that kind of environment. I could approach them appropriately.

I knew what I did worked in those days, and so I designed things to pattern after that. In those days it was important work, and it was, beyond a shadow of a doubt—the stuff that I did in those days, those experiences, regardless of whether it was a race riot or saving a kid who had a drug problem—it was overwhelmingly important to my colleagues and to the parents, to the community, and to the quality of life at that school. And it wasn't because I was applying some skill that I learned in college. It had nothing to do with that. I pushed from my heart.

It was very easy. I had arranged things in such a way that I would get feedback right away. All along I got an awful lot of feedback—psychic feedback—that this was working, that what I was doing was pretty important. It was improving life, and I tuned into it. All along I chose to do it—I really decided this is what I wanted to do against all odds.

My parents said I was crazy. My colleagues said, you're nuts to start a new program where you take kids out of school for two weeks on a backpack trip, male and female. In those days, 1967/1968, there were problems about forming coed patrols, but it worked. I had a volunteer female teacher and myself, and we did it. It worked, the darn thing worked so much that it became the most logical thing to do, to get kids out of that environment and challenge them.

It also turns them on to the point where they feel good enough to be able to contribute to others. They can leave their own gangs, and even contribute something back to their peers. The funny part is that right now there are kids of mine in the community who are managing stores who have actually been able to help me with donations of food for our backpacking outings. It's kind of a big recycling that is happening.

For me, service is kind of a primal urge to just live fully what I'm teaching. What I am teaching is way beyond the ordinary routine. And it wasn't that I wasn't qualified to teach biology. Boy, I'll tell you, I was a scientist! I went to South America and spent three months on the side of a mountain collecting birds. Shooting them, labeling them, weighing them—and I brought back a whole collection to the museum. But I just couldn't stay with that museum work—it wasn't enough. I loved collecting in the wilderness, and dealing with people in Third World countries was great, but I had to lead from the heart.

I mean when the school board questioned what I was doing I gave it to them in triplicate. There were close votes to shut my program down several times. But then there'd be some logical person on the board who'd say, well, let's give him a chance. That's all I needed. That's all these young people need.

Basically, there's an incubation period the kids go through in all these challenging experiences. When they finally get there, they are okay, and finally they get to a point where they don't really notice how well are doing. There's an arc of learning and a whole scheme of getting better that they don't even see. And finally one day they'll get approached by, say, a group of kids that want to do something, and they will realize they have information, they have skills, they have ability that others want. At that point, they realize, hey, I'm so good, I'm good enough to give a little bit, good enough to offer what I have. I've got answers. People need my answers. And that is kind of the same thing that was true for me. I can make something happen here. I have a purpose.

I think that's a real big one, to get to the point where, one way or the other—it's got to come from the outside, it's got to be undeniable—they feel okay. It's a feeling of saying, I'm okay here, I found my spot, I found my place. I am needed. I'm not hurt, I'm not lost, I'm not confused when I'm doing this. It's kind of like beyond logic, this kind of thing. It's uplifting, it's human, it's basically an offering that someone can make without even feeling like it's an offering. And it energizes them a lot.

What I get personally, and I think what some of these kids get, is a sense of intimate achievement and personal worth, a sense that I matter, I count, I've lived through something, I've got an answer. I'm not going to solve all the problems, but I'm a piece of the puzzle. That's the way I consider myself as a teacher. I'm one of the people during their course of living at the school that will count, that will get them on their way. I help them help themselves . . . that's all.

For someone who wants to get involved in helping other people, the big thing is they have got to begin. And to begin they need to take a break from what they are doing every day. They need to just realize their worth as a human being. They basically need to look at what really interests them. And that means any organization, from a group of people trying to save the butterflies on some hill to some traditional operation. They have got to get to the point where they feel the connection. It's got to be hands on—heart-felt and hands on. I mean, right from the heart, and from the hand, and, of course, they must use their head, too. But if they would just take that small step, acquire a little chunk, become involved in one thing—they have begun.

What I have done over the years is—being on the Outward Bound board, the YMCA board, a volunteer leader with Operation Raleigh—I mean, it's all the same stuff over and over. We all have skills. Every person has skills. It's just a matter of really looking at what is the mission of the operation they want to get involved in; what are they really trying to do.

Just so they feel that it's totally connected to them. They have got to be utilized in such a way that they feel that it is a releasing experience. A lot of these people come from jobs that are pretty routine. They are confined. So it should be a situation where they feel like they have an opportunity to express their specialness, a step toward winning fully. It is about life expression.

They went to school, they trained, and now they are going to get to use this stuff. It's something that forces them to look at a problem in a new way. It's kind of like the search and rescue. For years I was a search and rescue volunteer, and now I'm a volunteer fireman. You don't know what's going to jump out of the box. I mean, you get a call, and you've got to respond *now,* and you train as best you can, but it brings out the best in you. It is the truth, and it must be handled.

It brings forth an unconstrained and liberating feeling. It's almost like it brings forth the warrior. Again, it's the outside threat, and you've got to answer. It could be anything. You could save the whole operation from sinking because of a couple of decisions or actions or some real creative suggestions for ways of doing things.

Betty Ballard: *A secretary for twenty-eight years, Betty Ballard had tried other volunteer involvements before becoming involved in Literacy Volunteers of New York City about six years ago.*

I've always felt that people with families have a tremendous responsibility toward society, to raise their children to become productive citizens with good values, and that those who do not have families should look around for some way of contributing. So I was sort of looking for something to do.

But I was also looking for something to enrich my own life. Having had some experience with volunteering—without tremendous success, but having had a taste of it—I found that it helped my life a little bit. When I bumped into the Literacy Volunteers phone number, I called and registered and was invited to a workshop.

Reading is one of my major interests. I read voraciously, all kinds of books. It just pained me to think of people who could not read. I really focused more on the pleasure side of it than on the functional side, which is something I learned about fairly quickly—the problems. The average person just doesn't think about the functional problems the nonreader has.

When I went through the workshop, there was a lot of focus on the functional aspects of reading. And there were more revelations after that. I've been in the program for six years, and you constantly hear people say that you get so much more than you put into it. But you don't really understand what that means until it happens to you. Then it becomes a really specific thing.

As you get to know the people who come to this organization for reading help, one of the things that strikes you is the courage that it takes, and how different they are from other people who have the same problem but do not reach out for help.

I remember once, a few years ago, I got my wallet lifted out of my purse while I was on my way to tutor, after work—pressured day, I'm on the subway, I'm late, panting and puffing—somebody stole my wallet. It didn't have a lot of money in it, but I was mad. And the last thing I wanted to do was hold class.

I was working with a group of students who had been around for a while, in a special course on job applications, although it was more than that. We were talking about skills, translating those into work ideas, job ideas. They were a wonderful, steady group who were really making the class as good as it was. When I arrived, there they were, on time, waiting for me, ready to go to work. And it struck me that if I didn't do what I was supposed to do that night, the person who ripped me off was also going to rip them off.

I thought if anybody might have ended up out there on the streets ripping people off, it was them. Many have such a terrible time getting work, because of their problems with literacy—they can't fill out a job application. So I looked at them and I thought, this would be very wrong for me not to go through with class this evening. It really came home to me, how special these people are.

The first student that I worked with, a beginning reader, was in the Olympic class for championship archery. I was just blown away—he really taught me a lot about it. We decided to do some taping of some of his books, and I taped some things on an auxiliary microphone at my house on my little stereo. He came back laughing at me a week later. He said, you know, you really don't know how to record, all I got was the dog barking next door. And he told me how to set the recording levels on my machine to avoid that problem.

As I got to know him, I learned that he was able to build a house from the foundation to the chimney, without a blueprint. As time went by I met more and more people like that, and I learned to really listen to them and really know them. I think I was patronizing before, but really listening, really knowing, really getting inside someone else changes that.

I grew up with values that said people are equal, but most people are prejudiced even though they claim not to be. Truly getting to know someone takes careful listening and real caring and sharing, and then all that stuff is erased, wherever it may be. You can go through life thinking you're not prejudiced, but if you take a real hard look at it, you're going to find it somewhere in yourself.

At first, I tended to look at our students as disadvantaged, and I just don't anymore. They can be disadvantaged in the sense that they might not have opportunities—obviously some don't have opportunities, for all kinds of reasons. But certainly in what I've seen, in terms of the richness of their lives, they're not disadvantaged at all levels. People who are living in severe circumstances obviously need help, but there's a richness in people's lives. You can't go in assuming that people are disadvantaged. It's important to see how people perceive themselves.

It's a very gratifying thing to watch, students and tutors getting together and getting to know one another and getting to be friends, and helping each other with all sorts of things. It becomes a learning partnership.

For me, finding the right involvement was trial and error. I was always looking for something to do that would give me a sense of making a contribution. I floundered around and looked at several organizations, and they didn't work out for one reason or another. It's a good idea to research, but you absolutely must care about the cause. As I look back over the other things I did, I realize that I didn't always care very much about the cause. I often had to manufacture that caring; it wasn't very real.

As time goes by, Literacy Volunteers gives you an opportunity, if you want it, to be very creative. I could go on for an hour about the list of things you can do on your own, once you get to know the staff and they see that you've internalized the strategies. You can grow and grow and grow, as I have, and as many of the tutors and students have.

There are many tutors who do other kinds of volunteer service for the organization, in areas like public relations, fund-raising, workshop training, orientation of new students, testing, math classes, and materials research. Students become volunteers, too. There are also a number of people on the paid staff who began as volunteers. The assistant director was formerly a volunteer, for example. And many staff members still volunteer.

The friendships that I've made in Literacy Volunteers over the past six years are solid and will last all my life. I can name at least five people who I am certain I will have as lifelong friends. Some are students, others are tutors. And there will be more as time goes by.

I don't know what does it, maybe it's birds of a feather, I don't know. But the people in this program understand about commitment and about getting to know each other. We do with each other the same things we do in getting to know students—careful listening, really knowing someone, sharing, understanding, not judging. That works in your personal life as well, it works in your friendships. It's wonderfully rewarding.

I no longer think of this work as volunteering. It's a part of my life now. When people say, oh, isn't it wonderful that you do that— it sounds so alien to me to hear that. It's not wonderful that I do it—it's a part of my life, a very important part of my life. I can't look at it as "volunteering" anymore. It just sounds like a weird word to me.

Another thing it has done for me is that it has made me take a look at a career change. Not long ago, I said I wanted to make a career change, but that I didn't really know how or what, somebody—and they didn't know me that well—said to me, what is it in your life that you like doing so much that you would do it for nothing? Bingo, here it is. I like doing this so much that I've done it for nothing for six years. And so it's gotten me to thinking about how I might get into teaching, combining my business background and my teaching experience.

I would like very much to find a way to get into teaching clerical and typing skills to people who have marginal opportunities. And talk to them about attitude, what employers want from them— how they can get ahead, how to grow. I would probably make half of what I could make in a corporate law firm, but I don't care. To do what you really want to do, there's nothing better.

This has been such a bonus in my life—it has changed my life. I have been a secretary for twenty-eight years and I've hated it, and I've never known how to change it. Coming here gives me a sense of being able to take charge of my life.

Susie Fisher: *A senior vice president for the private banking firm Manufacturers and Traders Trust Company, Susie Fisher runs a division that lends and provides banking services to people with high net worth.*

On a personal level, I find work in the nonprofit world enormously rewarding. We all have opportunities, especially as we advance in business, to serve many different organizations and, as a business person, I have a personal need to make New York and the community a better place. I feel very gratified at the opportunity to have done that through many different kinds of organizations. I have also tried to diversify that involvement.

For the past couple of years I have been president of the **Columbia Business School** alumni board. I have been on the board for many years at the **National Choral Council,** which furthers the art of choral singing in this country. I think that this music makes a difference in the world in terms of providing enjoyment and furthering the art form. I have a similar involvement in the **Dance Notation Bureau.** I have recently joined the board of **WNYC Public Radio and Television,** and I feel that I am making a contribution to a better life for New York City through these public broadcasting stations. For many years I have been on the board of the **Women's Division of the Jewish Guild for the Blind.** I have a great respect for the organization and feel very good about the direct impact that it has on people who have visual and other handicaps.

The other side of this involvement has been exciting, positive rewards in business. I have met many clients through particular boards, like the Columbia board. For a year I was president of the board of the **Financial Women's Association,** and the people that I met have made major differences in my personal career and have provided a great deal of business for me. I'm very concerned about our country and our government. I am actively involved in the **Republican party.** My political involvements recently almost led to my moving to Washington, which is a goal that I still hold for the future.

My mother didn't work, and her major activities were her non-profit involvements. I remember that she set up a hotline in Westchester for people with problems. She taught Chinese students to speak English, which fascinated me, since she didn't speak a word of Chinese. My dad was very active in the community. He was an active Republican, and I was a Tyke for Ike. I had quite an education in college—I went to Columbia Business School, having been a Columbia graduate in mathematics in 1968—and was extremely moved by working on the president's advisory council. I was very upset watching Mark Rudd and his team try to destroy the university without having a positive plan to improve it.

My social life is closely related to my business life. Because so many of my friends are clients and because I get involved in their lives, the nonprofit organizations I get involved in are often through friends and clients, and it's also helpful to business. Outside of my family life, I probably spend 80 percent of my time on some combination of business and nonprofit work, with maybe 40 percent related to nonprofit work. If being involved with something like the **Museum of the City of New York Friends of the Theater Collection** is through a client, when I get very involved I spend time in the office, which I consider to be partly business as well.

This firm tends to support our clients and their efforts, and I will be the one who will often try to make a difference for a client in an outside effort, because in the long run it's good business and we do think about where we put our resources. Our purpose is to make a difference all the way around, and that is one of the ways we do it.

While a lot of my nonprofit work is connected to my professional life, not all is. My involvements go way beyond my working hours. I spend many nights of the week at functions that support nonprofit events—ones I'm involved in as well as others.

My children and I talk a lot about the fact that not everybody is as fortunate as we are and about what we can do from a personal and political viewpoint to make a difference. At the holiday season we always pick presents with the children to wrap for other children, and when there are events and opportunities—as at WNYC—for my children to join me, I always take them and talk to them about an organization and what it does, because I really want them to take their own roles in service as soon as they can. I try to involve them, and I like them to know as much about what I am doing as possible.

Nonprofit work provides a tremendous reward and sense of satisfaction. I try very hard to choose the organizations where one can make a difference. Over the years, I have learned that there are some organizations in which, because of their structure and politics, I would not be able to make a difference in terms of where they are and where they are going. I look very carefully at what an organization does, what its goals are, before I get involved. It's not that different from business, in that you like to achieve your goals.

But the excitement for me—with something like Columbia or

the Guild for the Blind—is seeing the people we're helping and how we are doing it and making New York or America a better place, actually improving people's lives. I think that when you are fortunate to have been successful and to have a lot, it's a privilege to be able to give it back.

CHAPTER SIX

CORPORATE SERVANT LEADERS

ON Sunday, November 1, 1987, Bill Phillips started fast-walking at 8:45 A.M. and eight hours and six minutes later finished the New York Marathon in the company of a man who did the course with one leg. Bill, chairman and CEO of the **Ogilvy Group,** parent of **Ogilvy & Mather,** one of the world's largest advertising agencies, and Stephen Wald, a former Wall Street investment manager, had formed a support group of two for Dick Traum, president of the **Achilles Track Club,** an organization that coaches and assists disabled persons to participate in recreational jogging.

As Bill put it, the faces of those along the way as they realized that Dick had only one leg, and their spontaneous outpouring of joyous support, made the marathon a continuing celebration of the human spirit—in the road and on the neighborhood sidewalks.

Bill is a servant leader—he is making a life as well as a living. His business and volunteer lives blend and complement each other. An avid outdoorsman and mountaineer, he serves as vice chairman of Outward Bound USA and as chairman of the board of the newly formed New York City Outward Bound Center, whose mission is to serve urban youth in urban Outward Bound experiences.

Combining his outdoor hobbies with work in a nonprofit organization that is engaged in providing outdoor education, Bill serves in a way he finds personally rewarding. When we think about corporate good citizenship—and without canonizing Bill—we often think of him as a role model.

Bill traces his working and volunteer lives back to his first job with **Procter & Gamble,** a company that takes a very big role in community service. As a young man, Bill was encouraged by the company's policy and its corporate culture to work on the **United Way Fund.** He later went to work for David Ogilvy, who was running a small advertising agency and was looking to hire people who were, as he put it, both "civilized"—people who were publicly inclined and who viewed business in a broadly responsible way—and motivated by "fire in their bellies." Ogilvy's billings were $17 million when Bill joined the agency in 1959. In 1987, they reached $4.5 billion, in a company now operating in forty-eight countries.

From the start, the Ogilvy Group has stated as one of its guiding purposes "for its companies to earn the respect of the community—wherever we are in the world." The Ogilvy Group spends a lot of time on representation of nonprofit clients, because they feel that it represents enlightened self-interest—that there is a high return for both the corporation, as a member of the community, and the groups and individuals involved.

In its public service work, Ogilvy & Mather contributes salary time at no cost—pro bono publico, that is, for the public good. With strong support from Ogilvy & Mather and other groups like Time Inc. and *Reader's Digest,* Outward Bound's enrollment has grown from 8,000 students to 18,000 in five years.

Ogilvy's advertising for the **City Volunteer Corps** (CVC), a youth service organization in New York City, is another success among many that have convinced the firm that good advertising makes an important contribution to voluntary recruitment. A campaign that used radio broadcasts and transit posters to secure awareness of the CVC has accounted for about 60 percent of applications. After advertising started, the number of high school graduate applicants increased from 12 to 30 percent of those applying.

In addition to his very significant involvement with Outward Bound, Bill has been a trustee of **Wells College** and he's been active in working for **Cornell** and **Northwestern** universities; in the 1970s, he was a leading member of the **Big Apple Advertising Campaign,** a communications program promoting the virtues of New York City, and he has been a director of the **Volunteer Con-**

sulting Group. His experience on a personal level has been that in service work you spread your net, meeting people you perhaps wouldn't meet in the narrower confines of your business life. You encounter unique people, sharing experiences with them that often result in lasting friendships, the kind that enrich your life.

Bill Phillips fears that corporate America is in danger of being turned over to the "number tumblers"—managers who are promoted only because they can cut short-term costs and improve the bottom line. Working in an isolated way, behind the scenes, they never have to have big ideas, lead, or fire someone face to face. As they cut the payroll by the hundreds or even the thousands, it's a little like dropping a bomb from 50,000 feet—they don't see the people they destroy.

A strong proponent of a public-spirited corporate ethic, Bill believes that management should have a deep concern and a strongly felt commitment not only to the welfare of the people in their companies but also to the good of the country at large. He notes that some CEOs stand up and say all the right things about public service and values but don't put those ideals into practice in their personal lives. It's Bill Phillips's conviction that a business leader who espouses an involved stance in terms of corporate citizenship must live according to those tenets, must be involved and be a servant leader himself or herself.

Bill is not unusual in his combination of personal and professional service or in his leadership by example in his job. John Whitehead, when senior partner and cochairman of Goldman, Sachs, spent a full *one-third* of his time on volunteer service activities. Within the American business community, many CEOs and other leading figures in management, through their personal activities as well as the policies they formulate, guide their companies—those mentioned in this chapter and many, many others—in formal and informal programs of community service.

THE RATIONALE FOR CORPORATE COMMUNITY SERVICE

Perhaps the most often cited reason for corporations becoming involved in community service is that "it's the right thing to do." While this phrase generally has a moral or ethical connotation, and while many corporations take a moral or ethical attitude toward their community outreach efforts, there are in addition many practical, almost tangible, benefits that come to involved corporations. The motivations and the returns—ethical and practical—have their roots in two groups: the community and the corporate employees.

The Community

Involved corporations feel a sense of responsibility to the community. They participate in community problem-solving in an effort to build healthy communities in which to live and in which to find workers and customers.

The contributions that corporations can make to private non-profit groups are many. The first thing that we think of is probably money, but beyond financial resources, corporations can and do donate products, services, and the energies of their employee and retiree populations. Through loaned management personnel, they can lend sophistication in long-range planning, in marketing, in advertising and public relations. With employee volunteer programs, they can infuse organizations with new talent and energy, as well as low-cost solutions to problems and answers to needs.

Attention to the community—whether we mean a city, a neighborhood, or a national cause—is in the long-term economic self-interest of a corporation. Service work forges new channels of communication with the community, through which the company can tie itself more closely to the network of community decision-makers: social activists, citizen lobbies, social service organizations, political bodies, etc.

Just as with the efforts of individual volunteers, the community in which the company does business is improved. And while the work of a corporation is built with single units of personal effort, the cumulative and focused efforts of a large company often make for a rather dramatic demonstration of giving.

Which leads kind of naturally into the aspect of good community relations. Again, as with individuals, we doubt that the reflected "good image" that can result from service work is enough to motivate companies to get involved. Nevertheless, one result of service work can be a gaining of public respect, an enhancement of the corporate image.

"The underlying philosophy of corporate philanthropy is that it is good business to be an enlightened corporate citizen. It doesn't make sense to talk about successful corporations in a society whose schools, hospitals, churches, symphonies, or libraries are deteriorating or closing." —*Clifton C. Garvin, Jr., former chairman of the board and chief executive officer of Exxon Corporation, in an essay in* Corporate Philanthropy: Philosophy, Management, Trends, Future, Background

The Employees

A corporation whose leadership exemplifies basic values and concern for the community and the nation is more likely to attract and hold personnel with good values and to exhibit concern for those people.

Corporations often get involved in the community because their employees want them to, and because the company learns that such participation works to the benefit of individual employees and, by extension, of the corporation. Involvement helps morale. Psychic income accrues when employees—whether members of the community, workers for local nonprofits, members of a volunteer committee, or initiators of a corporate matching grant—sense a spirit of cooperation from the company.

As does anyone involved in service work, an employee who takes part in a corporate volunteer program stands to improve his or her skills, knowledge, and contacts, particularly in leadership and participatory decision-making. When **Federal Express** surveyed members of its **Corporate Neighbor Team,** more than half reported that they had developed better skills in teamwork, the ability to motivate others, organization, and leadership. Working toward a common goal can help a company internally, by involving management and nonmanagement in shared projects, and getting diverse departments working together.

> Business does not flourish in a vacuum. Nor does professionalism. "Personal development includes not only fulfillment in the workplace," says Harry Witt, managing partner of the Touche Ross New York Metro region. "It means being active in the community. By volunteering time and talent, we lead a richer life, help build a more stable, prosperous community, and add value to the firm.
>
> "The process of becoming a partner in a Big Eight accounting firm requires not only the development of technical skills, but the personal broadening and business contacts that occur when one becomes active in charitable efforts. The fact is that business leaders are involved in charitable activities, and those committees and boards become a prime source for developing future business."

CORPORATE CASH GIVING

In 1986, corporations gave $4.5 billion, an amount that was 1.91 percent of corporate pretax net income and about 5.2 percent of total giving in this country. The great majority of companies contribute, and 80 percent of those with assets of more than $25 million make contributions.

Kenneth Dayton, who served for many years as chairman and CEO of the **Dayton Hudson Corporation,** had this to say about leading his company to establish their annual giving at 5 percent of their taxable income:

> I think it helped to formalize our program, to make us more professional in the way in which we gave. It made us more effective givers in the community. Secondly, it encouraged others to give more generously. And thirdly, it encouraged those who were already giving generously to speak about it. Eventually the Five Percent Club was formed in Minneapolis to recognize the fact that there were many corporations giving that much but no one knew about it.

Corporate giving has increased at a faster rate (257 percent) over the past ten years than has giving from all sources (179 percent); corporate giving grew three times faster than did pretax profits (72 percent).

But this growth may have peaked. The **Conference Board** has conducted a survey of 439 companies that represent 40 percent of corporate giving and reported that contributions for 1986 were down by 2.5 percent, the first decline in fifteen years. While the **American Association of Fund-Raising Counsel**'s annual report for the year found an increase of 2.5 percent, its figures reflected a rise in giving on the part of smaller companies included in its sample, and the overall rise does not dispel fears that some of the largest corporations may be backing off on cash contributions.

It's possible but by no means assured that as oil and steel companies reduce their contributions, donations will increase from food, pharmaceutical, and telecommunications concerns. And it may be that a myriad of pressures on American business could work against corporate cash philanthropy in the coming years: foreign competition, restructurings, mergers, buy-outs, declining profits, changing managements, changes in location. The pressures for earnings per share and the push for short-term profits may have a negative effect on corporate giving.

An important responsibility falls on the shoulders of corporate giving officers and CEOs—both of companies that have a history of community service and those that are yet to become involved— to keep the broad view in focus when planning participation in community affairs.

"I've come to believe that by working together as a team, the business community, private voluntary organizations, and, from time to time, government, can best develop and run effective social programs—programs to improve the quality of life not only of those who directly receive benefits and assistance but, by extension, the rest of us as well."—John M. Richman, chairman and chief executive officer, Kraft, Inc., in remarks delivered at the Second Harvest Conference, in Chicago, May 1987

According to the **United Way of America**'s 1987 environmental scan, *What Lies Ahead: Looking Toward the '90s,* corporate contributions of noncash gifts are projected to increase. In 1984, noncash gifts were 22 percent of corporate giving, as compared with 11 percent in 1983. And apparently noncash gifts are not being used to substitute for cash contributions but are an addition to traditional forms of support.

Corporate attention to basic human care needs—clothing, food, and shelter—is expected to grow significantly, and, according to a Conference Board study, 40 percent of companies plan increased support for human services not previously heavily funded (for example, services that deal with drug and alcohol abuse, domestic violence and child abuse, and programs for the elderly).

IN-KIND AND OTHER NONCASH GIVING

The Conference Board has reported that, in 1985, 20 percent of the contributions of more than 400 major corporations was in a form other than cash. Products made up more than half of the donations, the rest consisting of property and equipment.

Most such gifts are directed by donors to the "ill, needy, or infants." As a general rule, this stipulation qualifies donors for the maximum allowable tax deduction for in-kind gifts: cost, plus one-half of the difference between cost and the fair market value, not to exceed twice the cost value. (Because of the complexity of the tax laws, potential donors should consult an accountant or tax adviser.)

In addition to the tax benefits, in-kind contributions enable donors to reach a wide group of individuals and organizations with gifts that provide continuing assistance. Gifts of inventory also help to free warehouse space, reduce costs of holding inventory, and stimulate production. Product gifts can also be an effective long-range marketing tool. When IBM, Apple, and Xerox donate equipment for schools, they create familiarity with such office products on the part of students who can become potential buyers as adults. An effective way to put quality products to good use, in-kind giving gains visibility and goodwill for the donating company.

Gifts in Kind, Inc.

Created by the **United Way of America**, **Gifts in Kind, Inc.** (700 North Fairfax Street, Suite 610, Alexandria, Virginia 22314; telephone: [703] 836-2121) works to improve the efficiency and expand the capacity of nonprofits to deliver voluntary services. It provides assistance to enable companies to give in-kind resources—products, goods, services—to qualified voluntary organizations. Gifts in Kind uses the nationwide United Way system active in more than 1,300 communities to coordinate donations and provide administrative assistance to corporate donors.

Since the program began in the fall of 1983, more than $100 million in product donations have been distributed to more than 40,000 not-for-profit organizations. As gifts become available, Gifts in Kind helps donors distribute quality products in large quantities nationwide, regionally, or within states. *All services are free of charge to donors.* Gifts in Kind collects the tax documentation that verifies that the gifts will be used as intended by the applicable government regulations.

Many needy individuals nationwide have been helped by gifts from **Sara Lee** companies, including thousands of **Hanes** shirts, thousands of pairs of women's hosiery from **L'Eggs Products,** and tens of thousands of hats, scarves, and gloves from **Aris Isotoner. Electrolux Corporation** has donated more than 80,000 vacuum cleaners to thousands of nonprofit agencies. The **Greater Plymouth Association for Retarded Citizens,** of Pembroke, Massachusetts, is using some of these donated machines to teach mentally retarded people cleaning and maintenance skills geared to help them qualify for janitorial jobs.

The Albuquerque, New Mexico, court system's DWI (Driving While Impaired) Offender Screening program uses a donated **Apple** computer to screen first-time offenders charged with drunk driving for possible referral to treatment. As a result of the donation, the program, sponsored by the **National Council on Alcoholism,** has been able to reduce the number of repeat offenders and provide assistance to problem drinkers who need help. The program evaluates up to 300 offenders a month and tracks the progress of those with a drinking problem through completion of treatment.

The **United Way of the Texas Gulf Coast** recently received part of a nationwide donation of more than a million toothbrushes and other dental products from the **Gillette Company** coordinated through Gifts in Kind. One of the agencies that received the products, the Fort Bend office of **Early Childhood Development,** used them to sponsor a program targeted to children of low-income families, who were given instructions on good dental care.

The **Greenwich, Connecticut, Boys Club Association** is using a donated **Digital Equipment Corporation** letter-quality computer printer to help "turn kids on" to reading and writing. A newsletter for kids and by kids is being produced in an after-school program for eight- to twelve-year-old youths with volunteer help from local high school students.

Second Harvest

Incorporated in 1979 as an outgrowth of a local food solicitation and distribution agency in Phoenix, Arizona, **Second Harvest** (343 South Dearborn, Suite 410, Chicago, Illinois 60604; telephone: [312] 341-1303) was funded as a demonstration project of the federal government until 1984. Since then, it has been funded by the food industry, food banks, foundations, and corporations, and today receives no government funding.

Second Harvest's goal is to feed the hungry by soliciting surplus food and grocery products from America's food industry and distributing these donations to a nationwide network of certified food banks. The food banks in turn distribute the food to community charities, day care and senior centers, and church groups with meal programs for the needy.

In 1986, food donations from 265 national companies were distributed to a network of 82 member and 123 affiliate nonprofit food banks throughout the United States. Approximately 352 million pounds of food, valued at nearly $500 million, were channeled through the network to 38,000 charitable feeding programs.

And it's not just the food companies that support Second Harvest. Among other financial support, in 1986 the organization obtained a $630,000 grant commitment from the **Prudential Foundation.** The **Dallas Morning News** and the **Kroger Company** joined forces to combat hunger in north Texas through Second Harvest member food banks. The *News* inserted brown paper bags in its Sunday edition for readers to fill with food for distribution to three food banks in the region. Customers were asked to fill the bags with such items as tuna, soup, applesauce, mixed vegetables, peanut butter, and macaroni and cheese, and to bring the bags to a local Kroger store or the main lobby of the *News* building. Nearly 40,000 pounds of food were donated by Dallas residents.

Second Harvest and the **Greater Chicago Food Depository** were the beneficiaries of proceeds from the **Run to End Hunger,** sponsored in Chicago by the **World Runners International Foundation.** This ten-kilometer run, the first event of its kind ever sponsored by the group, attracted more than 800 participants. Runners were encouraged to enlist individual sponsors and bring canned goods to the site. **Leo Burnett U.S.A. Advertising** and **Bell & Howell Corporation** were the event's corporate sponsors.

On Sunday, June 22, 1986, about 25,000 people joined hands to demonstrate concern for needy citizens and to raise money to support the work of the **Houston Food Bank.** Hands Across Houston was a joint project of **KTRC-Channel 13, KRBE-FM Radio,** the **Houston Police Department,** *The Houston Chronicle,* and the **Houston Food Bank,** in cooperation with **Ticketron** and **Joske's** of Texas. Support from Houston's corporate community played a pivotal role, with fifty-nine companies each donating at least $1,300.

Independent Sector has published a resource for corporations who want to enter the world of in-kind giving or to expand their involvement in it and for nonprofits who want to take advantage of it. In *Resource Raising: The Role of Non-Cash Assistance in Corporate Philanthropy,* authors Alex Plinio and Joanne Scanlan discuss the new roles for corporate giving officers in this growing area. Covered are how grantees should think about and solicit noncash assistance; brokerage services; and the legal and tax aspects of noncash assistance.

One appendix in the book discusses forty-seven examples of noncash corporate giving. Another provides a model for a one-day workshop for discovering what types of noncash gifts can be used by a nonprofit and are available from corporations, and for devising strategies to gain access to products, people, and services. Two others describe brokers and distributors, and legal, tax, and accounting resources. *Resource Raising* is available for $10 from Independent Sector (see chapter 3 for address).

EMPLOYEE VOLUNTEER PROGRAMS

Businesses of all kinds—insurance companies, manufacturers, utilities, banks, energy companies, retail stores, discount outlets, transportation systems, hotel chains—have instituted programs that tap a tremendous source of energy: *people*—their commitment and ideas, their expertise and skills, their warmth and willingness to help. Many annual reports are centered around what company employees are doing in the world of service. Corporations are proud of this involvement!

The **United Way** reports that the number of firms with organized programs encouraging employee involvement in community service has increased 60 percent since 1979.

In 1984, 200 U.S. companies reported that 300,000 employees volunteered 50 million hours in a collective effort worth $400 million, according to **VOLUNTEER—The National Center,** which exists for the sole purpose of promoting and supporting more effective volunteering. During the past ten years, VOLUNTEER has played a major leadership role in helping companies to create and sustain high-quality employee volunteer programs.

VOLUNTEER's 1985 "Workplace in the Community" survey took a look at employee volunteering nationwide. Two hundred ninety-four companies responded, from a universe made up of the Fortune 1000 and Forbes 500 lists, 600 companies that are members of local corporate volunteer councils, and 300 companies that had responded to previous surveys. This survey, plus VOLUNTEER's work with involved companies, resulted in *A New Competitive Edge: Volunteers from the Workplace,* a sourcebook that describes in detail the corporate programs and the service work of employees in twenty-five companies and labor unions.

All types of companies have employee volunteer programs: Fortune 500 and small firms, those that meet the public and manufacturers that never do, urban and rural companies, as well as labor unions. They operate an astounding variety of programs, which we'll attempt to broadly categorize and describe below. Long-standing programs are often made up of activities from several of these categories.

We ask you again to bear in mind that, as in chapter 3, "A Service

Sampler," we're presenting these programs and companies to provide a sampling of what some companies do. In no way is this an evaluative assessment or an attempt at a definitive statement on corporate involvement programs.

Clearinghouses

Ninety-five percent of the corporations in **VOLUNTEER**'s survey encourage employees to serve on nonprofit boards; 61 percent provide information to employees about volunteer opportunities; 46 percent refer employees to agencies that place volunteers; and 33 percent sponsor an actual clearinghouse operation to match employees with volunteer jobs.

In New York City, **Metropolitan Life's Employee Volunteer Program** places volunteers—employees and retirees—with more than 300 community agencies in ongoing and short-term projects that serve the disabled, the disadvantaged, the elderly, the homeless, and the poor, as well as in programs that support cultural institutions and education. The program's administrator, Bruce Lentini, told us how it works:

> Our program will have been in place for ten years as of the spring of 1988, and more than 1,800 people have come through it. We work with them in a number of ways. Some people are interested in doing things on a regular basis, once a week for a period of six months to a year. Some are interested in doing things once or twice a year, something like the **March of Dimes Walk,** which is once a year, or **Channel 13** [PBS] telethons, which are three or four times a year, or something that's sporadic, based on their own schedule.
>
> We try to match and basically do a pairing process. I do a pre-screening with the employee. They come in and say, I want to do something, and they list about twelve different things. And I ask them, how much free time do you really have? We sit down and get an idea of what they really want to do, what their interests are, what their backgrounds are, do they want to do things that they are directly doing on the job, redirecting it to the nonprofit, or do they want to do something very, very different?
>
> At that point, we look to maybe three or four types of organizations, and suggest two or three of those that may be of interest to

them. We will make the referral and set up interviews, but we don't make the decision. That is made by the employee and the organization itself. They're the ones who are going to make it work, who are going to see if this pairing, this matching, is actually going to succeed.

Group and Partnership Projects

Many corporations have found great success in mobilizing teams or troops of employees on behalf of large projects—ongoing or one-time—and establishing partnerships with nonprofit groups and other corporations. These activities have taken the following forms, among countless others: blood drives; cooperation with local **United Way** projects; walkathons; telethons, in which the company donates phones or people or both; telephone reassurance projects (once-a-day calls to elderly or mentally ill people); cooperation with **Junior Achievement** and other youth groups; food collections and distributions, as well as other types of collections (of toiletries, baby food, old trophies that can be refurbished and reawarded); on-site or school-based tutoring; career counseling; writing a pamphlet for a community agency; neighborhood organizing for an environmental issue; participating in a neighborhood cleanup; mentoring programs, such as **Career Beginnings,** in which a corporate mentor guides an inner-city high school junior through his or her senior year, a summer corporate internship, and toward employment or a college decision.

Members of **Tenneco's Volunteers in Assistance** (VIA) program participate in a variety of special one-time projects during the year. Among the most visible are the many runs and walks benefiting such groups as the **March of Dimes, Leukemia Society,** and **Muscular Dystrophy.** VIA also assists numerous telethons and membership drives for the local public broadcasting station, **Easter Seals,** and the **United Negro College Fund.**

Volunteers, both men and women, in a program called Tenneco Creations turn out about 500 items each year for donation to infants and the elderly, ranging from quilts and lap robes presented to nursing home residents to tiny kimonos, blankets, dresses, shirts, caps, and sweaters for premature babies at a local hospital. Each item bears a tag reading, "Made Especially for You by Tenneco Volunteers."

Ripley House, a multiservice center for the Hispanic community in Houston, has benefited from its partnership with Tenneco since 1980. More than 100 Tenneco volunteers serve in a variety of capacities, including sponsoring a neighborhood youth boxing program, assisting individuals in preparation for becoming naturalized U.S. citizens, teaching classes in personal development, and career counseling. Tenneco volunteers plan, coordinate, and host the center's Christmas party, at which needy families receive food baskets, gift certificates, toys, clothing, refreshments, and entertainment.

About seventy **General Mills** employees have "adopted" Hamilton Manor, a senior-citizen high-rise in Minneapolis. They sponsor bingo parties, social events, and one-to-one friendships with residents. Each year forty to fifty employees of **Johnson & Johnson Baby Products Company,** at their plant in Las Piedras, Puerto Rico, donate their time to decorate dolls collected by the **Salvation Army.** The dolls are distributed at Christmas to children who might not otherwise receive a gift.

The Special Olympics Family Day is an annual **Honeywell**-sponsored athletic event in conjunction with **Minnesota Special Olympics.** The day-long event gives the mentally handicapped an opportunity to participate in athletic events with support from family and friends. Honeywell volunteers, as friends for a day, are paired with Olympians. According to one volunteer, the requirements weren't difficult to meet: "All you had to do was hug a lot, and that was something I could do easily."

In **Time Inc./Odyssey,** an educational partnership project with **Time Inc.** and the Washington, D.C., public schools, two students from each high school read about and discuss heroes in literature and then research and write about present-day heroes in the Washington community, finally producing a feature magazine, *Looking for Heroes.* Professionals from *Time* magazine and Time-Life Books work with the students and teachers throughout the year, providing seminars, tours, and internships.

Loaned Personnel and Pro Bono Assistance Programs

Seventy-six percent of the companies in **VOLUNTEER**'s survey lend personnel to nonprofits and government agencies. Such loans include upper-level executives and mid-level personnel who are "management and technically skilled" employees, as well as released time for any level of employee to participate in ongoing company projects. Sixty percent offer released time to assist volunteering during regular work hours, usually on company premises and for company-approved projects.

The **Volunteer Consulting Group,** founded in 1969 by the Harvard Business School Club of New York, assists other nonprofit organizations via programs focused on strengthening the governing ability of nonprofit boards. VCG's Board Recruitment Program addresses the need of nonprofit boards for help in finding knowledgeable corporate men and women who wish to serve as directors. The Board Consulting Program addresses the full spectrum of issues and concerns regarding board development, management, reorganization, recruitment, and board/staff relations.

VCG's Nonprofit Leadership Education Program offers seminars to which trustees and senior staff are invited to learn about a broad range of governance and management issues from practitioners in the field. Another program focuses on corporate leadership—case-based education for inclusion in management training programs extant within the corporate community.

IBM and **Xerox** have been leaders in lending personnel. Later we describe IBM's program, called Social Service Leaves, and following this chapter Xerox's former CEO Peter McColough describes how he started Xerox's program of one-year leaves for employees at all levels.

In 1981, **Aetna Life & Casualty** instituted the nation's first volunteer lawyers' project for the elderly staffed by corporate legal department employees. Cited by the American Bar Association as a model for other corporate law departments, the program offers free legal assistance to low-income, elderly people who live in the Greater Hartford area.

Ketchum Communications offered a substantial portion of its services on a pro bono basis when **Second Harvest** launched a multifaceted awareness program in 1986.

Retiree Programs

Sixty-nine percent of companies encourage retirees to be volunteers, through how-to seminars, involving them in the planning and administration of company volunteer activities or programs, and creating separate volunteer activities for retirees.

The PLUS in the name **Retirement PLUS** stands for People Lending Unselfish Support. It is an idea conceived at **General Mills** in early 1984 to help keep retirees in touch, to recognize their knowledge and expertise, and to encourage the use of their talents through voluntary service to other retirees and their communities. Retiree drivers provide transportation for other retirees to the doctor's office or grocery store; retirees handle an annual sale of items made by the handicapped; they join active employees in a team effort to recondition the houses of senior citizens who are less fortunate; they become part of the local **United Way** campaign, doing telephone follow-up work to fellow retirees and others in the community, and assisting with the auditing of the funds received.

The **Honeywell Retiree Volunteer Project** (HRVP) provides more than $1 million in assistance each year to community agencies through retired employees. HRVP maintains a skills data base to match the interests of retired volunteers with community needs. Since its inception in 1979, HRVP has placed approximately 1,000 Honeywell retirees with more than 230 nonprofit organizations.

Donated Honeywell thermostats have been installed at several nonprofit agencies by HRVP teams in a special weatherization project guided by the **Urban Coalition of Minneapolis**. When a local correctional institution requested assistance in setting up light assembly-type work on a subcontract basis, HRVP provided production line consultants. Several nonprofit agencies have used HRVP retirees with camera skills for slide show, brochure, and videotape work.

Matching Funds and Monetary Grants

Fifty-one percent of companies have such programs, according to **VOLUNTEER**'s survey. In "matching funds" programs, the company doubles or triples dollar contributions by the employee. Sometimes such grants are part of volunteer recognition in which honored employee volunteers receive a small memento and their agencies or organizations receive a cash award.

Through the Employee Matching Gift Program, **Kraft, Inc.**, will match any employee contribution from $25 to $5,000 per year to a qualified charity, including health agencies, social welfare and community service organizations, and art and cultural groups. If it's a qualified educational institution, the company will match any contribution up to $500 on a two-for-one basis. During 1986, the company donated more than $361,000 by matching employee gifts.

The **Honeywell Foundation** provides matching grants for employee gifts to public and private colleges and universities, and to public radio and television. Employee gifts are matched dollar for dollar, up to $2,000 per employee. Matching gifts totaled $625,000 in 1986.

Special Projects and Approaches

The categories above don't begin to capture the many innovative and remarkable charitable and philanthropic undertakings by corporations. Some examples:

Industrywide Projects. The **National Association of Accountants** conducted a nationwide economic consulting project to aid minority businessmen. One thousand accountants contributed 30,000 hours over a three-year period.

Responses to Emergencies. **Harris-Teeter Super Markets,** of Charlotte, North Carolina, hauled and stored hay for southeastern farmers devastated by the severe drought in the summer of 1986. The company cooperated with the **National Guard**, **FCX Railroad,** hotel chains, state highway departments, and many others to provide an estimated 2 million bales of hay from forty-six states and Canada. The company, which stayed involved until the crisis ended in October, provided its own convoy of trucks, drivers, employees, and vendors, as well as warehouses for hay storage, round-the-clock security, and insurance to protect and cover any losses.

Special Achievement Grants. The **Clairol Take Charge Awards** honor women who have overcome obstacles and taken charge of their lives after the age of thirty, with an end result of making significant contributions to their work or their community. The awards are part of the company's public service program supporting the efforts of women. In 1988, the company named twenty-five winners, each receiving $1,000.

Fifty teens from across the United States recently won **Sea Breeze Awards,** a public service program of Sea Breeze, a division of Clairol. The award winners are young people who campaign against drug and alcohol abuse, who care about the hungry and homeless, who take risks to save a life, who are companions to the elderly, who help the sick and the handicapped. The award carries with it a $500 grant.

Cooperative Efforts with Other Corporations. The **Corporate Angel Network** (CAN), based in White Plains, New York, arranges free transport of cancer patients to and from U.S. treatment centers, using available seats on corporate aircraft being flown on business trips. Four hundred corporations are involved. Founded in 1981, by the end of 1987 CAN had logged its fifteen hundredth flight.

COMPANIES THAT SERVE

We've collected not mini-profiles, but really just snapshots of some of the activities of a half-dozen involved corporations. Our aim— far from presenting the total picture of the service work of these companies—is to provide examples of elements of some interesting corporate programs. And do remember that these are companies with a history of involvement and with sizable ongoing programs. They started small, and so can your firm.

IBM

IBM is in the business of providing information processing systems, equipment, and services. The company develops, manufactures, markets, and services computer systems, as well as related programming and products. IBM is also a leader in support for social services, education, and the arts.

Community Service Assignment Program.   This program enables an employee to take a paid leave of absence to work for a nonprofit, tax-exempt community service organization. Groups benefiting from this program range in size and scope from the **American Red Cross** to a local youth center. Since the program began in 1971, more than 900 employees have been granted leaves, usually for one year and with full pay from IBM.

John Scudder took a one-year leave to work at the **Student Assistance Program** in Crystal Lake, Illinois, an assessment and counseling referral program for students with alcohol or drug problems. His work there, he says, "can be pretty rough, and very stressful, but it's well worth the effort." In the program, which focuses on elementary and high school students, John talks at length with both children and parents, then refers them to the appropriate specialists. His work is as meaningful to him as it is to the young people he helps. "Nothing has ever been this important to me," he explains. "I feel like I'm doing something that can really make a difference to these kids."

Fund for Community Service.   Financial support is available from IBM for specific purchases and activities of nonprofit groups with whom employees, retirees, and their spouses are actively involved. Since 1972, grants totaling more than $32 million have funded more than 21,000 projects, as disparate as purchasing cooking utensils for a soup kitchen and supplying ambulance electrocardiogram equipment.

Programmer Rob Schwab is enthusiastic about his game, wheelchair tennis. "It's really exciting to play—and even to watch," he says, explaining that the only difference in rules is a provision allowing the wheelchair player two bounces of the ball instead of one. Because there was no group organizing wheelchair tennis tournaments on the East Coast, Schwab formed the **Eastern Wheelchair Tennis Association,** and in 1985 the association hosted the Eastern National Championship in New York City with more than sixty top wheelchair tennis players competing. To help with the cost of getting players to and from the tournament site, IBM contributed $5,000 through a Fund for Community Service grant.

Job Training Programs. Since IBM began its affiliation with job training centers in 1968, more than 25,000 people have graduated from seventy-one major centers throughout the United States. And more than 80 percent of the graduates have found jobs with a variety of firms, mostly in text processing and data entry. Located in areas of high unemployment, the centers offer training to students of all ages who cannot afford to attend commercially available programs. IBM also helps support thirty-one smaller job training centers that teach basic typing skills.

> "We welcome the opportunity to contribute where we can. While no corporation has the resources to solve society's major problems, we strive to do our share as a company and to encourage and support employees in their activities. Because these investments benefit IBM and its people by benefiting the larger community in which we all live and work, our participation makes good business sense. We believe it is also the right thing to do."—*John F. Akers, president and chief executive officer, IBM*

Scientific Centers and Partnerships. IBM teams up with universities, research groups, and government agencies to address problems by developing new computer applications. In the Philippines, for example, work has been undertaken to develop disease-resistant strains of rice. Meanwhile, researchers at IBM's Scientific Center in Paris are working with the **French National Institute for Deaf Children** to use personal computers to help teach deaf children to speak and "hear" through electronic enhancement of sound. Other research programs range from energy conservation in the United States, to hurricane forecasting in the Caribbean, to satellite image processing for agricultural and environmental purposes in Latin America, Spain, and Africa.

Faculty Loan.   Since 1971, IBM has loaned more than 800 employees to colleges, universities, and high schools with high enrollments of or programs geared to minority, disadvantaged, or handicapped students. Employees are encouraged to participate in this program, and the company pays their regular salaries during the loan period. With assignments usually covering a full academic year, participants have aided faculties at more than 197 schools, teaching business administration, math, computer science, engineering, and other courses. They have also worked in planning and administration, counseling, financial consulting, and outreach programs.

Mellon Bank

The twelfth-largest bank holding company in the United States, **Mellon Bank** provides a comprehensive range of financial services to domestic consumer and commercial markets and to selected international markets. The bank has committed a full range of resources in its support of nonprofit organizations. In 1986, Mellon valued at $14,949,371 its cash grants, underwriting of programs and benefits, indirect and in-kind support (such as tuition reimbursement and the value of donated furnishings), and associate support (**United Way,** gift matching, collections, walkathons, etc.).

One very interesting project that Mellon has developed is *Discover Total Resources: A Guide for Nonprofits,* described as "a descriptive checklist to be used as a guide, or self-audit, by boards, staff, and volunteers to assess the degree to which they are tapping a full range of community resources: money, people, goods and services." (See "For Further Reading.")

The company practices what it preaches, extending its reach into community service in a great variety of ways that are not limited to cash contributions. Here are a few of them:

· Twenty-six inner-city Philadelphia high school students put their business skills to work at Mellon in the summer of 1986 through

Phila-a-Job, one of the nation's most successful minority summer employment programs, chaired by a Mellon vice chairman.

· Philadelphia's Martin Luther King High School developed a quality business curriculum with the help of a **Business Education Advisory Committee,** staffed in part by three Mellon associates.

· In central Pennsylvania, Mellon employees record monthly checking account statements on cassette tape for blind customers. In Pittsburgh, Mellon is the only bank that provides monthly Braille statements, a service requested by more than 100 southwestern Pennsylvania customers.

· To help women improve financial skills and make better financial decisions, Mellon cosponsored a seminar with the **United Jewish Federation of Greater Pittsburgh.** Financial advisers from Mellon participated.

· Mellon bankers frequently are asked to speak before audiences varying from schoolchildren to senior citizens. In central Pennsylvania, an organized speakers bureau of more than 100 Mellon professionals gave 150 speeches, workshops, and panel discussions during 1986 on topics such as wills, electronic banking, personal money management, and personal credit.

· The bank participates as a lender in the **Philadelphia Mortgage Plan,** a citywide program to help low- to moderate-income residents become homeowners.

· For World Food Day, Mellon linked Philadelphia's **Food and Agriculture Task Force** with Delaware Valley food industry executives to find local solutions to hunger. Mellon is a corporate leader in the implementation of Philadelphia's progressive municipal food policy, through which the city has launched a pilot nutrition program to reduce infant mortality in the inner city. Mellon created a new land trust to dedicate vacant lots for urban gardening.

· Mellon donates staff and equipment to count and verify coin and currency contributions during special fund-raising drives. In 1986, such services were donated to **KDKA-TV** for its annual December Children's Hospital drive, the **Pittsburgh Make-A-Wish Foundation,** and the **Salvation Army.**

Levi Strauss & Co.

Levi Strauss & Co. is the world's largest producer of branded apparel, marketing a broad range of clothing, most of it leisure-oriented, to customers throughout the world. Levi Strauss contributes to the needs of communities worldwide where its manufacturing plants are located, channeling its support through two major vehicles: Community Involvement Teams (CITs) and Special Emphasis Grants.

Community Involvement Teams.   CITs, made up of employee volunteers within their workplace, undertake a wide variety of fund-raising and community service projects to benefit nonprofit organizations.

In the San Antonio, Texas, jail system, 80 percent of the female prisoners are unmarried and have young dependents whom they must be able to support upon their release. The local Levi Strauss CIT adopted an agency called **Bexar County Detention Ministries** and secured a $13,000 grant to help initiate Project MATCH (Mothers and Their Children) in the local detention facility. The project includes an on-site visitation program, and emphasis is placed on parental training and using available community services—like health care, child care, transportation, counseling, and tutoring—to support families in creating productive lives after the mother's release.

When the unemployment rate in Price, Utah, reached 22 percent in August 1983, the community created a food bank. During a period of short workweeks and layoffs at their factory, CIT members cleaned and painted donated warehouse space and stocked the shelves with donated food. They also assisted with shopping and bookkeeping, fund-raising and food drives, volunteering a total of 300 hours to the project. Their efforts resulted in a $10,000 foundation grant to purchase refrigeration equipment and pay staff salaries. The food bank has since expanded to conduct classes in cooking and nutrition, and serves as a referral agency to other community social services.

Special Emphasis Grants.   The program focuses on five key areas: aging, community development, families, and Hispanic and women's issues.

The **Southside Growers Association** works to stimulate the local agricultural economy in the historically depressed area of Farmville, Virginia. Through cooperative marketing and distribution of vegetable crops produced by individual growers, the program aids a seven-county rural area with a population of 83,500. In 1984, the Levi Strauss Foundation made a two-year grant of $40,000 to support this effort to increase the family incomes of small-scale vegetable farmers.

The **Women's Shelter of Corpus Christi, Texas,** has provided temporary shelter to more than 1,400 women and 4,000 children since it opened in 1977. In addition to emergency refuge, the shelter provides a twenty-four-hour hotline, referrals, group therapy, advocacy, and other services for battered women. In 1984, the foundation awarded a two-year, $60,500 grant toward start-up support for the shelter's Project Phoenix, a group counseling program for male batterers.

In South El Paso, Texas, the **Centro del Obrero Fronterizo** is a self-help program for low-income women. In 1983, the foundation made a $27,000 grant to support La Mujera Obrera (The Working Woman), a long-term business development project to create a membership-supported workers' services center and benefits package for women working without adequate health insurance or other benefits. In 1984, the foundation provided an additional $28,000 to develop a pilot program to provide primary health service for fifty women, improve utilization of existing health services, and develop a coordinated strategy with local health providers, the business community, and local foundations.

Shell Oil Company

Shell Oil Company is an oil, gas, and chemical company with a primary focus on U.S. operations. In 1975, Shell conducted an employee survey that confirmed many employees would be glad to pitch in and help their community if they only knew what was needed of them. So, with the support of top management, Shell Employees and Retirees Volunteerism Effort (SERVE) was formed with the purpose of matching employees, retirees, and their families with volunteer opportunities that would best utilize their time, talents, and energy.

The SERVE Community Fund Grant Program is an extension of the SERVE Program. It provides special project funding to

Houston-area volunteer organizations in which Shell employees and retirees are active volunteers. Grants range from $100 to a maximum of $1,000 and have helped meet many special needs, such as emergency apparatus for volunteer fire departments and playground equipment for disadvantaged children. Through this grant program, volunteers have directed more than $325,000 to community betterment agencies.

SERVE volunteers are primarily recruited through a bimonthly flier, *SERVE Classifieds,* which advertises volunteer positions in the community. Below are some sample opportunities, as listed in the issue of June 1987.

A car, a sack, and a smile! These are all that you need to become a volunteer with a new program at **Houston Metropolitan Ministries** (HMM) called Food for Seniors. Volunteers will meet one Saturday a month at HMM, located in the Montrose area, to sack donated groceries for each senior citizen in the program and then volunteers will deliver the groceries to 5–10 homes in a specific area. Friends and family members are welcome to participate together.

Share your technical skills. Volunteers experienced in DBase III Plus or writing procedures/guidelines are in demand at the **Houston Society for the Prevention of Cruelty to Animals** (HSPCA). Computer volunteers will be composing how-to's on things such as kennel and adoption procedures. Both evening and weekend shifts are available at the HSPCA offices located in the Heights.

Be part of the solution. As a volunteer with the Houston Police Department you can assist the Theft Division in its work by inputting information on the computer or by working in the newly formed Call-Back Program for auto theft victims. Both opportunities take place at HPD headquarters near downtown and are available evenings and weekends. Training is provided.

Help develop a child's potential. Volunteers are needed to serve as scout leaders for small groups of handicapped youngsters and adults wanting to participate in the scouting experience. Troops are available throughout the city and troop assistants as well as leaders are needed. Your time commitment can be as little as an hour every two weeks. All the programs are geared to the special needs of the children and training is provided.

The Pillsbury Company

The Pillsbury Company is a diversified international food and restaurant company. In fiscal 1987, Pillsbury, to use their word, "invested" $7.5 million in nonprofit organizations and donated 5.4 million pounds of product seconds, worth $5.4 million, to food banks across the nation. The company focuses their grant-making on two areas: youth, aiming their programs at positive development for low-income young people who have the highest risk for unemployment or underemployment; and hunger, which they fight by supporting emergency programs that provide food assistance but also seek to address the underlying causes of chronic hunger and malnutrition.

Career Beginnings, mentioned earlier, has a chapter (one of twenty-five across the country) at the **University of Minnesota's Center for Youth Development and Research.** With support from Pillsbury, it provides more than 200 disadvantaged high school seniors with career and academic counseling, summer work experience, and business mentors. An eighteen-year-old woman gave this testimonial: "Self-control and self-expression, that's what Career Beginnings has taught me. Before, when I had a problem, or when I got tense, I'd yell. I'd lose control. Now, I stay cool."

In 1986, Pillsbury made its first national youth grant, to the **Quest National Center** of Columbus, Ohio, to develop a career-oriented curriculum and mentor program for about 9,000 ninth and tenth graders nationwide. Pillsbury was also the lead funder for "I'll Take Charge," a **Minnesota 4-H** program to help rural young people develop career goals.

The Urban Coalition's **Smart Start** in Minneapolis received Pillsbury support to improve the educational performance of minority children who fall behind in school. The company funded **Project Destiny,** a Minneapolis youth mentor program; **Fresh Force,** the Minneapolis youth voluntarism project; and the **Center School** ("NA-WAY-EE"), an American Indian alternative school in south Minneapolis.

On June 24, 1987, some 2,000 people were expected for a catered banquet at the World Congress Center in downtown Atlanta,

Georgia. Only 1,200 showed. Long serving tables of fresh, sparkling salads and ethnic entrees were left untouched. But the food, which once would have been destined for dumpsters or animal feedlots, was whisked within hours to the sites of meal programs for the hungry throughout the city, in a new effort called **Atlanta's Table.** This public-private partnership underwritten by Pillsbury's **S&A Restaurant Corporation** salvages extraordinary amounts of surplus prepared food from dairies, hotels, institutions, and restaurants. Organizers hoped to save some 100,000 pounds of prepared food during 1987.

Pillsbury underwrote four national hunger efforts in 1987:

- Research into malnutrition among children by the **Physician Task Force on Hunger in America**;
- The **National Ad Council**'s Food Stamp Awareness Program;
- The **Food Research and Action Center**'s promotion of school breakfast programs;
- A marketing program to enable **Second Harvest,** the nationwide surplus food clearinghouse, to solicit throughout the food industry for contributions of product and services.

Pillsbury is also active in supporting education. **Cities in Schools, Inc.,** supported by a major grant from **Burger King Corporation,** is a Washington, D.C.–based nonprofit clearinghouse for agencies serving thousands of disadvantaged young people each year with counseling, tutoring, and preemployment skills training. In three years, Burger King's Crew Educational Assistance Program had paid more than $500,000 in college and vocational-technical expenses for more than 3,100 eligible crew members.

In 1987, the company sponsored 127 scholarships in 67 communities where Pillsbury does business and matched 683 employee and director contributions to colleges and universities, as well as providing scholarships to 134 children of employees.

Primerica Corporation

Primerica Corporation, formerly American Can Company, is engaged in financial services and specialty retailing, having undertaken since 1982 a dramatic shift away from manufacturing and into the service sector of the economy.

William S. Woodside, president of Primerica Foundation, sets the tone for the organization's work:

> Businesses can, because of their own urgent challenges, back away from social and public responsibilities. What is called for, however, is not withdrawal, but action and leadership. The very leadership, imagination, energy and commitment which American business is demonstrating to reshape itself for the nineties and beyond must also be applied in collaborative efforts with other sectors to help revitalize our society.

The foundation conducts its activities in four principal areas: national themes; general grants; local contributions; and employee-related programs. In 1986, the foundation contributed $3.7 million to carry out its programs of awarding grants for charitable purposes. In its major activities, Primerica seeks selectivity, aiming to make significant grants, rather than multiple minor ones. It seeks innovation in the creative, well-managed use of funds; involvement beyond the specific contribution; and specificity in considering results and timing.

National Themes.   At the heart of the Primerica Foundation are its National Themes programs, in three focus areas: economic transition, hunger and nutrition, and public education.

Among the foundation's economic transition projects launched in 1986 was a three-year grant of $100,000 to the **Center for Business and Government of Harvard University** to explore and analyze through four case studies methods of effecting economic recovery in small and midsize communities.

The foundation awarded a grant of $54,339 to the **Corporation for Enterprise Development** in Washington, D.C., to identify, examine, and assess community-based initiatives that benefit low-income women. A two-year grant of $70,000 was awarded to the **Rural Coalition** to examine the successes and failures of rural economic development efforts and to propose effective public policies for rural development.

The **College of New Rochelle School of New Resources** received a grant of $60,000 to begin dissemination to other academic institutions of **Project ACCESS (Adult Career Counseling: Education and Support Services),** a career-counseling model developed expressly for women returning to college for a liberal arts education. The **Structured Employment/Economic Development Corporation** (SEEDCO) was awarded a grant of $43,125 to provide support to the community redevelopment plan proposed by Texas Wesleyan University in the Polytechnic area of Fort Worth—one of several innovative model projects SEEDCO is supporting to promote the use of public and quasi-public institutions as anchors for community revitalization programs.

In 1986, public awareness and public policy analysis remained as the cornerstones of Primerica's work in the area of hunger and nutrition. Among other grants in 1986, one of $50,000 went to the **Harvard University School of Public Health** to underwrite the third report by the **Physician Task Force on Hunger in America,** which helps document the benefits and progress of the federal food stamp program. A grant of similar size went to the **Food Research and Action Council** to develop and sponsor an advocacy training program for emergency food providers and antihunger advocates in three pilot cities.

Primerica is supporting several initiatives to address and alleviate the dropout problem among public school students. They will also seek to learn more about those youngsters who stay in school. The foundation made a grant of $54,263 to **Children's Express** to enable student journalists aged eight to fourteen to investigate and report on the issues, problems, and people that influence school dropouts.

Another effort addresses the same issue by seeking to improve the quality of education of at-risk children who stay in school. The foundation has awarded a grant of $60,000 to the **Bank Street College of Education,** which will report on how community-based organizations in New York City work with the public schools to confront the problems of youth at risk of dropping out.

General Grants. The Big Apple Circus, the professional performing company of the nonprofit **New York School for Circus Arts,** received a $10,000 grant to provide underprivileged and handicapped children an opportunity to see the circus free of charge. In 1986, the foundation provided sole sponsorship of a national tour of the exhibition "Lost and Found Traditions: Native American Art 1965–1985," organized through the **American Federation of Arts.** Primerica has been involved with this project for five years, supplying approximately $170,000 in funding for acquisition of more than 380 objects of traditional, but contemporary, Indian art.

Local Contributions Program.   Started as a pilot program in 1984, the Local Contributions Program placed "investment decisions" for supporting community agencies directly in the hands of a committee of local employees representing various levels of management. In 1986, more than 150 Primerica employees were involved in the decision-making grant process as members of thirty-four Local Contributions Committees.

Michigan Bulb's committee, in Grand Rapids, funds three major programs: **Capital Lunch,** an all-volunteer community effort to provide more than 300 hot meals daily for those in need; **Respite Care,** which offers weekend care for handicapped children, providing the youngsters with some special adventures and enabling parents to take a brief break from the normal care routine; and **Ears for the Deaf,** which trains dogs to assist people with severe hearing impairments.

PennCorp Financial, in Santa Monica, California, helped establish counseling and placement services at two agencies that help homeless people. In addition, this committee works with youth gangs and supports child care and substance abuse programs, by funding such organizations as **Connections for Children,** the **United Stoner Youth Foundation,** and **Turning Point.**

Employee-Related Programs.   In 1986, Primerica awarded scholarship funds to nearly 200 children of company employees and retirees. Because of donations made by employees and retirees, the Matching Grants to Higher Education Program sent 864 grants to 341 colleges and universities, for a total of $232,684.

CORPORATE VOLUNTEER COUNCILS

In forty cities nationwide, involved corporations have banded together in what are most often called Corporate Volunteer Councils, which promote volunteerism and serve as communications vehicles between corporations and the nonprofit sector. They identify developments and new opportunities in employee and retiree involvement, and serve as resources for companies that are developing or expanding programs. Among member companies, the councils foster cooperation and communication, with an aim to realizing common objectives and identifying solutions to common problems.

In "A Report to the Community" for 1986, the **Corporate Volunteerism Council of the Minneapolis/St. Paul Metro Area** provided a profile of the involvement of their forty-nine members. They found that a slight majority (57 percent) of corporations had formal volunteer programs. Most companies (83 percent) had ongoing relationships with specific individual agencies, the most common being **Junior Achievement** and the **United Way.** Only 22 percent had a specific focus area, such as education or youth, but many mentioned that they would be identifying such an area in the future. A majority indicated that they participate in cooperative projects and partnerships.

Many corporations indicated that they are currently striving to include all employees in volunteer opportunities, including those previously reserved for upper management. Most companies (73 percent) indicated that they provide volunteers for boards and commissions, 55 percent for fund-raising, 65 percent for management and technical assistance, and 59 percent for loaned executives (almost exclusively for the United Way).

The September 1987 newsletter from the **Business Volunteer Council,** in Dallas, Texas, carried the following items:

> *While ARCO Plays Games . . .* Sixty-two **ARCO** volunteers supported the **Regional Jesse Owens Games** in Dallas, the largest volunteer group to work the games to date. The ARCO group, with the **Dallas Parks & Recreation Department** staffers, operated the annual track and field event for a group of 300 youngsters. . . . Volunteers met planes arriving from Midland and Lafayette and buses arriving from Houston and Longview. The volunteers assisted emergency treatment professionals, manned check-in tables, kept ice water available, measured students for uniforms, and served as spotters, photograph assistants, and award assistants.
>
> *Coors Brings the Beach to Land-locked Dallas.* The original Coors/KZEW Dallas Beach Party rocked Dallas in June. This downtown

Dallas tradition, begun in 1984, raised $60,000 for the **Muscular Dystrophy Association.** More than 50,000 people attended the event. Event planners dumped 420 tons of beach sand onto City Hall Plaza, turned City Hall's fountain pool into a swimming hole and added tanned, muscle-bound lifeguards, inflatable sharks, and sand volleyball courts. Sandcastle-building contests and continuous live entertainment were featured.

The **Texas Society to Prevent Blindness** will provide training to the LaPlaza Community Relations Team. This group of **Southwestern Bell Telephone** volunteers serves the Hispanic community and performs vision screening for young children. Trained team members will go to school campuses in the fall to assist school health professionals in an effort to detect possible vision problems before severe damage occurs.

The **Corporate Employee Volunteer Council of Jacksonville, Florida,** in July 1987 conducted an extraordinarily successful food drive with the theme "Some People Are Starving for Attention." Twenty-two participating companies collected thirty-five tons of food—twice the amount planners had anticipated—for the **Lutheran Social Services Food Bank,** which each month provides a three-day supply of food to about 375 families who have an emergency need. **Southern Bell** was the leader, collecting twenty-two tons. In food donated per person, **Sun Bank** was highest, averaging eighteen pounds per employee.

Contacting your local corporate volunteer council is an easy first step in creating an employee volunteer program or expanding an existing one. Because the officers of these councils change periodically, we can't give current addresses and telephone numbers. However, volunteer councils and their names are listed below alphabetically by state and city. Contact your local voluntary action center, United Way office, or chamber of commerce, or **VOLUNTEER**—The National Center, for the location and telephone numbers of current officers.

Huntsville, Alabama: Corporate Volunteer Council of Huntsville and Madison County, Alabama
Los Angeles, California: Corporate Volunteer Council of Los Angeles/ Orange County
Pleasanton, California: Valley Community Volunteer Council

Redwood City, California: Corporate Partnerships Program of San Mateo County

San Francisco, California: Bay Area Corporate Voluntarism

San Jose, California: Corporate Council of Santa Clara County

Hartford, Connecticut: Corporate Volunteer Committee*

Stamford, Connecticut: Corporate Volunteer Council

Washington, D.C.: Corporate Volunteer Council of Washington, D.C.

Jacksonville, Florida: Corporate Employee Volunteer Council

Orlando, Florida: Central Florida Council on Corporate Volunteerism

St. Petersburg, Florida: Pinellas Volunteer Corps*

Tampa, Florida: Employer Volunteer Council (EVC) of Hillsborough County

Chicago, Illinois: Corporate Volunteerism Council of Chicago

Montgomery County, Maryland: Montgomery County Corporate Volunteer Council

Boston, Massachusetts: Corporate Volunteer Council of Greater Boston

Detroit, Michigan: Southeastern Michigan Corporate Volunteer Council*

Duluth, Minnesota: Duluth Corporate Volunteerism Council*

Mankato, Minnesota: The Greater Mankato/North Mankato Area Volunteer Council

Minneapolis-St. Paul, Minnesota: Corporate Volunteerism Council of the Minneapolis/St. Paul Metro Area

Kansas City, Missouri: Corporate Volunteer Council of Greater Kansas City

St. Louis, Missouri: St. Louis Corporate Volunteerism Council

Albany, New York: Albany, New York, Corporate Volunteer Council*

New York, New York: Corporate Volunteers of New York

White Plains, New York: Westchester Corporate Volunteer Council

Akron, Ohio: Akron Corporate Volunteer Council

Cincinnati, Ohio: Corporate Voluntarism Council

Cleveland, Ohio: Business Volunteerism Council*

Tulsa, Oklahoma: Corporate Volunteer Council of Greater Tulsa

Portland, Oregon: Oregon Corporate Volunteer Council

Philadelphia, Pennsylvania: Corporate Volunteer Council

Memphis, Tennessee: Corporate Volunteer Council of Memphis

Austin, Texas: Austin in Action

Dallas, Texas: Business Volunteer Council

Houston, Texas: Corporate Volunteer Council of Greater Houston, Inc.

San Antonio, Texas: Business Volunteer Council*

Salt Lake City, Utah: Corporate Volunteer Council of Salt Lake City

---

* Council names followed by an asterisk were in the development stage as of fall 1987.

Fairfax County, Virginia: Corporate Volunteer Council of Northern Virginia

Richmond, Virginia: Corporate Volunteer Council*

Milwaukee, Wisconsin: Southeastern Wisconsin Corporate Volunteer Coordinators Council

VOLUNTEER—The National Center in late 1986 merged with the National Council on Corporate Volunteerism, thus becoming the primary national resource organization working in support of companies with employee volunteer programs. In 1986, the staff handled information requests from approximately 230 companies and conducted major consultations with **Bradlees, Atlantic Richfield, Union Carbide, Mellon Bank,** American Can (now **Primerica**), **McDonnell Douglas,** and **IBM.** The people at VOLUNTEER love to hear from corporations who want to involve their companies in community service. Their address and telephone number, along with many other resource organizations, are listed in chapter 3, "A Service Sampler."

* Council names followed by an asterisk were in the development stage as of fall 1987.

IN THEIR OWN WORDS

"I am particularly pleased that many of my goals and objectives are noneconomic. The satisfaction of seeing your effort pay off for other people is one of the richest rewards a person can have."

—Arthur Levitt, Jr.

"No matter how well a corporation may do within the narrow context of its own business, it's dependent on the surrounding society, and if the society is not as happy as it should be economically, if it's not politically stable, it's not going to have much of a future."

—C. Peter McColough

"If your principal occupation is to be a businessman, as mine was, by involving yourself in all these [volunteer] activities—aside from the merits of the activities themselves—you are a better businessman, because you see your business dealings from a variety of different vantage points instead of the narrow point of view that comes from being involved in business activities alone."

—John Whitehead

"There was one very funny line. [After four days out in the woods,] we're standing on top of a rock and wearing helmets and everyone is wearing their harnesses and all. Arlene was standing sort of near the edge, and one of the kids says, 'Be careful, Mrs. Mark, don't fall. I wouldn't want you to fall because then, there goes college . . . ege . . . ege . . . ege!' "

—Reuben Mark

Arthur Levitt, Jr.: *Chairman and chief executive officer of the American Stock Exchange, Arthur Levitt, Jr., is a member of the board of the Rockefeller Foundation and of Williams College, and is on the board of the New York State Council on the Arts.*

I became involved in volunteer service when I got out of the Air Force in 1954. I came from a family that was involved in all kinds of community activities. My grandmother, for instance, used to travel every day to the Brooklyn Home for the Incurable. My mother and father were both active in a whole variety of nonprofit programs and impressed on me my responsibility to do the same in order to give something back to society.

My efforts in the nonprofit arena provide me with the satisfaction of knowing that what I am doing is relevant and that it's important to people other than myself. I am particularly pleased that many of my goals and objectives are noneconomic. The satisfaction of seeing your effort pay off for other people is one of the richest rewards a person can have.

Try to involve yourself in activities that perhaps you have had no experience with before, because such involvement can be one of the greatest learning opportunities imaginable. If you have never worked with the elderly, becoming associated with a project involving geriatric care can be an extraordinary experience.

One thing I would advise is not to spread yourself too thin. Don't get overcommitted. Select one or two organizations as the ones that you will devote most of your effort and time to rather than having six or seven that you give a very little time to. If you're involved in development for an organization, be sure that your commitment goes beyond merely fund-raising. Be sure that you understand the institution and what its goals and objectives are.

In balancing the nonprofit, the business, and the family parts of life, my advice would be to try to get your family to support the same causes that you support. Balancing those interests is important. Be the kind of person who can lead a structured life rather than the kind who shoots from the hip. Be well organized. You must be absolutely ruthless in your ability to say, I *will* undertake this, and I *won't* undertake that. By doing that, you develop greater values for your family and your business in your voluntary pursuits. Don't be the kind of person who accepts anything that comes down the pike.

C. Peter McColough: *C. Peter McColough stepped down as chief executive officer of Xerox Corporation in 1982, having held that post for fourteen years. He joined Xerox thirty-three years ago, when the company had 600 employees. Currently, Xerox has some 120,000 employees, and Peter McColough was the architect of that growth. A natural leader in the nonprofit world, he was chairman of the United Way of America.*

From the corporate side, I've always strongly believed and encouraged people from Xerox to get involved. It seems to me that a large slice of the talented, educated, vigorous, helping people work for corporations both large and small. I've tried all my life to encourage these people to get involved, whatever their choice may be, in the public sector, to try to make a difference.

One rationale, which I think is very important, is that if the corporate people do not get involved, you're really leaving a very small slice of people in society to do those jobs, which is just not going to be manageable. You're withdrawing far too many people from those activities. Second, it seems to me that if people don't get involved here in the United States or in any country, you're not going to have a very healthy society—culturally, economically, politically, and so forth.

Therefore, no matter how well a corporation may do within the narrow context of its own business, it's dependent on the surrounding society, and if the society is not as happy as it should be economically, if it's not politically stable, it's not going to have much of a future. So there is a direct, I think almost selfish, interest on the part of the corporation to get the people involved in the society in all sorts of activities. These people can probably make all the difference in making the society more successful.

At Xerox, we have stated policies for employees, and communications to try to encourage them to get involved. We mount big efforts to encourage them to get involved in the United Way Fund, just to give one example. I used to travel, as most officers do, and meet with all sorts of employees around the country. At almost every talk, regardless of what I was speaking about, I would try at some point to urge them to get involved one way or another in the affairs of their community.

After a talk, people used to come up to me and say, it's all right for you to be involved, because you're the head of the company, and you can take time away from work; I'm just so busy, I don't know how I can do that. I pointed out to them that after you've taken on the first job, you are usually more willing to take on the second one, because it forces you to organize your time better. Taking on a second assignment outside the company is usually easier than taking on the first one.

Still I had a lot of objections from people who said they just couldn't do it, they didn't have enough time. Really in part to smoke them out of that, we came up with a Social Service Leave program, which we have had now for at least ten years. People can apply to go on leave from the company with full pay and benefits for up to a year, to serve some social purpose.

We do this through a procedure in which a rank and file committee of employees oversees the selection of those who go on Social Service Leave. This rotating committee meets once a year and all the applicants who are interested put their applications through them. The committee has almost a week-long meeting in which they interview these people, see what they are planning on, how serious they are, and how well they have thought through what they might like to do. Most people don't take a year. Usually it's shorter, six months or something like that. They get the full benefits, their full pay, and we guarantee that when they come back to the company they will get their old job back or the equivalent job.

The interest in the program is across a very broad range, from clerks to salesmen to all sorts of people. They want to help in a prison, they work in the ghetto areas. Before, they really never felt that they had enough time, or they couldn't afford to quit their job or take a leave without pay to do it. The people who have done it are in a very broad cross-section, including some pretty important managers of the company. We select about thirty people a year.

Years ago on the request of an executive recruiter at Ward Howell I went to see Joe Wilson [son of the founder and CEO of the Haloid Company, which later became Xerox Corporation]. He spent an afternoon with me, describing what he wanted to do with the technology, what he hoped to do, which was more promise at that point than anything else. I was really very intrigued with his views on the need to contribute to the quality of life, to good education, good health. He felt a real obligation to give something back, and I think that what persuaded me as much as anything else to accept the job offered by Wilson was his view of public service. I was tremendously impressed by his sense of dedication. In fact, I took a 50 percent salary cut to go to work for this man.

The very best training you can get is outside the company in a volunteer organization. Within the company you don't really lead, or shouldn't lead, by giving orders. There is a higher type of leadership. Companies, corporations are perhaps more disciplined, more highly organized than anything else in our society, more than the church, the government. So there is that hierarchy that can be seen as giving orders, but that is not a very good way to lead.

Outside the company, it just seems to me that if you go to work in the United Way campaign or go on the board of Outward Bound, nobody gives a damn what your title is back at Exxon or Xerox. You only lead by persuasion, by innovation, by your ideas. And if you can learn to lead that way, that is the very best training to bring back to your company. I think that the individual gains a great deal, not only in the sense that he is doing something that is worthwhile, but also in terms of the training in how to lead.

As for caveats in volunteer service, I think that you want to stay clear of going on a board of an organization that is really run by another group or an individual, where the board just ends up as a rubber stamp. There are some organizations of that sort, and I personally always want to stay away from that. You're not really going to play a role. The other thing is, don't do it unless you are going to do the job. Sometimes people accept things and they don't really try to do anything for the organization. They just never really pull their own weight.

You get a great satisfaction from trying to be helpful to other people and making other people's lives better in some way. I think we should examine our consciences—I find this particularly as I get older—to see whether we are really doing the positive things in terms of putting something back into society; if you have advantages, whether you just stay there and take them or have met your further obligations to try to serve your fellowman. It's a tremendous satisfaction to have done something in a positive way.

Service has really been an important part of my life. I would not want at this stage of my life—in the mid-sixties—regardless of how much money I had made, to think that I had done nothing but be a corporate man. I think it would be a very empty feeling, and I think I would have a very selfish view of myself. Volunteering was an easy decision—even though it can make the days and weeks a lot longer sometimes.

John Whitehead: *Deputy secretary of state in the Reagan administration, John Whitehead was for many years cochairman at Goldman, Sachs & Company. Long active in a variety of service organizations, he is a member of the Board of Overseers of Harvard University and former chairman of the Board of Managers of Haverford College. He was previously a trustee of the Carnegie Corporation and the Carnegie Foundation for the Advancement of Teaching. The former president of the International Rescue Committee, he was also a director of the New York City Partnership, the New York Chamber of Commerce, the Economic Development Council of New York City, the American Productivity Center, Junior Achievement, and Outward Bound.*

I guess I've done it all my life, even when I was a teenager, so I don't really think of volunteer service as something I started at a particular time. The motivation, the reasons are sort of complex, especially since it goes back so long. I just have always found it a necessity for leading a full life, leading a life that has breadth as well as depth, and not overly concentrating on one thing, like my studies when I was in college or my job. I've always felt the need to broaden and enrich my life.

I don't know exactly where it came from. My parents were always involved in a lot of community activities, and I guess I saw that as sort of a model, but more than any of that, I think I was just inwardly motivated—that I felt this need to do more with my life than just to put in my time.

During my life there have always been activities that have had major meaning for me. One, which I was involved with for thirty years, is the **International Rescue Committee.** I was also very active with my college—Haverford—after I graduated. I was on the board for close to twenty years and was chairman of the board for ten.

People ask me how I broke down my time during my last ten years with Goldman, Sachs, when I was senior partner and cochairman. I spent about a third of my time on nonprofit activities, a third of my time on being a board member of other business corporations, and only a third of my time running Goldman, Sachs. If I were advising someone, that would be the ideal proportion. I really wasn't shortchanging the firm because the other activities gave me the perspective to make better business decisions.

When I retired from Goldman, Sachs I had been there thirty-seven years, and somehow I thought the time had come for a change, both for my own good and for the firm's good. You can be head of an organization too long. After I left and before I came to Washington, I was actively involved in a variety of nonbusiness activities that I hadn't had enough time for before.

As an example of how to become involved, or at least how I became involved: in 1956, I was on vacation in Vienna with my wife, having breakfast in a little restaurant with a Viennese friend, and suddenly a sort of disheveled young man burst in, seeking out our friend. Just that night, he had come across the border from Hungary, fleeing from the Soviet invasion of Hungary, which had taken place a few weeks earlier.

The young man was appealing to our breakfast companion for help in providing radios to permit communications between the various bands of freedom fighters still holding out in Hungary. It was an exciting moment, and I got caught up in the activity. We cut short our vacation and went back to New York. I sort of conned RCA into providing the radios that he needed and conned Pan Am into flying them over. Within forty-eight hours, I had a plane full of ham radio equipment going back to Vienna. My friend received it at the airport and he arranged for trucks. To make a long story short: within a couple of days all the radio equipment had gone into Hungary to help the freedom fighters.

I felt that this was an exciting cause. I was caught up in the emotion of these Hungarians fighting Soviets oppression. So I looked around for an organization that could help me with that new interest of mine. I found the International Rescue Committee, and that is how I got involved in it. If you believe something is important, there probably is an organization out there somewhere through which you can fulfill your hopes.

For me, the main benefit of service work is the experience and the exposure created by being involved in a whole variety of things. I'm a much more well-rounded person for it, and when you become well rounded you see problems from the perspectives of people who are involved in different activities. I think it makes you a better judge of situations.

If, your principal occupation is to be a businessman, as mine was, by involving yourself in all these activities—aside from the merits of the activities themselves—you are a better businessman, because you see your business dealings from a variety of different vantage points instead of the narrow point of view that comes from being involved in business activities alone.

You find yourself associating with other leaders in other fields, and it turns out that, while it has not been your motivation, it is good for business, too. You meet other people who are helpful to your business career, and you meet them on a different plane than if you just met them in business. You are meeting them as colleagues trying to benefit whatever cause the activity is involved in.

My advice would be: don't do it for the prestige, do it because you want to. Pick activities that you are really committed to and that you really want to make a contribution to. How to do it is just like anything else, like a business career: you start at the bottom. You should find out what you can do today to help—some rather lowly chore or menial activity.

Just go to it and learn what the organization is about, how they operate. Don't feel you have to go on the board of trustees the first day. That will come along—if you show the other people involved that you are really committed and that you are effective.

When I went to work at the State Department, the job is such an all-consuming one that I simply couldn't do any outside activities, and there were conflicts of interest involved with many of them. I ended up resigning, to my amazement, from thirty-seven organizations that I had involvement with as a board member or some active membership.

You don't realize how many things you can and do become involved in. You find that they help each other. Additional responsibilities in a new organization do not take as much time or effort as the first one. They work together. You know how to get things done. You find that you helped one organization with one problem, and that took a lot of time, but when that same problem comes up in the next organization, you know how to do it much more efficiently because you have already seen how best to solve that problem. You educate yourself as you go along in how to be effective in nonprofit organizations.

Reuben and Arlene Mark: *Reuben Mark, chairman and chief execu-tive officer of Colgate Palmolive, is on the board of directors of Phoenix House, a drug rehabilitation center. Arlene Mark is a school psychologist who works with adjudicated youth in New York City and New York State. The Marks, who are on the board of the I Have a Dream Foundation, partially finance and run a program for a group of special education children within the I Have a Dream program. Reuben Mark was chairman of the Outward Bound benefit dinner held in New York City on October 20, 1987, at which a record $380,000 was raised to support the work of Outward Bound USA.*

Reuben: We've been involved for many years in volunteerism in terms of boards and charitable work. Right now we're involved in a particular and most intensive educational situation. Arlene and I had read about Eugene Lang's I Have a Dream program and got quite interested in it. Through mutual friends we met Gene.

Arlene: His original class was being educated and was on its way to graduation. In the meantime, he was getting other kids started. Within two sixth-grade classes on the Lower East Side of Manhattan there was a group of twenty-six students who were considerably behind in reading and math and who were classified as special education students. The sponsors of these programs didn't know what these students would need in order to catch up, to graduate, or even if it was possible for them to take advantage of what the I Have a Dream sponsors were providing.

I could see that these were students who had experienced failure for many years and who got no sense of their competence in school. They often tried to obtain their self-esteem out of school. These were the kinds of students who could wind up in places like Lincoln Hall, the facility for juvenile offenders where I have worked for the past two years.

Reuben: The thought occurred to Gene to put these special education students together in one class and let somebody who is professionally trained help them. That is how we got involved. Arlene and I are splitting the cost of this with Colgate Palmolive.

There are now twenty-three kids in the class that we are working with. The statistics say the probability of these kids staying in high school is about 95 percent against them. We have agreed that we will support these youngsters both emotionally and scholastically for ten years. They are between fourteen and sixteen years old now. We started with them in the sixth grade and will stay with them for six years until they graduate high school and then through four years of vocational training or college, if that is a possibility.

Arlene: We now have high hopes for the students because they have become motivated to graduate and are really enthusiastic about the program. We decided that this was something that was worthwhile as a project, not only for these students, but we hoped it might also become a model of how to get other inner city kids who have been failing back into the system.

On Saturday mornings we leave home at about 7:30 and get to the Grand Street Settlement House on the Lower East Side at about 8:30. The students arrive between 8:30 and 9:00 for one-on-one tutorials, provided by learning specialists, high-level professionals, whom we obtained through the Bank Street School of Education. After the tutoring, the children are scheduled for different activities. They can go off to sports—basketball, whiffle ball, or aerobics. We have a wonderful artist there, too, and we are seeing incredible drawings that these kids are doing, drawings that they never thought possible because they had never been exposed to big artist pads, charcoal, and talented instruction. The kids are learning and having fun—discovering things that they have never really known about themselves before.

Reuben: In addition we see them at various times during the week—evenings and on various trips. This morning, for example, I took one of the kids to visit an alternative school. He is a very troubled kid who has a lot of difficulty in school and out of school. Arlene thought this new school might be good for him. He sat in on an English class and spent some time with the principal and in an electronics class, just to get a feeling whether it was something he would like to do. That doesn't happen every day, but in addition to the group efforts there is a lot of individual help and support.

Arlene: Our own children are involved to some extent. One of my sons, Steven, went to Grand Street with us once or twice and happened to play a game of checkers with one of the most resistant students, and the student beat Steven. This boy, who is one of the ones who is very difficult to motivate, had such a good time with Steven and has in a sense identified with our son. He comes to tutoring but he fools around—it's always a power struggle. One day we arranged for the tutor and this boy to go for a ride in the Jeep, and during this ride the tutor and the student wrote Steven a letter at the University of Virginia. He was very motivated to do that and since then he's become more and more involved.

Our son Peter is very involved in helping me design a newsletter on his computer. He has all these good ideas on how to involve the kids more. Our twenty-three-year-old daughter Lisa has recruited her peers to become big brothers and big sisters. She believes that if each dreamer has one person as a young role model, he or she can call them when they have something they'd like to do with them. So the Peer Pals are all involved in an informal way to try to advise and help the kids, who are relatively close to their age.

Reuben: We arranged one special project because we thought that these were the kind of kids who could react strongly to an Outward Bound type of experience in which they are being pushed a little closer to their limits than they had normally been, in a situation where they depend upon each other. We arranged for a Project U.S.E., Outward Bound–style trip, a five-day wilderness experience in New Jersey. It was November so it was a little bit cold. We got twenty of the kids to come.

These are kids who act out much of the time. There is a lot of violence, a lot of profanity, a lot of unsocial behavior, but it really did, I think, make a very significant impact on several of them. I think that it was kind of a life-shaping experience for them, even though there was a certain amount of pain and anguish that went into it. They went through the various confidence courses—the ropes course, rock climbing, some rappelling. But the activities— such as cooking food and building the tents and getting to know one another a little better—that was the most important part.

There was one very funny line. We're standing on top of a rock and wearing helmets and everyone is wearing their harnesses and all. Arlene was standing sort of near the edge, and one of the kids says, "Be careful, Mrs. Mark, don't fall. I wouldn't want you to fall because then, there goes college . . . ege . . . ege . . . ege!"

It was a lot of strain, because there was a tremendous amount of intervention that we had to perform. I went into it with great expectations, very excited, and initially I was somewhat let down by it, but when it was done I really thought it was extremely positive.

Arlene: What it did was make the kids much better friends and much more supportive of each other. The name-calling decreased and when we go to Grand Street now, the level of noise and the level of fighting is incredibly decreased. They are just more comfortable with each other. They have experienced each other in a setting with the tents and they carried potatoes and pots and pans. They shared the load and did all of that, so in a sense it's desensitized them to a lot of things and somehow it's better.

Reuben: Colgate-Palmolive is quite community-minded and believes you should always give back to the community in which you operate. We had some of the kids working at Colgate last summer. They had internships, in which we tried to match each kid with a job where they had mentors and supervisors. It was a very exciting thing for them and a pretty exciting thing for the people at Colgate.

Arlene: We want to show them what is out there. Everything we offer them is based on their earning it in class. Last year the kids who became interns were the ones who really showed progress in attendance, in their schoolwork, and in their effort and behavior. Right after the beginning of the year, we are going to start skills training, helping them to understand how you go to an employer and behave during the day.

Reuben: This work with I Have a Dream is probably the most intensive thing that I have done. We are finding that we are actually getting involved in the kids' lives—certainly not to the extent that you are involved in your own children's lives, but not far from it. This is a very frustrating but at the same time gratifying thing. Occasionally things happen that make you feel very good about the project, and we are seeing sufficient glimmers that we may be able to make some difference, to change those statistics somewhat.

My feeling in terms of my own personal satisfaction is that sitting on a charitable board and approving programs and raising funds is important, but I feel I can personally contribute more by getting involved directly with the kids.

Arlene: In a sense it's like the Outward Bound philosophy. There is a challenge there for us, to see that these students, who have such frustrations in their lives, are getting their education, coming to school daily and doing things that regular kids do.

As for the kids, I don't know that they see it as a challenge. They don't really quite understand, they just know that there are some people around—a lot of people—who believe in them. They see that a lot of adults are supporting them, saying they can do this and actually giving them the tools to do it with.

They have got to feel good about themselves. Those pats on the back when the tutor says, that was so good, you did that, look at that—the kids just beam, and that good feeling is such competition for that street stuff where they get their self-esteem from stealing or getting in trouble or getting suspended. We are seeing that some of the kids are falling away from the street-smart kids.

Reuben: The return that you get from a project like this one for I Have a Dream is a combination of having, at least in a modest way, some positive effect on the lives of people who have had difficulties, and introducing people who have never experienced success—at anything, in school or at home—to some possibility of feeling a little better about themselves, of experiencing some degree of success in some area. There is considerable satisfaction in seeing that, yes, there is a bit of progress and seeing the glimmer where there has been very little before.

Inevitably as you move on in life, you feel both emotionally and practically that there is an obligation to pay back some of the good things that have happened to you. Also you see situations with your own children that you might do differently or things you've learned that you might want to pass on. Finally and most importantly, once you get into it, it's a very exciting thing that draws you in, despite the frustrations and problems. It's something that builds and that you increasingly look forward to.

CHAPTER SEVEN

SERVICE AND YOUR LIFE

$\mathcal{W}$E hope that by this point you've gotten a solid and intriguing introduction to the world of service work: the kinds of activities and organizations, and the different roles to be performed. We've led you through a thought process about choosing the right activity for yourself and given you, through their first-person accounts, the feelings of volunteers about their experience of service.

In this final chapter, we want to come back to some of the benefits of service work:

· How it can become an integral and most meaningful part of your life;
· The connection it can have with your career;
· What it can mean for relationships and values within your family;
· How it enriches the lives of the entire age spectrum from young to retired people.

Service adds a unique dimension of quality and value to your attitudes, actions, and relationships. When you choose your service work wisely and strike a reasonable balance among the various aspects of your family and business lives, you're very likely to feel, as have many people we've talked to, that you've finally found the mix of activities that will help you feel good about life.

THE PLEASURES OF SERVICE

Service brings us needed psychic income—in the form of satisfaction, refreshment, recreation—and fun, too! As we get involved in the lives of others, we often bear our personal burdens more lightly. We feel moments of quiet joy when a project takes off or a strategy starts to show results. And, beyond the quiet pleasure of satisfaction, service can mean the thrill of exercising our talents—either existing skills or ones that we discover. In opening avenues, we're likely to encounter new and exciting parts of ourselves. As our friend Dale Coudert, author, mother of two, and nonprofit worker, says, "It makes you feel good! Whatever you give, you get back tenfold."

In service work, we can apply our abilities in ways that we had never thought about but that make wonderful sense. An animal lover can join a pet-assisted therapy program. A musician or actor can perform for patients in hospitals, people in prison, assemblies of schoolchildren. A sports enthusiast can do her thing while bringing self-esteem and excitement into the lives of kids in programs like the Special Olympics. The person devoted to gardening can get his workout in the dirt while beautifying the town square.

Creating a new dimension for interests and activities is often especially appealing to people middle-aged and older who have developed their skills around a certain focus and want to broaden their application. An accountant who is tired of keeping track of widgets may get involved with the budgeting for the PTA's fashion-show fund-raiser. A corporate lawyer may want to give time pro bono for a favorite social service cause.

John: *Other people use service as a way to embark on and enjoy activities unrelated to their working lives. As a young auto dealer, I sought to keep my mind from turning to chromium by volunteering to teach modern poetry for the University of California at Berkeley extension service. I found myself conducting seminars with Allen Ginsberg, Brother Antoninus, Lawrence Ferlinghetti, and the whole North Beach, San Francisco, movement. Talk about unrelatedness and literary ferment!*

We learned about a woman retiree from Metropolitan Life in New York City who had had to flee Nazi Germany as a girl in the late 1930s, abandoning her studies in science and astronomy. Through the employee volunteer clearinghouse at Met Life, she heard about the volunteer program at the Hayden Planetarium of the American Museum of Natural History and now takes enormous pleasure from her work there. She has contact with important people in the field and meets lecturers and experts who come to town. Her work has been so energizing to her that she has now also started volunteering at a hospital in her community. This kind of catalytic effect of service is not at all unusual.

A SERVICE VIGNETTE

Here's an example of a short-term group service project that left the volunteers feeling particularly good about themselves:

About fifty middle-aged and teenaged alumni of the New York City Outward Bound Center and other Outward Bound schools met at Youth Action Program's home offices in East Harlem on a beautiful, crisp December morning. First, everyone loosened up with some Outward Bound games. Then, after listening to some inspiring words, they split up into teams to tackle five different service projects in the area.

Four projects were undertaken in conjunction with Youth Action Program. One team installed fiberglass insulation in the ceiling of a building being renovated into apartments for homeless youth. Another cleaned up a vacant lot to create a playground for homeless infants and toddlers. A third gave a birthday party for a little girl at the Young Mothers' Cooperative of the Homes Away from Homes Program. And a fourth did construction work to create office space for the East Harlem Cadets housed at Youth Action Program. The fifth team took men from Create House, a shelter for homeless men, ice-skating in Central Park and to the Museum of the City of New York.

At the end of the afternoon, everyone returned to Youth Action Program's offices to have a party, share their thoughts about the projects with the group, enjoy a slide show, and indulge in a giant group hug. Everyone felt a sense of achievement and gained a broader understanding of the kinds of service we can provide to others in New York and to ourselves when we get involved.

If you've been reading the accounts in the sections called "In Their Own Words," you probably don't need further convincing about the fact that service brings friendships that most people call the most important of their lives. In service, we not only meet new people, *we meet the best in people.* Friendship is the one pleasure that seems to be almost guaranteed in service work.

Far from taking the gift of good health for granted, Americans in the late twentieth century are in earnest and conscious pursuit of it. We try to eat well and exercise regularly in order to maintain our physical well-being. Medical research suggests that service work can help. It's not really a farfetched piece of logic. By increasing our self-esteem and involvement with other lives and greater causes, service reduces stress and loneliness, which have been implicated in various diseases.

Kenneth Dayton of the Dayton Hudson Corporation has been an enthusiastic member of the large community of corporate servant leaders in the Minneapolis area. In addition to his work in formalizing the community service programs at Dayton Hudson, Ken has served on the boards of several cultural organizations and commissions and is currently national chairman of American Public Radio. When we asked him to describe the return he gets from being civic-minded, he responded, "It's just immeasurable. It's just so much fun to participate in something that's important to the community or to the nation, to help it grow and be of greater service to its clients."

The activities are diverse and the types of involvement are many, but in the end service gives us one return in common: *an increase in the overall quality of our lives.*

SERVICE AND YOUR CAREER: DOING WELL BY DOING GOOD

You may wish to keep your service work separate from your job, or you may find that your career and your not-for-profit interests can relate, formally or informally. How the two coexist in your life will depend on many individual, personal factors.

Our thesis is that service work brings benefits to the person who performs it, benefits that we like to think of as psychic income: the freedom to act on our best instincts and impulses, the sense of making a difference and of empowerment, personal growth through discovering new abilities and making new friendships, and a feeling of being connected to a larger community or cause. The energy and confidence that result from this psychic income not only bring great pleasure, they also make you a more dynamic and interesting person—as a spouse, parent, friend, and colleague and employee.

So, even if your approach is to keep job and service separate, your working life will very likely be affected in one or more of the following ways:

- · The feedback you get from helping other people or doing something that you believe in can energize you for your work.
- · Because service is likely to give added dimension to your life, it may complement your job and make you like it better.
- · By improving your self-image, service can help your on-the-job performance.

While the intangible far outnumber the tangible rewards, we would be remiss if we were to ignore some of the very good things that can happen in your professional life through service. *Simply put, working in a nonprofit organization can directly help your career.* Through service work, you meet and work with new people, people who hold the same values and truths that you do. They get to know you, you get to know them, and a mutual trust evolves. Very often, because of the camaraderie that is built up, you will do business. You may gain clients from among the people you meet, or you may gain insights into profitable avenues to explore—new opportunities in your field, even new fields and new careers.

At the same time that nonprofit work does good for others, it is good for your visibility. If you are at a senior level within your company, membership on a nonprofit board may lead to a seat on a corporate board. If you make a real contribution as a fund-raiser or the head of a local education campaign, you may hear from a nonprofit coworker about an executive spot opening up within his or her company. This most intangible quality, visibility, can bring unplanned, unexpected rewards of a similar kind at every level of service.

Ellie: *As an executive recruiter, I know that employers place a high value on the service work of job candidates. Most of my colleagues believe* *that if you never become involved in service activities and just do your job, you really are not a multidimensional person. Recruiters like candidates who have done a lot of nonprofit work because, in general, such involvement is a big plus in the eyes of the company doing the hiring.*

Recruiters try to put up as candidates people who have more than just the job criteria. What they're looking for is the added edge, which very often is energy. And energy frequently shows up in résumés as the things people do in their nonprofessional lives, in how they spend their time outside the office. Those activities also very much reflect a person's self-image. A person is a superior candidate if his or her activities reveal someone broad-gauged, someone who finds time to give something back, to do something different and energizing.

In 1982, the **Mayor's Voluntary Action Center of New York City** conducted a survey of private-sector employers operating in the metropolitan area. From a cross section of 144 companies that hire recent college graduates, they learned that:

- More than 80 percent recognize volunteer experience as a consideration in their employment decisions;
- Roughly one-fifth recognize volunteer work as equal in weight to other hiring criteria;
- More than 76 percent look for it on résumés;
- More than 37 percent have space for it on their job applications;
- And 72 percent ask about it in their interviews.

The above information is from *Volunteer to Career: A Study of Student Voluntarism and Employability,* by Jeremy Bentley-Kasman. The Mayor's Voluntary Action Center, New York City, 1983.

There are practical reasons why employers like to see community service on candidates' résumés. Service teaches you things. Gerry Ulrich retired from her public relations business seven years ago when she had a child. Now engaged in a variety of volunteer activities, among them fund-raising for St. Thomas Aquinas College in Sparkill, New York, Gerry says:

> Boy, am I learning—which is the fun part of becoming a trustee of a college. You get involved in so many areas in which you may have

had no prior experience. Suddenly I'm interested in compensation and pension plans for faculty and staff, demographics, and long-range planning for an academic institution. The more involved I get, the more I learn, the more I begin to feel a part of the college and begin to have my own vision of its future. It can only happen if you jump in and get your feet wet.

As you interact with people in nonprofit situations, on boards, committees, or in direct service, you learn skills to augment your present ones and new ways to apply what you already know. You can learn how to lead, according to former Xerox chairman Peter McColough:

> The very best training you can get is outside the company in a volunteer organization. Within the company you don't really lead, or shouldn't lead, by giving orders. There is a higher type of leadership. . . . Outside the company, it just seems to me that if you go to work in the United Way campaign or go on the board of Outward Bound, nobody gives a damn what your title is back at Exxon or Xerox. You only lead by persuasion, by innovation, by your ideas. And if you can learn to lead that way, that is the very best training to bring back to your company. I think that the individual gains a great deal, not only in the sense that he is doing something that is worthwhile, but also in terms of the training in how to lead.

The list that follows, which is long but by no means exhaustive, will give you an idea of the kinds of perceptions, skills, and experiences you can gain from service work:

- The person who chairs committees and heads projects is perceived as a leader, someone who has meaningful supervisory and management skills.
- You may gain experience in writing reports for board meetings.
- Fund-raising can develop your latent talents in selling and marketing.
- You can learn how to prepare a budget and a business plan.
- Helping to plan innovative methods of producing income may bring out the dynamic entrepreneur who has been lurking within your quiet exterior.
- The person who can plan, organize, and run an efficient meeting will often emerge as a business leader.

- Skills you develop in training other volunteers and running workshops can translate directly into a corporate position in human resources.
- Service work often provides experience in public speaking, a skill that is of tremendous benefit in all professions.
- Poise and presence, spin-offs of dynamic interrelating with other people, are assets in all walks of life.
- Special event promotion and public education campaigns provide valuable experience in publicity: in planning strategy, designing releases and ads, distributing and placing materials.
- Service can help develop and refine your problem-solving skills.
- You can learn to lobby legislators.
- You can gain experience in purchasing.
- You can become skilled in administration, personnel management, recruitment, and counseling.
- Work in community service can lead directly to a corporate job in community relations.

Write Service into Your Résumé

Don't make the mistake of omitting your service work from your résumé. Many employers include sections for it on their application forms and specifically ask questions about it in interviews. They want to know about these activities for people at all levels.

Entry level. When employers evaluate a student applying for a first job after high school or college, they examine the applicant's academic record, personal recommendations, and extracurricular activities. These data tend to follow certain patterns and may give little insight into the personal qualities of the individual. A brief report on the young person's service work—which can reflect initiative, commitment, how well he or she gets along with others—can be the factor that sets the applicant apart.

Women reentering the job market. In the late 1980s, the topic of women and work is extraordinarily complex. We'll grossly simplify to make a point here: if a woman stops working for a while to raise a family and later returns to the job market, her community involvement can provide prospective employers with a sense of the continuity of her growth, as well as of her energy and creativity. (*This was certainly true in my case!*—Ellie)

Ellen Phelan taught at a community college before her children were born. When she stopped working, she volunteered in the public schools, teaching and serving as president of the parent-teacher association. Thinking about going back to work, she says, "I will probably use my volunteer experiences in trying to get a job. I'll be able to show that, maybe I haven't been working, but I have been active and involved. All the organizing that I've had to do will be a benefit. I'll be able to say, I've been able to do this, I've been able to apply for grants and get them, I've been able to start a program and follow it through."

Moving up the ladder. We spoke above about what a person's record of service can reveal to an employer. In a similar way, corporations and professional firms want to advance those people who have the strongest skills in working with other people, in problem-solving, in vision and leadership. The service portion of the résumé can bring talents into focus, can highlight a person as someone special, with the energies and qualities for sustained success.

At the top. We haven't seen any studies on this, but we feel absolutely confident in saying that the majority of senior-level executives are engaged in service work. The experiences of John Whitehead, Bill Phillips, Peter McColough, and Kenneth Dayton are not exceptions but the rule. The point is not whether service work "helped" them in their careers; it is that service has become an essential part of the lives and personalities of many people in top positions.

The most common format for résumés is the chronological listing of titles and organizations, with brief descriptions of what the jobs entailed. Generally, a longer section on paid employment is followed by a bare-bones listing of community or association work. We feel that if your work for particular organizations has been substantial, you should provide, as in the section on paid work, brief descriptions of your responsibilities and accomplishments.

An alternative format is the functional résumé, which lays out, with four or five lines of description for each entry, your talents, skills, or areas of expertise, followed by the chronological history of your paid employment, service work, and education. If you choose this format, which is useful for women returning to the work force or when an unusual career path or erratic pattern of employment exists, you should integrate the skills and expertise gained from service work with those you derived from paid jobs.

Mary Gittings, program director of the Piton Foundation, in Denver, Colorado, gave us this account of her career:

"I started the Denver Women's Career Center, primarily motivated because I was widowed in 1976 and had the firsthand experience of what women deal with when they become single heads of families. The purpose of that organization, which is still operating, is to help women reenter the work force. I also got involved in Rocky Mountain Planned Parenthood, which is one of the largest service providers of family planning in the country. We oversee the operation of thirty-five family planning clinics.

"I've been on many other boards that were most significant in teaching me skills that I transferred to my profession. I went on to the national board of the Junior League, representing the thirty-seven Junior Leagues in the western part of the country.

"Then, because of those experiences, when the Piton Foundation was being formed ten years ago, they sought me out and started by asking me to work as a consultant in helping to develop their program areas in projects that served women. So I started on a very part-time basis doing that kind of work and over the years worked into the position of program director."

In preparing for interviews, be sure to think carefully about your service involvements so that you can describe not just your position but your contributions as well. If you are very proud of an aspect of your service work, if you feel that it reflects something about you that you want an employer to know, and particularly if it directly relates to the job in question, find the right moment to bring it into the conversation. Don't be shy: any sincere interviewer wants to know as much as possible about your best qualities.

The people you work with in nonprofit organizations can be excellent references for prospective employers. As with all references, be sure to let these people know that you would like to give their names for this purpose.

WOMEN AND SERVICE

In the early 1970s, NOW (The National Organization for Women) issued a resolution that urged women to limit their volunteering to groups that worked for feminism and social change. Women were encouraged not to join community service organizations, because—the idea went—these male-dominated groups simply used them as cheap labor. Women were advised to get jobs so they could receive "real" pay and "real" professional credit. This pronouncement, which the current leadership of NOW has not followed up on, did considerable harm to the cause of volunteerism.

Today most women, avowedly feminist or not, take a more complex view of the world, or perhaps we should say worlds, for many women feel that they are engaged in a juggling act, trying to keep several balls in the air at once. Some women have kept as their goal a kind of superwoman image: they will be career women and mothers, plus find the time to create additional personalized fulfillments for themselves. Many, however, have found that trying to do too much means not doing anything well, or at least not enjoying it; or it often leads to a feeling of coming apart at the seams.

At the end of the 1980s, some women who can financially afford to are leaving corporate life. The reasons are many: the desire to be a greater influence on their growing children, discouragement about whether they will be allowed to advance to the top layers of management, or a feeling of disappointment in the values of the corporate world.

In the last century and the earlier parts of this one, women who volunteered were often from wealthy or at least comfortable families. During a period when most women worked in the home, these individuals had the time to devote to, and the resources to support, nonprofit projects and causes. Service work was a focus for their energies, a place where their ideals could find fertile ground and their projects take root.

> "The unthinking pursuit of money and respectability—until recently, largely a male obsession—has sapped the nation's strength. It has forced many of our most talented people into vocations of little or no use for the rest of us, and fostered selfishness and narcissism. Whenever possible, men *and* women should try to do what satisfies them most. This not only means that women should continue to volunteer; perhaps more important, it means that men should volunteer much more. And rather than reject voluntarism, women should see its revival as an opportunity for leadership in areas in which they've long excelled—not just caring for family, but caring for others as well."—*Kathleen Kennedy Townsend, "Americans and the Cause of Voluntarism," in* The Washington Monthly, *October 1983*.

Before feminism, there was voluntarism, and through their service involvements, women showed themselves to be inspirational leaders: they raised money and funded large projects and institutions, and brought muscle to their compassion. Voluntarism was good for women, and women did an immense amount of good for the world through voluntarism.

The fact that, thirty years ago, a large number of women volunteers were in supportive rather than leadership roles was not the fault of voluntarism, for the same syndrome prevailed throughout the world of work outside the home. Business, education, the arts, religious organizations, not-for-profit groups—all had failed to encourage women to become leaders. Today attitudes have changed and more openness prevails. The result has been a proliferation of opportunities for women to contribute and to lead, in ways that are less socially dictated and more of their own choosing.

A complex world encourages complex responses. Women today have a solid sense that they have contributions to make, so many contributions, in fact, that they may not be able to act on all their impulses at once. If her financial situation permits, a woman may work for a few years, then take time out to have a family, perhaps working part-time, perhaps going back to work later. A growing number of women are leaving corporations to form free-lance consultancies or to start their own businesses, and professional women can sometimes adjust their client load in response to family responsibilities. (*In fact, that is exactly what I did.*—Ellie)

Service work can complement the work and family lives of women in whatever role or combination of roles they choose, allowing a deepening of focus or a broadening of perspective, a way to keep skills sharp and to meet people in expansive situations.

Wendy Kaminer has written a lively and fascinating book on this subject. In *Women Volunteering*, she provides this way of looking at the situation of women today: "Liberation won't mean 'having it all'; it will mean choosing our compromises instead of having them chosen for us. And, in a feminist world, when women are free to work for money, they should feel free, once again, to volunteer."

SERVICE WORK AFTER RETIREMENT

In 1985, 43 percent of people between ages sixty-five and seventy-four, and 26 percent of people over age seventy-five, volunteered, according to a Gallup survey commissioned by Independent Sector. Their stories and their words are the strongest testimonials that exist for the value of service in providing fulfillment and involvement in the later years.

Jimmy and Rosalynn Carter, in their book *Everything to Gain: Making the Most of the Rest of Your Life*, write frequently about the importance of working for and with others. In this passage, they describe one of the most significant rewards of service for older people:

> For us, an involvement in promoting good for others has made a tremendous difference in our lives in recent years. There are serious needs everywhere for volunteers who want to help those who are hungry, homeless, blind, crippled, addicted to drugs or alcohol, illiterate, mentally ill, elderly, imprisoned, or just friendless and lonely. For most of us, learning about these people, who are often

our immediate neighbors, can add a profound new dimension to what might otherwise be a time of too much worrying about our own selves.

During her tenure with the **Peace Corps,** retired teacher Virginia Spray helped Liberian children receive a better education by conducting teacher-training workshops in a town not far from Monrovia. How did she like it? "I had a marvelous experience. Age is so looked up to, you suddenly feel important again."

Here are some comments from people who participate in the **Retired Senior Volunteer Program** run by ACTION, the federal domestic volunteer agency:

"You get a lot more out of volunteer work than you'll ever have to give. I'm always the lucky one—not the agencies I work for."

"I again feel needed and wanted, a part of society, rather than filling time by sitting around playing solitaire, turning on the radio or television for a while, taking a walk, hoping that somebody will notice you."

"Volunteer work does more for me than it does for the people [I help]."

"I got bored after retirement. I think a person's first reaction to retirement is: 'Wow! Now I can stay in bed in the mornings.' That wears off pretty fast. Life needs an objective. Otherwise, the gray matter just doesn't function anymore."

"Eighteen months ago I was stagnated and depressed. Now things are different: I love what I'm doing. Everyone cares about everyone else, and I am active and involved and happy."

The **International Executive Service Corps** (IESC) recruits retired executives and technical advisers to share their years of experience with businesses in the developing nations.

Volunteer Theodore P. Zoli, former president of Torrington Industries, Inc., assisted an Egyptian contractor in the area of construction machinery maintenance.

Mildred H. Callaghan, president of her own company when she retired, helped a Peruvian hotel reach its occupancy goal.

Edward P. Folley, a retired executive with Johnson & Higgins, helped a Salvadoran printing and packaging company update its insurance program.

Thomas Hurst, for many years an executive with A. E. Staley Company, worked with an Ecuadoran grain company to develop new corn products.

Hyman S. Edelstein, a retired materials manager with Stanhome, Inc., advised a Santo Domingan manufacturer of toiletries and pharmaceuticals on the efficiency of their labeling process.

Cambridge G. Edgreen, a former production supervisor for Pierce Glass Company, advised a Philippine company on the start-up and training necessary to operate the firm's manufacturing equipment.

As a former client observed, "All good and experienced advisers work from the mind but the IESC executive brings an extra dimension . . . he works from the heart, too."

In chapter 3 See "Groups of Interest to Senior Citizens and Retired People" for several organizations of particular appeal to older people.

SERVICE DURING SCHOOL AND AFTER GRADUATION

Independent Sector's 1985 Gallup survey showed that 52 percent of people ages fourteen through seventeen volunteered, a figure that was about even with one reported in a similar survey made in 1980. *However, whereas in 1980 54 percent of people ages eighteen through twenty-four volunteered, in 1985 only 43 percent did. And of single people of all ages, 58 percent volunteered in 1980, but only 39 percent did so in 1985.*

Around the country, many junior and senior high schools have established programs requiring community service work, and at many colleges student groups have formed to work against the problems of hunger and homelessness, and in support of other social issues.

In his book *Outward Bound USA,* Josh Miner, the organization's first president, reprints a prescription for education created around 1930 by the innovative founder of **Outward Bound**, Kurt Hahn:

Give children the chance to discover themselves.

See to it that children experience both success and defeat.

See to it that there are periods of silence.

Train the imagination, the ability to anticipate and to plan.

Take sports and games seriously, but only as a part of the whole.

Free the children of rich and influential parents from the paralyzing influence of wealth and privilege.

The **Campus Outreach Opportunity League** (COOL) is a national nonprofit organization that promotes and supports student involvement in addressing community needs (see page 128). COOL's network includes more than 400 campuses and 150 national, state, and local organizations. In August 1987 at Duke University, participants at COOL's summit meeting issued a paper called the Durham Statement, which contains the following key paragraphs:

There is a growing movement among college students in the United States. It affects no one particular college or region, and it is not singularly ethnic or religious, reactionary or radical. It is based on a quiet but strong commitment to make American life better for people in need. Across the country we see college students staffing after-school recreation programs, organizing and maintaining shelters for the homeless and foodlines for the hungry, tutoring illiterate adults, working to clean up and protect the environment, and providing companionship to the elderly. . . .

It is our hope that by the end of this decade every college and university student in the United States will be challenged to make concerted service efforts in their communities. To do this, service leaders—whether in the student body or the administration—must design programs which help students and those they work with discover dignity and self-determination. . . .

The opportunity to participate in community service is fundamental to a student's education, intellectual growth and personal development; it is our goal to challenge every student to participate in the student service movement.

The **Rice Student Volunteer Program** at Rice University is only two years old but has had great success, offering students thirty programs in the Houston area in which to work, including big brother/big sister activities, a food bank, a recycling center, a tutoring program for runaway and homeless youth, an alcohol awareness group, peer counseling, and refugee tutoring.

Brown and Stanford universities award scholarships to students who take time off from college to volunteer for public service, and dozens of other schools are studying ways of making community service a formalized part of the education process.

Campus Compact: The Project for Public and Community Service is a coalition of college and university presidents established to create public service opportunities for their students and to develop an expectation of service as an integral part of student life and the college experience. The members work to create incentives for student involvement in service, heightening awareness about the value of community service, and providing information and technical assistance to campuses across the country (see page 128).

In the spring of 1987, students at Vanderbilt University took an Alternative Spring Break. One group of about twenty visited a Sioux reservation in South Dakota to paint and tile a YMCA center. Others helped build a church in Juárez, Mexico, or went to Appalachia to plant trees and work on construction projects. Students who stayed in Nashville worked with Cambodian refugees.

In 1985—the year of "We Are the World" and Live Aid, which generated a lot of energy on campus about the hunger issue—the **National Student Campaign Against Hunger** was started by the **Public Interest Research Groups** in cooperation with **USA for Africa.** The campaign assists students in organizing educational, community service, and fund-raising programs on their campuses and in their communities.

The resurgence of community involvement on campuses is encouraging, but why the drop-off of participation after college graduation? Is it that our schools and families have not been consistent in laying a foundation for volunteering, or that other forces—materialism, workaholism, a desire to make more money sooner—are displacing the impulse to be involved? We're not equipped to offer reasons why, but it seems clear that at mid-decade the service ethic had lost its appeal for a sizable group of young people and of single people across the board.

Brian O'Connell, president of Independent Sector, offered this point of view in an April 15, 1987, article in *The Chronicle of Higher Education:*

> Part of the problem lies in the fact that one can go through a full and supposedly thorough formal education without ever hearing or reading about the major role the voluntary sector plays in American life. Alan Pifer, president emeritus of the Carnegie Corporation, reviewed more than 50 textbooks used in civics, history, social studies, and the like and found no reference to philanthropy or voluntary organizations.

Later in the article, O'Connell reports that the situation is changing at a number of schools:

> Universities such as Yale, with its Program on Non-Profit Organizations, and Duke, Indiana, and Tufts, which are planning centers to study public service in the non-profit sector, are educating a new generation of public servants sensitive to the enormous contribution made by organizations and individuals in the voluntary sector.

Another major and even more obvious source of impetus for service work is the family, and we'll discuss below some ideas for working together in service as a family and passing along these ideals and values in a dynamic fashion.

Before moving on, however, we want to restate our strong belief in the value of service for young people embarking on careers and family life, providing that they can manage to strike a healthy balance of involvement inside and outside the home. We're speaking directly from personal experience when we say that the service work we did when we were in our twenties provided us with exposure to and close participation with people who were on a higher level of responsibility and to projects, planning, and budgeting that were larger and more sophisticated than those we were involved with in our business and personal lives.

So if what keeps some younger people away from service is an intense career orientation, *they are unwittingly missing out on one of the greatest methods available of advancing their careers.* We have to honestly say that the most meaningful rewards are of the intangible variety. Nevertheless, the knowledge and skills one can develop running a committee, raising money, or doing publicity for not-for-profit groups, as well as the contacts and visibility within the organization and the larger community, can be worth far more than a pattern of working late four nights a week.

THE FAMILY THAT SERVES TOGETHER . . .

The Cozza family believes that a community functions best when its members give of themselves. Silvino Cozza, an engineering assistant at Ethicon, a Johnson & Johnson company, and his children—Louis, Laura, David, and Steven—have given a combined forty-five years of service to the volunteer rescue squad that serves Bound Brook and several adjacent central New Jersey towns. As a family, they devote approximately 250 hours per month to the squad, practicing rescue techniques, attending meetings, and responding to calls for help.

John: *Volunteerism is catching. I'm sure that my own value formation process, the reason I was heavily involved in charitable work in my twenties and then came back to be very active in it and to work full-time in it in my fifties, is that my father was a very active deacon in the church and that my mother, a dedicated volunteer, was, during the Second World War, the unpaid head of the Red Cross canteen program in Minneapolis.*

Ellie: *My grandfather, a politician and historian, was deeply involved in all sorts of nonprofit organizations. His main credo—doing for others—is what kept him going. Being raised by him during my teenage years was a broad influence on my views of service and personal and business ethics.*

Children growing up in the late twentieth century are the inheritors of a world that is truly mind-boggling in its complexity and contradictions. In such a world, young people are at risk of becoming alienated, of losing motivation, of falling into an attitude of "The world is a mess; what's the point of trying?"

Service provides a perfect setting for passing along values from generation to generation, and the family is an excellent vehicle for demonstrating ideals in action and for letting young people feel the satisfactions and personal growth that derive from service work.

Arthur Levitt, Jr., chairman of the American Stock Exchange, was influenced by his family:

> I became involved in volunteer service when I got out of the Air Force in 1954. I came from a family that was involved in all kinds of community activities. My grandmother, for instance, used to travel every day to the Brooklyn Home for the Incurable. My mother and father were both active in a whole variety of nonprofit programs and impressed on me my responsibility to do the same in order to give something back to society.

We also like his statement that "in balancing the nonprofit, the business, and the family parts of life, my advice would be to try to get your family to support the same causes that you support."

Carol Noyes feels the family tie in her service work:

> My parents didn't teach me except by example, but I got involved in Planned Parenthood, I suppose, as a legacy, because my mother had been involved. I suppose they said, there's Carola's daughter, let's nab her. I certainly haven't belabored the idea of giving back with my children. I think the best that one can do in that area is to do it by example. At the time of my birthday last year, apart from the beautiful pin they gave me, everybody made a contribution, in my name, to something they thought was important. Which means that they had gotten the message.

When families work together, they bring a number of important qualities to a service activity. The project or organization benefits from the variety of approaches the group provides, and individual family members support and complement one another's efforts. The very fact that they are a family can be vitally important in certain situations. An intact, relatively healthy family unit can serve as a model in work with troubled families, and such an environment has often been the key factor in the success of visiting or companionship programs with the ill and elderly.

What families get from volunteering far outweighs what they give. An obvious benefit is the additional time spent together, time that is "quality" time in several ways. Not only do children receive psychic income. In service work, family members share experiences, a phenomenon that has largely passed out of many family's lives. And because a project is likely to be one that all family members have entered into at the same time, it truly belongs to all equally.

Service projects often provide family members with new ways of relating, ways of creating patterns to replace old ones that no longer work. They exist as forums in which the interests and talents of individual members can thrive and be rewarded. Parents and children see one another in a new light, noticing talents and qualities that they hadn't seen before or that hadn't been called into action before.

Some children, especially teenagers, are chronically unhappy with their parents, their lives, their possessions. Volunteering can show them how good their lives really are, how much they are truly loved and cared for, how much more they have—of material and emotional well-being—than so many others.

Volunteering is also a good way to combat parental feelings of dissatisfaction with their children—cranky teenagers, underachievers, or kids with minor emotional problems. Volunteering, especially with groups that work with troubled children and teens, can show parents that their kids are not unique in having problems—and where those problems can lead if they're not properly addressed. The most likely result will be, of course, for parents to realize that their own kids aren't really so bad, after all!

The way that service calls out the best in people—in terms of compassion, innovation, leadership—is one of the most important of its benefits for families. It helps children know that they are needed and important for who they are.

A wide range of opportunities exists for families: ongoing commitments and one-time projects; activities that are primarily physical and ones that mainly involve emotional support; projects to be done indoors or out, in the city and the country. Here are some examples of projects that you and your family can get involved in:

- Cleanup campaigns in neighborhoods, playgrounds, parks, beaches
- Opening your home as a place to stay for out-of-town visitors to local hospitals or prisons
- Walkathons for charity
- Manning local collection sites, for example at a mall or supermarket, for donations of money, food, or clothing
- Nature activities, such as helping to build hiking trails, and planting trees and gardens
- Work in soup kitchens and shelters, particularly those that help other families
- Assistance at special events: setup, ushering, ticket and refreshment sales
- Handing out fliers at malls or on street corners
- Doing chores for the elderly and handicapped: yard work and gardening, small repairs, housecleaning
- Running a booth at a block association or church fair
- Helping an immigrant family get integrated into the community
- Hosting a holiday dinner for a needy family
- Joining a summer visitors program for inner-city children, such as New York City's Fresh Air Fund
- "Adopting" an elderly or handicapped person, visiting and helping them in an ongoing relationship
- "Adopting" a student in a program such as A Better Chance, Upward Bound, or other programs that provide tutoring help or preparation for college

Some activities, such as door-to-door fund drives, scouting, and some sporting activities, may not be suited to a large group but are perfect for sharing by a parent and one or two children.

Children learn values from their parents' example, rather than in the abstract, and they respond to tasks. Children want to feel needed. Through service projects, families can keep values alive, making them part of a living tradition that provides all members with valuable tools for meeting the challenges we face as individuals and as members of society.

GIVING FIVE: A NATIONAL GOAL

The fact that large numbers of Americans volunteer time and contribute money to service organizations is profoundly important to the members of Independent Sector, a nonprofit coalition of 650 corporate, foundation, and voluntary organizations, who provide services to the public, operate voluntary agencies, and otherwise represent not-for-profit activity throughout the educational, scientific, health, welfare, cultural, and religious spheres of our national life.

After thorough study and long deliberation, an Independent Sector task force has put forth a challenge: *that Americans collectively double their charitable giving and increase volunteering 50 percent by 1991.* The campaign, officially called "Daring Goals for a Caring Society," sets goals not only for individual giving, but for foundations and corporations as well.

In cooperation with the Advertising Council, Independent Sector is promoting an individual standard of "Give Five." The campaign asks all Americans to join the 20 million people who already give 5 percent of their income and the 23 million volunteers who give five or more hours per week. To quote from one public service ad: "If we all gave just five hours a week to the causes we care about, it would be like mobilizing a force of more than 20 million full-time volunteers. If we all gave just 5 percent of what we earn, it would come to $175 billion a year."

This exciting campaign—which carries the tag line "What you give is five. What you get back is immeasurable"—puts into very persuasive language some of the points we've tried to make in this book:

"One person may not be able to make that much difference. But 200 million people can make all the difference in the world."

"That minor change in your family budget could be the start of some major changes in your family's world."

"It could be the most productive five hours you'll ever spend."

"That small investment could change somebody's life. And it's hard to imagine a better return than that."

The implications of the "Daring Goals for a Caring Society" program are immense. It is a blueprint for helping to solve local and national problems in a direct and satisfying way. For the charitable community, it can mean the development of new and enlarged sources of financial and volunteer support. For all Americans, it can become an affirmation of the spirit and practice of active citizenship and personal community service.

SERVICE GIVES YOU MORE THAN YOU GIVE IT

We've returned to this somewhat inelegant phrase, above, which we asked you to bear in mind at the end of chapter 2. It's not beautiful in a literary way, but it is absolutely true.

We keep hearing the comments of the people we spoke to for this book:

"There is just some sort of warmth that comes through in knowing that you really are doing something, that there is some action. I believe in action, that you can make a difference."

—Millie Harmon-Meyers

"It brings forth an unconstrained and liberating feeling. It's almost like it brings forth the warrior. Again, it's the outside threat, and you've got to answer. It could be anything. You could save the whole operation from sinking because of a couple of decisions or actions or some real creative suggestions for ways of doing things."

—Reno Taini

"My advice to anyone with an opportunity to get into a significant volunteer spot would be to do it. It certainly has enriched my life more than I could ever have dreamed of."

—Debbie Scott

"You get a great satisfaction from trying to be helpful to other people and making other people's lives better in some way. I think we should examine our consciences—I find this particularly as I get older—to see whether we are really doing the positive things in terms of putting something back into society; if you have advantages, whether you just stay there and take them or have met your further obligations to try to serve your fellowman. It's a tremendous satisfaction to have done something in a positive way."

—Peter McColough

Millions of Americans have discovered service work as a marvelous source of satisfaction and fulfillment. They are supporting causes and taking part in the lives of other people as a way of making a life, instead of just working at jobs to make a living. They are helping themselves by helping others. Can 89 million people from all walks of life be wrong? Won't you also give service a try? You have almost nothing to lose and so much to gain.

FOR FURTHER READING

America's Voluntary Spirit: A Book of Readings, edited by Brian O'Connell.
New York: The Foundation Center, 1983. Forty-five selections that analyze and celebrate the strengths and variety of the service sector. Contributors range from Tocqueville, John D. Rockefeller, and Thoreau to
Erma Bombeck, Vernon Jordan, and Lewis Thomas.

The Board Member's Book: Making a Difference in Voluntary Organizations, by
Brian O'Connell. New York: The Foundation Center, 1985. Written for
board members who wish to make the most of their volunteer efforts.
A practical guide to the essential functions of voluntary boards, offering inspiration, advice, and time-tested solutions to the problems and
challenges board members face.

Careers in the Nonprofit Sector: Doing Well by Doing Good, by Terry W.
McAdam. Washington, D.C.: The Taft Group, 1986. Within the context
of helping the reader find a job in the vast and fascinating world of the
nonprofits, this book explains the sector and discusses the organizations and the people who work in them.

*Community Resources Directory: A Guide to U.S. Volunteer Organizations and
Other Resource Groups, Services, Training Events and Courses, and Local
Program Models,* edited by Harriet Clyde Kipps. Second edition.
Detroit: Gale Research Company, 1984. For the person who is thinking
about becoming involved, information on selected local volunteer pro-

grams. For the volunteer in a new or growing organization, descriptions of resource groups, publications, and training programs.

Corporate Philanthropy: Philosophy, Management, Trends, Future, Background. Washington, D.C.: The Council on Foundations, 1982. Forty brief essays that are substantial food for thought for corporate policymakers.

Discover Total Resources: A Guide for Nonprofits. Pittsburgh: Mellon Bank Corporation, 1985. A descriptive checklist to be used as a guide, or self-audit, by boards, staff, and volunteers to assess the degree to which they are tapping a full range of community resources: money, people, goods, and services. (Available by writing to Mellon Community Affairs Division, Room 368, One Mellon Bank Center, Pittsburgh, Pennsylvania 15258-0001.)

Encyclopedia of Associations, edited by Karin E. Koek and Susan Boyles Martin. Twenty-second edition. Detroit: Gale Research Company, 1988. Addresses, telephone numbers, and contact names for more than 25,000 national and international organizations, with a concise description of their objectives, programs, and publications.

The Endangered Sector, by Waldemar A. Nielsen. New York: Columbia University Press, 1979. A lucid and literate discussion of problems confronting the "third sector," with suggested remedies. Detailed attention is given to higher education, basic science, health, culture, and social action.

The Grassroots Fundraising Book, by Joan Flanagan. Chicago: Contemporary Books, 1982. A wealth of ideas for special events: how to choose the right strategy, raise money, and build the organization at the same time. Includes a listing of 100 books and articles on fund-raising.

Handbook of Special Events for Nonprofit Organizations: Tested Ideas for Fund Raising and Public Relations, by Edwin R. Leibert and Bernice E. Sheldon. New York: Association Press, 1972. Specific step-by-step advice for planning and running a variety of events. Includes sample budgets and timetables, and provides case histories.

Making Things Happen: The Guide for Members of Voluntary Organizations, by Joan Wolfe. Andover, Massachusetts: Brick House, 1981. How to plan successful programs, run meetings, raise money, get publicity, keep committees alive and well, make board meetings fun, and manage the time demands of service work. Lively, refreshing, down-to-earth advice.

A New Competitive Edge: Volunteers from the Workplace, by Cynthia Vizza, Kenn Allen, and Shirley Keller. Arlington, Virginia: Volunteer, 1986. An excellent sourcebook. Describes in detail the corporate programs and the service work of employees in twenty-five companies and labor unions.

Philanthropy in Action, by Brian O'Connell. New York: The Foundation Center, 1987. A collection of stories of several hundred philanthropic gifts that made, and continue to make, a difference in American society and throughout the world.

Promoting Issues and Ideas: A Guide to Public Relations for Nonprofit Organizations, by Public Interest Public Relations, a Division of M Booth and Associates. New York: The Foundation Center, 1987. An all-in-one guide to public relations, offering proven strategies that will attract the interest of the people you wish to influence and inform.

Resource Raising: The Role of Non-Cash Assistance in Corporate Philanthropy, by Alex J. Plinio and Joanne B. Scanlan. Washington, D.C.: Independent Sector. A report on the many ways corporations have discovered that their assets, products, services, and personnel can play important roles in extending corporate giving.

Securing Your Organization's Future: A Complete Guide to Fundraising Strategies, by Michael Seltzer. New York: The Foundation Center, 1987. An information-packed handbook that offers a step-by-step approach to creating and sustaining a network of funding sources. Includes case studies and worksheets.

Servant Leadership: A Journey into the Nature of Legitimate Power and Greatness, by Robert K. Greenleaf. New York: Paulist Press, 1977. Inspiring insights for business leaders and prospective board members.

The Successful Volunteer Organization: Getting Started and Getting Results in Nonprofit, Charitable, Grass Roots, and Community Groups, by Joan Flanagan. Chicago: Contemporary Books, 1981. The author, a nationally recognized expert on leadership development and organizational management, has compiled the advice of hundreds of community leaders into this comprehensive, easy-to-use manual.

Tested Ways to Successful Fund Raising, by George A. Brakeley, Jr. New York: Amacom, 1980. Expert tips from one of the nation's best-known fund-raisers.

Volunteers from the Workplace, by Kerry Kenn Allen, Isolde Chapin, Shirley Keller, and Donna Hill. Washington, D.C.: National Center for Voluntary Action, 1979. Valuable detailed discussion of many types of corporate social service involvement.

What Volunteers Should Know for Successful Fund Raising, by Maurice G. Gurin. New York: Stein and Day, 1982. Guidance for those who ask for annual gifts, seek gifts of capital, make campaign decisions, or lead an organization.

Women Volunteering: The Pleasure, Pain, and Politics of Unpaid Work from 1830 to the Present, by Wendy Kaminer. Garden City, New York: Doubleday, 1984. Some history, many interviews, and a thoughtful analysis celebrate the contributions of volunteers to both the feminist movement and American community life.

ABOUT THE AUTHORS

John F. Raynolds III is president of Outward Bound USA, the world's largest and oldest nonprofit adventure-based educational organization, which has expanded in recent years into many social service and business settings. Eleanor Raynolds is a partner in the executive search firm Ward Howell International, a former president of the British-American Chamber of Commerce and is a Commander of the British Empire. Both long active in service work, the Raynoldses live in Connecticut, work in New York, and travel extensively nationally and internationally.

Additional copies of *Beyond Success* may be ordered by sending a check for $19.95 (including postage and handling) to:

MasterMedia Limited
333 West 52nd Street
Suite 306
New York, New York 10019
(212) 246-9500

The Raynoldses are available for keynotes, half-day and full-day seminars, and workshops. Please contact MasterMedia for availability and fee arrangements.

OTHER MASTERMEDIA BOOKS

The Pregnancy and Motherhood Diary: Planning the First Year of Your Second Career, by Susan Schiffer Stautberg, is the first and only undated appointment diary that shows how to manage pregnancy and career. ($12.95 paper)

Cities of Opportunity: Finding the Best Place to Work, Live and Prosper in the 1990's and Beyond, by Dr. John Tepper Marlin, explores the job and living options for the next decade and into the next century. This consumer guide and handbook, written by one of the world's experts on cities, selects and features forty-six American cities and metropolitan areas. ($13.95 paper and $24.95 cloth)

The Dollars and Sense of Divorce, by Dr. Judith Briles, is the first book to combine practical tips on overcoming the legal hurdles and planning finances before, during, and after divorce. ($10.95 paper)

Out the Organization: Gaining the Competitive Edge, by Madeleine and Robert Swain, is written for the millions of Americans whose jobs are no longer safe, whose companies are not loyal, and who face futures of uncertainty. It gives advice on finding a new job or starting your own business. ($17.95 cloth)

Aging Parents and You: A Complete Handbook to Help You to Help Your Aging Relatives Maintain a Full, Healthy, Rewarding and Independent Life, by

Eugenia Anderson-Ellis and Marsha Dryan, is a complete guide to providing care to aging relatives. It gives practical advice and resources to the adults who are helping their elders lead productive and independent lives. ($9.95 paper)

Criticism in Your Life: How to Give It, How to Take It, How to Make It Work for You, by Dr. Deborah Bright, offers practical advice, in an upbeat, readable, and realistic fashion, for turning criticism into control. Charts and diagrams guide the reader into managing criticism from bosses, spouses, relationships, children, friends, neighbors, and in-laws. ($17.95 cloth)

Managing It All: Time Saving Ideas for Career, Family Relationships, and Self, by Beverly Benz Treuille and Susan Schiffer Stautberg, is written for women who are juggling careers and families. Over 200 career women (ranging from a TV anchorwoman to an investment banker) were interviewed. The book contains many humorous anecdotes on saving time and improving the quality of life for self and family.   ($9.95 paper)